The Revels Plays
COMPANION
LIBRARY

E. A. J. HONIGMANN, ROBERT SMALLWOOD and PETER CORBIN
former editors
SUSAN BROCK, SUSAN CERASANO, PAUL EDMONDSON and GRACE IOPPOLO
general editors

For over forty years *The Revels Plays* have offered the most authoritative editions of Elizabethan and Jacobean plays by authors other than Shakespeare. The *Companion Library* provides a fuller background to the main series by publishing important dramatic and non-dramatic material that will be essential for the serious student of the period.

Three seventeenth-century plays on women and performance
eds CHALMERS, SANDERS & TOMLINSON
'Art made tongue-tied by authority' CLARE
Drama of the English Republic, 1649–60 CLARE
Three Jacobean witchcraft plays eds CORBIN, SEDGE
The Stukeley Plays ed. EDELMAN
Three Renaissance usury plays ed. KERMODE
Beyond *The Spanish Tragedy: A study of the works of Thomas Kyd* ERNE
John Ford's political theatre HOPKINS
The works of Richard Edwards KING
Marlowe and the popular tradition: Innovation in the English drama before 1595 LUNNEY
Banquets set forth: Banqueting in English Renaissance drama MEADS
Thomas Heywood: Three marriage plays ed. MERCHANT
Three Renaissance travel plays ed. PARR
John Lyly PINCOMBE
A textual companion to Doctor Faustus RASMUSSEN
Documents of the Rose Playhouse RUTTER
John Lyly: Euphues: The Anatomy of Wit *and* Euphues and His England
ed. SCRAGG
Pap with an Hatchet, *John Lyly: An annotated, modern-spelling edition* ed. SCRAGG
Richard Brome: Place and politics on the Caroline stage STEGGLE

Doing Kyd

Manchester University Press

THE REVELS PLAYS COMPANION LIBRARY

Doing Kyd
Essays on *The Spanish Tragedy*

EDITED BY
Nicoleta Cinpoeş

Manchester University Press

Copyright © Manchester University Press 2016

While copyright in the volume as a whole is vested in Manchester University Press, copyright in individual chapters belongs to their respective authors, and no chapter may be reproduced wholly or in part without the express permission in writing of both author and publisher.

Published by Manchester University Press
Altrincham Street, Manchester M1 7JA
www.manchesteruniversitypress.co.uk

British Library Cataloguing-in-Publication Data
A catalogue record for this book is available from the British Library
Library of Congress Cataloging-in-Publication Data applied for

ISBN 978 0 7190 8382 2 *hardback*

First published 2016

ISBN 978 1 5261 2715 0 *paperback*

First published 2018

The publisher has no responsibility for the persistence or accuracy of URLs for any external or third-party internet websites referred to in this book, and does not guarantee that any content on such websites is, or will remain, accurate or appropriate.

Typeset in Monotype Imprint with Scala Sans display
by Koinonia, Manchester

For Philip Edwards, in memoriam

CONTENTS

LIST OF FIGURES	page ix
GENERAL EDITORS' PREFACE	x
NOTES ON CONTRIBUTORS	xi
ACKNOWLEDGEMENTS	xvi

Introduction
Nicoleta Cinpoeș   1

PART I: 'Vindicta mihi'

1 Supernatural structures in Kyd and Shakespeare
   Philip Edwards   15
2 Enacting revenge: the mingled yarn of Elizabethan tragedy
   Jonathan Bate   25
3 Vindicating revenge
   Evghenii Musica   43
4 Gendering revenge in *The Spanish Tragedy*: feminine fury and the contagiousness of theatrical passion
   Kristine Steenbergh   53

PART II: *The Spanish Tragedy* in print

5 'Undoing Kyd': the texts of *The Spanish Tragedy*
   Simon Barker   75
6 Editing *The Spanish Tragedy* in the early twenty-first century
   Jesús Tronch   88

PART III: 'Chronicles of Spain' or tales of Albion?

7 How Spanish is *The Spanish Tragedy*? Dynastic policy and colonial expansion in revenge tragedy
   Clara Calvo   111
8 Kyd's use of Antonio Pérez's *Las Relaciones* in *The Spanish Tragedy*
   Frank Ardolino   129
9 *The Spanish Tragedy* and revenge tragedy in seventeenth-century Britain and the Low Countries
   Ton Hoenselaars and Helmer Helmers   144

PART IV: Doing Kyd

10 Staging Babel: *The Spanish Tragedy* IV.iv in performance
   Tony Howard   171
11 Hieronimo still mad: why adapt *The Spanish Tragedy* today?
   Tod Davies   195
12 'For what's a play without a woman in it?'
   Carol Chillington Rutter   201

PART V: Thomas Kyd bibliography 1993–2013
Nicoleta Cinpoeş   213

INDEX   233

LIST OF FIGURES

6.1 The fifth 'Addition' in Q1 and Q4 – parallel text   page 94
9.1 *Toneel der Engelsche Ellenden – The Stage of English Miseries* (Amsterdam: Hugo Allard, 1650). Courtesy of the Rijksmuseum, Amsterdam (FM2045a)   155
10.1, 10.2 The Spanish/Portuguese throne and the iron-maiden in Michael Bogdanov's production of *The Spanish Tragedy*. National Theatre, London, 1982 © National Theatre Archive / James McDougall   172
10.3 Siobhan Redmond (Bel-imperia) and Patrice Naiambana (the Ghost of Don Andrea) in Michael Boyd's production of *The Spanish Tragedy*. Royal Shakespeare Company, 1997. Malcolm Davies Collection © Shakespeare Birthplace Trust   176
10.4 Michael Bryant (Hieronimo) in Michael Bogdanov's production of *The Spanish Tragedy*. National Theatre, London, 1982. Photograph Laurence Burns. © ArenaPal   177
10.5 Peter Wight (Hieronimo) in Michael Boyd's production of *The Spanish Tragedy*. Royal Shakespeare Company, 1997. Malcolm Davies Collection © Shakespeare Birthplace Trust   178
12.1 Woodcut on the title page of the 1615 (Q7) edition of Thomas Kyd's *The Spanish Tragedy*. Manuscript C.117.b.36 © British Library Board   202

GENERAL EDITORS' PREFACE

Since the late 1950s the series known as The Revels Plays has provided for students of the English Renaissance drama carefully edited texts of the major Elizabethan and Jacobean plays. The series includes some of the best-known drama of the period and has continued to expand, both within its original field and, to a lesser extent, beyond it, to include some important plays from the earlier Tudor and from the Restoration periods. The Revels Plays Companion Library is intended to further this expansion and to allow for new developments.

The aim of the Companion Library is to provide students of the Elizabethan and Jacobean drama with a fuller sense of its background and context. The series includes volumes of a variety of kinds. Small collections of plays, by a single author or concerned with a single theme and edited in accordance with the principles of textual modernisation of The Revels Plays, offer a wider range of drama than the main series can include. Together with editions of masques, pageants and the non-dramatic work of Elizabethan and Jacobean playwrights, these volumes make it possible, within the overall Revels enterprise, to examine the achievements of the major dramatists from a broader perspective. Other volumes provide a fuller context for the plays of the period by offering new collections of documentary evidence on Elizabethan theatrical conditions and on the performance of plays during that period and later. A third aim of the series is to offer modern critical interpretation, in the form of collections of essays or of monographs, of the dramatic achievement of the English Renaissance.

So wide a range of material necessarily precludes the standard format and uniform general editorial control which is possible in the original series of Revels Plays. To a considerable extent, therefore, treatment and approach are determined by the needs and intentions of individual volume editors. Within this rather ampler area, however, we hope that the Companion Library maintains the standards of scholarship that have for so long characterised The Revels Plays, and that it offers a useful enlargement of the work of the series in preserving, illuminating and celebrating the drama of Elizabethan and Jacobean England.

J. R. MULRYNE, SUSAN BROCK, SUSAN CERASANO

NOTES ON CONTRIBUTORS

Frank Ardolino is Professor Emeritus at the University of Hawai'i, USA. He has published two books on Thomas Kyd's The Spanish Tragedy and contributes numerous articles on the play and Renaissance literature and drama to *Shakespeare Bulletin*, *Sixteenth Century Journal*, *Shakespeare Newsletter* and *Renaissance Quarterly*.

Simon Barker is Professor of English Literature and Head of the Department of English and Creative Writing at the University of Chichester, UK. His books include, with Colin Haydon, *Winchester: History and Literature*, and an edition of John Ford's *'Tis Pity She's Whore*. In 2002 he edited *Wartime Refractions*, a special issue of the journal *Literature and History*. He is co-editor with Hilary Hinds of *The Routledge Anthology of Renaissance Drama* (2003) and published *Shakespeare's Problem Plays* in 2005. Other books include an edition of Thomas Deloney's *The Gentle Craft* and *War and Nation in the Theatre of Shakespeare and His Contemporaries*, both published in 2007. He is co-editor, with Jo Gill, of *Literature as History: Essays in Honour of Peter Widdowson* (2010). Other publications include studies of twentieth-century theatre, television and music.

Jonathan Bate is Professor of English Literature at the University of Oxford and Provost of Worcester College, Oxford, UK. Before he was Fellow of Trinity Hall, Cambridge, King Alfred Professor of English Literature at the University of Liverpool in 1990, and Professor of Shakespeare and Renaissance Literature at the University of Warwick. Well known as a critic, biographer and broadcaster, Jonathan Bate has held visiting posts at Harvard, Yale and UCLA. Among his books are a biography of Shakespeare, *Soul of the Age*, and a history of his fame, *The Genius of Shakespeare*. He is on the Board of the Royal Shakespeare Company and was chief editor of the RSC edition of Shakespeare's *Complete Works*. A Fellow of both the British Academy and the Royal Society of Literature, he was made CBE in the Queen's 80th Birthday Honours.

Clara Calvo is Professor of English Studies at the University of Murcia, Spain. She is the author of *Power Relations and Fool–Master*

Discourse in Shakespeare (1991), co-author of *The Literature Workbook* (1998), with Jean-Jacques Weber, and co-editor, with Ton Hoenselaars, of *European Shakespeares (The Shakespearean International Yearbook*, 8, 2008) and of the special issue *Shakespeare and the Cultures of Commemoration* for *Critical Survey* (2011). Her articles have appeared in *Shakespeare Survey* and *The Year's Work in English Studies*, and in collections, her most recent being 'Thomas Kyd and the Elizabethan Blockbuster: *The Spanish Tragedy*', in *The Cambridge Companion to Shakespeare and Contemporary Dramatists* (2012). She edited, with Jesús Tronch, *The Spanish Tragedy* for Arden Drama (2013). She is a member of the editorial board of *SEDERI* and associate editor of *Cahiers Élisabéthains*. She is currently working on a research project on Shakespearian anniversaries and festival cultures.

Nicoleta Cinpoeş is Principal Lecturer in English – Shakespeare at the University of Worcester, UK, where she teaches Renaissance literature and film adaptation, and is co-director of the Early Modern Research Group. She is particularly interested in early modern drama in performance viewed as site-, time- and media-specific and her research takes place through reconstructing productions, writing theatre history and reading performance hermeneutics. She is the author of *Shakespeare's Hamlet in Romania 1778–2008* (2010) and of the open-access website *The Jacobethans*. Her work has appeared in the journals *Testi e linguaggi, Theatrical Blends, Shakespeare Bulletin, Studia Dramatica* and *SEDERI*, and in collected volumes. In the theatre, she has worked in several capacities from dramaturge to assistant director and translator. She is consultant to the International Shakespeare Festival, Craiova, Romania, sits on the editorial board of several journals, acts as the associate editor for Romania on *ReviewingShakespeare.com* and is collaborating on a new Romanian translation of Shakespeare's *Complete Works*, writing the introductions to: *Hamlet* (2010), *Titus Andronicus* and *The Comedy of Errors*.

Tod Davies is a screenwriter, adapter and writer. Her screenplay credits include *Three Businessmen* and *Revengers Tragedy*, which she also produced; she was co-writer for the screenplay of the adaptation of Hunter S. Thompson's novel *Fear and Loathing in Las Vegas*, and the uncredited screenwriter of *Catchfire* and *The Hot Spot*. She is the founder of Toxteth TV, an educational/media studio for young people, based in Liverpool, and also founder, editor and publisher of *Exterminating Angel Press*, an online magazine which became an independent press in 2009, where she published *Snotty Saves the Day* and *Lily the Silent*, both from *The History of Arcadia* series, and the cooking memoirs *Jam Today: A Diary of Cooking With What You've Got* and *Jam Today Too: The Revolution Will Not Be Catered*.

Philip Edwards (1923–2015) was Senior Lecturer at Birmingham, Professor of English Literature at Trinity College Dublin (1960–66) and the University of Essex (1966–74), and King Alfred Professor of English Literature at the University of Liverpool (1974–90) – then Emeritus. He held visiting positions at a number of universities around the world, among which the University of Michigan, All Souls Oxford, ICU Tokyo and Otago University. His publications include editions – *The Spanish Tragedy* (1959), *Plays and Poems of Philip Massinger* (1976), *Pericles* (1976), *Hamlet* (1st 1985, 2nd 2003), *Cook's Journals* (1999); books – *Sir Walter Ralegh* (1953), *Shakespeare and the Confines of Art* (1968), *Threshold of a Nation* (1979), *Shakespeare: A Writer's Progress* (1986), *Last Voyages* (1988), *Story of the Voyage* (1994), *Sea-Mark* (1997), *Pilgrimage and Literary Tradition* (2005); and numerous articles and contributions to books.

Helmer Helmers is Lecturer in Early Modern Dutch Literature and NWO Veni Research Fellow at the University of Amsterdam, the Netherlands. He has published widely on Anglo-Dutch cultural and literary exchange in the seventeenth century. His monograph *The Royalist Republic* (2014) discusses Dutch publicity on the English Civil Wars and regicide. He is currently working on a project on the development of Dutch news culture during the Thirty Years War.

Ton Hoenselaars in Professor of Early Modern Literature in the English Department of Utrecht University, the Netherlands. He is the author of *Images of Englishmen and Foreigners in the Drama of Shakespeare and His Contemporaries* (1992). He has edited, alone or with others, *Shakespeare's Italy* (1993), *The Italian World of English Renaissance Drama* (1997), *English Literature and the Other Languages* (1999), *The Author as Character* (1999), *Four Hundred Years of Shakespeare in Europe* (2003), *Shakespeare and the Language of Translation* (2004), *Shakespeare's History Plays* (2004), *Challenging Humanism* (2005) and *The Cambridge Companion to Shakespeare and Contemporary Dramatists* (2012). He is also the founding Chairman of the Shakespeare Society of the Low Countries, and managing editor of its journal *Folio*. He is currently writing a monograph on Shakespeare and Richard Wagner.

Tony Howard is Professor of English at the University of Warwick, UK, where he teaches on the English and Comparative Literary Studies programme. He has published on performance in its social and political contexts, primarily Shakespeare, contemporary British drama and East European poetry and theatre. His *Women as Hamlet: Performance and Interpretation in Theatre, Film and Fiction* (2007) is a seminal study of the shifting relationship of Shakespeare, culture and gender in many societies and ideological situations – from nineteenth-century Britain, America and France to Weimar Germany, Stalinist Russia and Eastern Europe during the fall of Communism. He has translated, with Barbara Bogoczek, many major works of Polish drama and poetry by writers such as Tadeusz Rozewicz, Maria Pawlikowska and Ewa Lipska. His collaboration with playwright Howard Brenton on *A Short Sharp Shock* (Royal Court/Stratford East) provided a prescient insight into the politics of Britain in the 1980s. His other theatre work, the drama-documentary *'I Have Done the State Some Service': Robeson, Othello and the FBI,* links to his current work as Principal Investigator for Multicultural Shakespeare, a major AHRC-funded project which aims to record the contribution of Black and Asian artists to the development of Shakespearian performance in the UK.

Evghenii Musica is an independent researcher in tragedy and psychoanalytic theory. He has written on spectrality and parodic adaptations of *Hamlet* in the context of Freud's seduction theory. He has also been contributing various entries on Freudian terminology to *The Literary Encyclopedia*. He earned a PhD in English at the University of Warwick (2007) and teaches at Bergen Community College, Paramus, New Jersey, USA.

Carol Chillington Rutter is Professor of Shakespeare and Performance Studies at the University of Warwick, UK, where she has also been Director of the CAPITAL Centre between 2006 and 2011. A regular contributor to *Shakespeare Survey* and *Shakespeare Quarterly*, and published in both Cambridge University Press and Blackwell companions to Shakespeare on stage, film and popular culture, her major publications include *Clamorous Voices: Shakespeare's Women Today* (1988), *Enter the Body: Women and Representation on Shakespeare's Stage* (2001), the Introduction to *Macbeth* (2005), with Stuart Hampton-Reeves, *Henry VI in Performance* (2006), and *Shakespeare and Child's Play: Lost Boys on Stage and Screen* (2007). She contributes to the RSC's Artists' Development programme, is a consultant to Northern Broadsides and patron to 1623 theatre company, and she's a regular contributor to BBC radio arts programmes. General editor for the Manchester University Press series *Shakespeare in Performance*, she sits on the editorial boards of *Shakespeare Bulletin, Great Shake-*

speareans and *Borrowers and Lenders*, and serves as a Trustee to the Shakespeare Birthplace Trust. Her current research project focuses on the life and diplomatic activities of Henry Wotton, appointed ambassador to the Venetian Republic by James I in 1604.

Kristine Steenbergh is Lecturer in English literature at the Vrije Universiteit Amsterdam, the Netherlands. Her current research project 'Moving Scenes' analyses the role of the theatre in thinking about the effects of emotions on an audience, in the context of the emerging public sphere in early modern England. With Willemijn Ruberg she has edited *Sexed Sentiments: Interdisciplinary Perspectives on Gender and Emotion* (2010).

Jesús Tronch is Senior Lecturer at the University of Valencia, Spain. He has edited *A Synoptic 'Hamlet'* (2002), authored a number of commissioned essays in book collections and articles in journals such as *SEDERI*, *Shakespeare Survey* and *TEXT*, and co-edited bilingual English–Spanish editions of *The Tempest* (1994) and *Antony and Cleopatra* (1999). Most recently, he edited, with Clara Calvo, *The Spanish Tragedy* for Arden Drama (2013). He is associate editor of *Cahiers Élisabéthains* and is currently collaborating in a project for an open-access multilingual collection of classical European theatre.

ACKNOWLEDGEMENTS

As its title announces, this book was born out of 'doing' Kyd. Back in 2005, this meant just designing the first open-access, interactive website on Thomas Kyd's *The Spanish Tragedy*, a project which has grown into a textual, critical, stage and bibliographical electronic resource that led the way in online playscript close reading and performance archiving. Since then, Kyd and his *Spanish Tragedy* have acquired a number of friends, out of whose willingness to share their 'doings' the current collection has taken shape. They include editors, translators, performance critics, screen playwrights, e-learning designers, directors, actors, stage designers, students, researchers, theatre archivists, librarians, readers and, last but not least, the publisher – Manchester University Press. My thanks go first to all these contributors to the volume, in each and every sense of the word: without them, *Doing Kyd* couldn't have happened.

Several institutions and people have aided Kyd and my journey in different but equally important ways. I am indebted to the University of Warwick for the opportunity to develop *The Jacobethans* open-access website and conduct the workshop 'Doing Kyd' in 2006, and to the University of Worcester for the encouragement and time granted to develop and complete this volume. For their unfailing support and patience, I am grateful to Gavin Clarke at the National Theatre Archives, to Susan Brock at The Capital Centre, to Helen Hargest at the Shakespeare Birthplace Trust, and to Matthew Frost at Manchester University Press. To my students, for their comments and proactive curiosity which have spurred me on, I owe special thanks. Finally, and most of all, I thank my family: your love and help have sustained me throughout.

Introduction
Nicoleta Cinpoeş

'*Vindicta mihi!*' are two of the most famous words of the 1590s. Some Elizabethans would have heard them uttered from the pulpit (Romans 12:19); others, cried out from the stage, with renewed pathos and urgency, by Hieronimo, father and Knight Marshal, whose only son has fallen victim to the murderous hands of the very power he faithfully serves. The play was Thomas Kyd's *The Spanish Tragedy*, the box-office and print success of its day. In the four months of Lord Strange's Men's first season at Philip Henslowe's Rose, the play – recorded by Henslowe as *Jeronymo* – was performed an extraordinary nineteen times, sometimes in tandem with a partner piece, 'the comodey of Jeronymo', and by 1597 had seen twenty-nine performances.[1]

Among the top three plays of the 1590s (along with Marlowe's *The Jew of Malta* and the now lost *The Wise Men of West Chester*), *The Spanish Tragedy* is a play which Shakespeare, a young, recent arrival in the capital, must have taken a good note of. It not only ran in repertoire with his *Henry VI* ('harey the vj') at the Rose but, being the blockbuster of the day, it served as a benchmark, informed his imagination and entered his theatrical vocabulary. Its shadow stretches through *Titus Andronicus* and *Richard III*, down to *Hamlet*. The track record of Kyd's dramatic masterpiece was impressive both on the stage and on the page. Between 1592 and 1604, it was put on by four of the most reputable theatre companies of the day: Lord Strange's Men, Lord Pembroke's Men, the Lord Admiral's Men and the Lord Chamberlain's Men (who later became the King's Men),[2] and the lead role, Hieronimo, was performed by the stars of the time – Edward Alleyn and, most likely, Richard Burbage. After the 1592 edition, the earliest survivor of the printed versions, but clearly not the play's first, as it boasts to be 'newly corrected and amended of such grosse faults as passed in the first impression', *The Spanish Tragedy* appeared in ten separate quarto editions before 1633, a record unsurpassed by any Shakespeare play. Some of these editions followed the 1592 text, others, particularly those which came out after 1602, advertised a play '[n]ewly corrected, amended, and enlarged with new additions of the Painters part, and others', an announcement which has sparked centuries of debate regarding the authorship of the Additions, with Jonson, Webster and William Shakespeare amongst the contenders.[3]

Apart from its huge stage success, the measure of the play's importance lies in its impact on Elizabethan playwriting. Though it drew on both Seneca and the Tudor morality play, *The Spanish Tragedy* was a singularly innovative play in its astonishing stage craft engaging the full potential of the public playhouses and launching a new vogue for revenge tragedy. Kyd's theatrical imagination influenced Christopher Marlowe, his writing partner, room-mate and star of the early Elizabethan stage, as well as several generations of playwrights, including Shakespeare, Webster, Middleton, Tourneur and Ford. Seminal at home, Kyd's oeuvre was also influential abroad. Well into the seventeenth century *The Spanish Tragedy* was on the boards in Germany, in the Low Countries and in Prague.[4] By the end of the Caroline period its popularity had turned it into a handy subject for pastiche and critique (by Nashe, Jonson), a kind of prolonged life with a comic twist. During the closure of the playhouses (1642–61), like all plays, *The Spanish Tragedy* disappeared from view. Its return can be traced through a brief entry in Pepys's diary: '24 February 1667/68 at the Nursery Theatre in Hatton Garden'. Lukas Erne comments on this Restoration revival noting a shift in status, from a 'play [...] performed by the leading actors on London's main stages for about half a century' to one 'played in a marginal and temporary playhouse by mediocre actors'.[5] After this, both Kyd and *The Spanish Tragedy* disappear from view and sink into anonymity.

Anonymity continued to be their fate until 1773, when Kyd's name was (re)connected with the play and its title restored; the discoverer was Thomas Hawkins, who paid attention to Heywood's (passing) reference to 'M. Kid, in the *Spanish Tragedy*'.[6] The late nineteenth-century interest in the medieval and Tudor periods resurrected the play for an academic reading public and attracted the interest of editors. Only in 1921 did it return to the stage owing to the enthusiasm of an amateur troupe, the Birkbeck Players (at Birkbeck College, University of London), who staged it again in 1931. Next followed a spate of Oxford productions: 1932 at Christ Church, 1937 at St Edmund Hall, 1951 at St John's College. Productions, put on by university dramatic societies, as the special correspondent of *The Times* noted, aimed to give life to 'dramatic masterpieces of the past', which 'could not survive the vulgar tests of the box-office'.[7] During the two following decades, the play's life was secured by amateur dramatics and radio productions, whose objective was to 'lift the curtains on unfamiliar plays'.[8] As a result, their shared approach was to 'rid the plays of [...] "anything that is indigestibly diffuse or archaic"', according to John Barton, then Fellow of King's College, Cambridge, who 'prepared the programme', 'arranged the plays for broadcasting' and 'introduce[d] each production' on BBC Radio in 1956.[9]

Unlike the first performances and editions of the play, the amateur and radio productions reached a rather different audience from Kyd's early modern one – not the ordinary spectator or reader of cheap quartos but the scholar, student and a specific group of radio listeners.[10] Outside scholarly exegesis (most notably Boas's *The Works of Thomas Kyd* (1901)), Kyd's play featured only in collections and anthologies (of minor Elizabethan dramatists or non-Shakespeare plays of the period) before appearing, again, as self-independent editions. In 1959, Philip Edwards's trailblazing edition finally reclaimed the play's position in the history of early modern drama, thus securing its presence in the curriculum, and a renewed interest towards it and its author in the second half of the twentieth century. A number of independent editions followed (Cairncross in 1967, Mulryne in 1970, Bevington in 1996 – all of which had reprints), as did specialised anthologies (of revenge tragedies or Renaissance plays). The play finally had its first modern professional stage production at the Mercury Theatre, London, in 1973.

While Kyd's presence in print steadily rose in the late twentieth century, *The Spanish Tragedy* has never again matched its initial page and stage success. Productions remained few and far between: only three professional stagings (Citizens Theatre, Glasgow, in 1978; National Theatre, London, in 1982 and 1984; and The Swan Theatre, Stratford-upon-Avon, in 1997); one radio production (1994) and a healthy number of amateur (university) ones. Academic interest and amateur performance can be credited with saving Kyd's play and allowing it to reach the point where it again becomes topical as ideas of revenge have gained a new currency in a world fuelled by war, conflict, cruelty, death, corruption and injustice.

Just as in the 1590s, in the twenty-first century Kyd's play is sharing the stages with *Titus Andronicus* (another play which has undergone a huge upsurge in interest). Productions engage head on with state politics, domination, religion, national identity, lack of hope. Whether set in the corporate world that tramples over individuals and their lives (as in the Doublethink production, Arcola, London, 2009), or focusing on war tearing families apart (as in the Lazarus Theatre Company, Blue Elephant Theatre, 2013), Kyd's play is treading the boards again and talking to us. In a number of seminal studies published during the first decades of the millennium, Kyd and his *Spanish Tragedy* have been at the forefront of critical and editorial debates regarding early modern stage practice, the emergence of the revenge genre in England, authorship, collaborative playwriting and the (re)distribution and attribution of plays from the period.[11] The play's presence in the English curriculum – albeit among the 'other', non-Shakespeare plays – has contributed to repositioning Thomas Kyd within the early modern period and to re-charting the socio-cultural practices of the period itself.

The current volume, *Doing Kyd: Essays on The Spanish Tragedy*, recognises the importance of the playwright and *The Spanish Tragedy* for the development of early modern theatre and beyond. It approaches the play and its author within their social and theatrical set-up by mapping out the context from which Kyd's dramatic work emerged. Its aim is to familiarise readers with the play which, literally, set the stage for the Elizabethan revenge tragedy boom. The chapters revisit theories of revenge, and examine the play's latest editions, stage productions and screenplay adaptations.

The novelty of the collection is threefold. Firstly, it 'does Kyd' in the broadest sense: in wide-ranging chapters contributors look at the play's immediate impact and its legacy, at textual and contextual reception, at genre and gender, at editing (for the page, stage and film), at stage productions; and, in addition, it offers a significant bibliographical update. Secondly, it 'does justice' to Kyd in that it explores what, to date, is still a less trodden territory: the stage life (and afterlife) of *The Spanish Tragedy*. Last, but not least, it 'undoes Kyd', as several of the contributors revisit their own professional encounters with the play and propose new interpretative avenues.

Part I, '*Vindicta mihi!*', engages with the revenge genre from its Senecan roots to its early modern Englishing and the problems around its reception. Its first chapter, 'Supernatural structures in Kyd and Shakespeare', by Philip Edwards, the play's 1959 editor, takes the reader on a rewarding journey from Kyd's Proserpine to Shakespeare's Prospero. He argues that, while Shakespeare's later work, especially *Macbeth* and *King Lear*, shows little or no direct influence of Kyd's play, it demonstrates how Kyd's scepticism continued to affect his plays. Setting the sixteenth-century aesthetic and theatrical scene, Jonathan Bate argues that Kyd's generation found tragedy 'classical' (Greek mediated through Latin) and left it 'English(ed)'. His 'Enacting revenge: the mingled yarn of Elizabethan tragedy' traces the (trans) formation of the genre from an imitation of a received aesthetic model into an indigenous exploration, both as topic and as form, from a static work of debate into public action and spectacle. Evghenii Musica's 'Vindicating revenge' interrogates the acceptance of 'revenge' as genre-designator in recent readings of tragedy in the context of ongoing investigations into the evolution of the term. He focuses on the relationship between *The Spanish Tragedy* and *Hamlet* – two plays which testify simultaneously to the paradigmatic consolidation and the dissolution of the genre. His argument posits and analyses the paradox of self-destruction and perpetuation of revenge within and beyond the context of its origin. Kristine Steenbergh concludes Part I by situating gendered representations of revenge in *The Spanish Tragedy* in relation to cultural frictions caused by the attempts of the Elizabethan legal system to eradicate extrajudicial traditions of revenge. Her 'Gendering revenge in *The Spanish Tragedy*: feminine fury and the contagiousness of theatrical passion' argues that the Inns of Court, one of the central legal institutions, which mediated the introduction of Seneca's revenge tragedies into Elizabethan culture, used their performances to shape an association between vengeance and uncontrolled feminine passion, thus strengthening the image of a masculine and rational law. Other plays emphasised the heroics and rationality of masculine revenge, a surmise that gendered representations of revenge were central to the stage's contributions to debates over retribution.

Part II, '*The Spanish Tragedy* in print', brings two personal editorial accounts on what it means to edit *The Spanish Tragedy* in the third millennium. Simon Barker's '"Undoing Kyd": the texts of *The Spanish Tragedy*' is a retrospective account, one of co-editing (with Hilary Hinds) *The Routledge Anthology of Renaissance Drama*, published in 2003. Beginning with a short preamble on the project and the editorial and critical issues that it gave rise to, the chapter explores the way in which 'the text' of *The Spanish Tragedy* has been (re)constructed by editors over the course of the four centuries since its first staging, with particular emphasis on twentieth-century editions and the *Routledge Anthology*. He argues that there is an analogous relationship between the management of the text and the critical, or introductory, material accompanying it in editions and in anthologies, where it is placed alongside other works from the period. Barker suggests that this most important of early modern texts has a very unstable history in print and in its encounters with various critical and theoretical movements, and that some recent textual and critical work has been 'undoing' the Kyd of earlier times. The chapter concludes with an analysis of Kyd's evolving literary reputation as a significant figure in his own right as well as a source for others, an interest partly produced by speculation about his life and his relationships with his contemporaries. Finally, Barker reviews this reputation with a plea for more critical attention to Kyd's minor work, an approach which will 'undo' the dramatist, but restore him as a key figure of the dramatic and non-dramatic literature of late Tudor England. Jesús Tronch's 'Editing *The Spanish Tragedy* in the early twenty-first century' started as the work in progress of an editor readying himself for the editorial enterprise by considering the principles and problems involved in producing a play-text that is 'new' and original in relation to previous critical editions. His account specifically focuses on the decisions and consequences of a modern-spelling edition based on the 1602 quarto, which pursues the socially oriented editorial aims of reconstructing the text intended by its publishers.[12]

Part III, '"Chronicles of Spain" or tales of Albion?', engages with issues of identity – English, Spanish, early modern – and new ideas regarding the play's complex relations with its political and cultural context of emergence and early circulation. Taking up the frequently asked question 'How Spanish is *The Spanish Tragedy*?', Clara Calvo's response begins with an analysis of *The Spanish Tragedy* in relation to other early modern English plays. Her cross-textual comparison evidences that, while other playwrights signalled national identity through a diverse array of dramatic means, including racial features, linguistic difference and attitudes to the world, Kyd did not avail himself of any of these practices, and that, in (textual) fact, there is little about the characters, the plot, the manners, the language or the play as a whole that can be seen as particularly Spanish or Portuguese, which suggests that national identity and the idiosyncrasies of national character are not the play's crucial concern. Instead, Calvo argues, Kyd grapples with the identity of monarchies and courts, and the clash of political and geographical entities. In this sense, his play rather encodes an anxiety as much to do with Spain and Portugal as with England, as it ends with two kingdoms without heirs to the throne. Her chapter, 'How Spanish is *The Spanish Tragedy*? Dynastic policy and colonial expansion in revenge tragedy', advocates a shift in the critical approaches to *The Spanish Tragedy*, away 'from debating whether the play reflects Habsburg Spain or Renaissance Italy to considering how it portrays Mediterranean culture (Spanish, Portuguese, Italian, French and Ottoman) in relation to early modern England and its desire to play a role in the European colonial expansion'. Calvo concludes that *The Spanish Tragedy* can be read as a play that grafts its English interest on to Iberian affairs (reaching beyond the Armada and the religious conflict) and that 'simultaneously favours a view of corrupt Mediterranean monarchies and contemplates future imperial dreams for England'.

Frank Ardolino, author of two books and numerous articles on Kyd and *The Spanish Tragedy*, looks at the play afresh and argues that, in the Pedringano hanging episode (III.v–vii), Kyd creates a political subtext which is related to the play's anti-Spanish theme. While acknowledging that the play is anti-Leicester – as others have suggested – he posits that Kyd combines aspects of the anti-Leicester tradition with the anti-Spanish black legend as primarily expressed in Antonio Pérez's *Relaciones*, first published in France in 1591, which perhaps did more to undermine Philip II's image as a responsible and prudent monarch than any work in the anti-Hispanist tradition. His chapter, 'Kyd's use of Antonio Pérez's *Las Relaciones* in *The Spanish Tragedy*', places the play firmly within the pro-Leicester context of the ideological war between Spain and England. It argues that *The Spanish Tragedy*, which has been regarded primarily as a 'blood and guts' revenge tragedy, was actually written to promote the Protestant politico-religious ethos, represented by Leicester, against Catholic Babylon/Spain under Philip II.

Ton Hoenselaars and Helmer Helmers discuss the European fortunes of *The Spanish Tragedy* during the seventeenth century, devoting special attention to the reception history of Kyd's play in the Low Countries. Their '*The Spanish Tragedy* and revenge tragedy in seventeenth-century Britain and the Low Countries' places three early Dutch translations and adaptations of *The Spanish Tragedy* in relation to other drama imported from England, such as Thomas Middleton's *The Revengers' Tragedy* (translated by Theodore Rodenburgh, in 1617) and *Titus Andronicus* (rewritten by Jan Vos as *Aran and Titus*, in 1638). Besides mapping the early impact of the English genre on Dutch drama, their contextual and cross-textual exploration seeks to illustrate how such early translations can be useful in 'un-editing' some of the versions of the playtexts currently in circulation. Such an analysis of the adapted plays, the two authors argue, may contribute to our understanding of the changing appreciation of the genre during the seventeenth century. As it entered the discourse of the English Civil War, the initially averse attitude to revenge in the Low Countries (marked by additions to the texts of the translated plays) was modified. Already during the 1650s, the stereotypical carnage at the end of the revenge play was in several instances replaced by happy endings, a cultural longing for the restoration of order, which appears only in post-Restoration plays in England. Considering the fact that Dutch adaptations of English texts dealing with revenge were often part of the propaganda effort of English royalists in exile, Hoenselaars and Helmer conclude that the changes made to the revenge genre in the Dutch Republic were part of the ongoing development of the English genre. In other words, not only did *The Spanish Tragedy* affect the literary scene in the Low Countries during the seventeenth century, but the Dutch revision of the genre, in its turn, gave a new lease of life to the English tradition in the post-Restoration period.

Part IV, 'Doing Kyd', engages with performances of *The Spanish Tragedy* – one chapter offers a spectator's first-hand experience of the play in what is the first extensive study of the professional stage life of the play in the twentieth century; the other explores some of the challenges adaptors face when turning it into a screenplay. Tony Howard's analysis of professional productions of *The Spanish Tragedy* in the United Kingdom discusses their ways of dealing with the play's metatheatricality. Howard shows how directors such as Robert David MacDonald (at Glasgow Citizens Theatre, in 1978), Michael Bogdanov (at the National Theatre, Cottesloe studio, in 1982), Michael Boyd (at the RSC's Swan Theatre, in 1997) and Alan Drury (BBC Radio 3, in 1994) pursued unique textual and interpretative strategies, illustrated by their approach to the play's catastrophe for which each created a different balance between tragedy, pathos, black comedy and horror. His analysis of Act IV of *The Spanish Tragedy* in the four productions demonstrates how intricate the relationship between language and action can be, and how these productions explored the power of performance to elucidate meaning in startling ways.

In 'Hieronimo still mad: Why adapt *The Spanish Tragedy* today?', Tod Davies argues that an adaptor of *The Spanish Tragedy*, not unlike its editors, is faced with the choice of multiple 'texts' and the 'technical problem' of dealing with the 'extraneous bits' – the 1602 Additions. That, she suggests, becomes more acute if the 'dominant theme' of the play, brought to the fore by the general plot streamlining and action pruning, is 'the theme of the tragedy of a well-intentioned, honourable man who believes in the justice of an unjust society – until it takes away the thing he loves most in the world'. In this chapter Davies takes a retrospective look at the adaptation of *The Spanish Tragedy* for film and considers 'historical interest' and current 'artistic relevance' as two, not unrelated, reasons for adapting an older play.[13]

Cued by the woodblock illustration on the title page of the 1615 edition of *The Spanish Tragedy*, Carol Chillington Rutter's '*For what's a play without a woman in it?*' provides an epilogue to Part IV in its review of some of Kyd's doings, namely 'the patterns' and 'precedents' it sets for his contemporary playwrights through the four characters portrayed – Horatio, Lorenzo, Bel-imperia and Hieronimo. Rutter's study, however, is particularly concerned with the 'fifth figure' which does not make it into the 1615 illustration and which can be regarded as much of a 'precedent' as the others. Much like Hieronimo, in his 'what's a play without a woman?' (IV.i.97), she challenges readers to see the woman *within* it. Her reading brings Isabella in the spotlight and remembers the work she does in the play, as a wife and as a mother, and the cultural work she has done since, in a survey of her long line of offspring – Shakespeare's Ophelia and Lady Macbeth, Sheridan's Tilburina, Stoker's Lucy Westenra, Williams's Blanche du Bois, O'Casey's Nora, Kane's *4:48 Psychosis* – thus functioning also as a prologue to 'doing Kyd' differently.

Part V, 'Thomas Kyd bibliography, 1993–2013', is a comprehensive, though by no means an exhaustive, account of all Kyd work done between 1993 and 2013. Continuing the Kyd bibliographic account – starting where José Ramón Díaz Fernández's 'Thomas Kyd, a bibliography 1966–1992' ended[14] – it captures the renewed and diverse interest in *The Spanish Tragedy* over the past two decades. The subsections aim to differentiate between the editorial, critical, performance and digital focus, while indicating (without any attempt at hierarchising) the type of the source and the play's presence in it. The bibliography, which includes editions of the play, single-authored books with Kyd as the exclusive focus, chapters in single-authored books, articles in collections and journals, unpublished material (i.e., doctoral theses), professional stage history (listing reviews) and a sample of electronic resources, brings up to date the record of 'doing Kyd'.

In the latest stage reincarnation of the play, 'Vindicta mihi!' (III. xiii.1),[15] these most recognisable words of *The Spanish Tragedy*, were not heard from the stage of the Blue Elephant theatre in Camberwell, London, 2013. This was one of a series of daring directorial interventions in the play, performed by Lazarus Theatre Company.[16] Other changes included casting a young Hieronimo, brother (not father) to Horatio, which brought a clearer sense that their fate was interchangeable, a female King of Spain and a Pedragina. This was a play of young and angry rulers, soldiers and servants, initially indistinguishable in the warm-up exercise which opened the production. The play's classical frame – the Ghost of Don Andrea and Revenge – was edited and inserted as flashbacks, into an unsettling story about war, corruption and competing interests, set against a background of vulgar victory celebrations and raucous entertainment. Hieronimo's *coup de théâtre*

– which struck dumb both the onstage audience and those sitting in the theatre – was not (only) his staging of *Soliman and Perseda* in pantomime key but the 'spectacle' (IV.iv.89) he unveiled by pulling down a curtain. His dead son's corpse stood propped up against the back wall on which a giant chalk inscription read: 'Vengeance is mine!' These words – an unclaimed, muted cry – remained in the spotlight after Don Andrea and Revenge consigned everyone to their fate. The words stared back at the audience, offsetting a stage littered with the remains of a wedding party – balloons, party hats, the script pages of Hieronimo's play, earlier handed around to the onstage audience. They haunted the theatre space in 2013 as they did in the sixteenth century, while stacked-up volumes of Marlowe's and Shakespeare's plays 'spectated' from stage left. Like this volume, Lazarus Theatre 'did' Kyd by acknowledging his central position in print and on the boards – both the modern and the early modern.

NOTES

1. Greg, *Henslowe's Diary*, pp. 13–14.
2. See Philip Edwards, *Thomas Kyd* (1966), and Clara Calvo and Jesús Tronch's introduction to the Arden edition of the play (2013).
3. The case for Shakespeare has been reopened in the recent years, with Warren Stevenson's book *Shakespeare's Additions* (2008), Brian Vickers's recent computer analysis evidence, in 'Identifying Shakespeare's additions' (2012), Douglas Bruster's further proof of Shakespeare's hand in the Additions in 'Shakespearean spellings' (2013) and the play's inclusion in Bate and Rasmussen's *William Shakespeare and Others: Collaborative Plays* (2013).
4. For more on the play's travels on the continent in the seventeenth century and its subsequent German and Dutch adaptations, see Philip Edwards, *Thomas Kyd* (1996), Ton Hoenselaars, 'The seventeenth-century reception' (1999) and Lukas Erne, *Beyond the Spanish Tragedy* (2001).
5. Erne, *Beyond The Spanish Tragedy*, pp. 134–5.
6. Thomas Hawkins was then editing a three-volume work, *The Origin of the English Drama*, when he discovered Thomas Heywood's reference, in his *Apology for Actors* (1612), to 'M. Kid, in the *Spanish Tragedy*'. See J. R. Mulryne's entry on Kyd in the *Oxford Dictionary of National Biography*.
7. *The Times*, 31 July 1937.
8. *The Times*, 24 September 1953.
9. *The Times*, 22 August 1956.
10. For more information on the performance history of the play – amateur, professional and radio – see my website *The Jacobethans*.
11. Part V of this book is indicative of the renewed interest in Thomas Kyd and his work after 2000. The increased number of single-author volumes

and extended critical articles on Kyd and *The Spanish Tragedy* signals the clear shift from highly specialised and/or sporadic interest, mainly in relation to other established names and/or texts of the period, to establishing Kyd studies in their own right.

12 Back in 2006, at the Doing Kyd workshop, University of Warwick, Tronch was working through the editorial principles and priorities of an edition yet to be accomplished; his and Clara Calvo's effort was released, in 2013, by the Arden Early Modern Drama series, as the latest edition of Kyd's play.

13 Following *The Revengers* [sic] *Tragedy* (directed by Alex Cox, 2001), *The Spanish Tragedy* is the second of nine plays that made Exterminating Angel's project JACOBEANS.NET™.

14 Díaz-Fernández's was the last Kyd bibliography published, in the *Bulletin of Bibliography*, the leading journal in bibliography which kept abreast with the world of research since 1897 but which sadly ceased publication in 2002.

15 All quotations from *The Spanish Tragedy* in this book are taken from Philip Edwards's edition, The Revels Plays (London: Methuen, 1959) and are referenced parenthetically in the text.

16 The production was directed by Ricky Dukes.

REFERENCES

Bate, J. and E. Rasmussen (eds), *William Shakespeare and Others: Collaborative Plays* (London: Palgrave Macmillan, 2013).

Bruster, D., 'Shakespearean spellings and handwriting in the additional passages printed in the 1602 *Spanish Tragedy*', *Notes and Queries* 60:3 (2013): 420–4.

Calvo, C. and J. Tronch (eds), *The Spanish Tragedy*, Arden Early Modern Drama (London: Arden Shakespeare, 2013).

Díaz-Fernández, J. R., 'Thomas Kyd: A bibliography, 1966–1992', *Bulletin of Bibliography* 52:1 (1995): 1–13.

'Early English drama: BBC series of monthly performances', *The Times*, 22 August 1956.

Edwards, P., *Thomas Kyd and Early Elizabethan Tragedy* (London: Longmans, Green, 1966).

Edwards, P. (ed.), *The Spanish Tragedy*, The Revels Plays (London: Methuen, 1959).

Erne, L., *Beyond The Spanish Tragedy: A Study of the Works of Thomas Kyd* (Manchester: Manchester University Press, 2001).

Greg, W. W. (ed.), *Henslowe's Diary*, Part I: Text (London: A. H. Bullen, 1904).

Hoenselaars, T., 'The seventeenth-century reception of English Renaissance drama in Europe', *SEDERI* 10 (1999): 69–87.

The Jacobethans, www2.warwick.ac.uk/fac/arts/ren/elizabethan_jacobean_drama/kyd/spanishtragedy/performancehistory/ [last accessed 30 January 2014].

Murlyne, J. R., 'Kyd, Thomas (bap. 1558, d. 1594)', *Oxford Dictionary of National Biography* [online].
'Oxford summer diversions', *The Times*, 31 July 1937.
Schuessler, J., 'Much ado about who: Is it really Shakespeare? Further proof of Shakespeare's hand in "The Spanish Tragedy"', *The New York Times*, 12 August 2013.
Stevenson, W. *Shakespeare's Additions to Thomas Kyd's The Spanish Tragedy: A Fresh Look at the Evidence Regarding the 1602 Additions* (Lewiston, NY, and Lampeter: Edwin Mellen Press, 2008).
'Third Programme plans: Lifting the curtain on unfamiliar plays', *The Times*, 24 September 1953.
Vickers, B. 'Identifying Shakespeare's Additions to *The Spanish Tragedy* (1602): A new(er) approach', *Shakespeare* 8:1 (2012): 13–43.

PART I

'Vindicta Mihi'

CHAPTER 1

Supernatural structures in Kyd and Shakespeare
Philip Edwards

This chapter is largely retrospective and looks at the work I have done on Thomas Kyd since the preparation for my edition of *The Spanish Tragedy*. The year 1959 is a long time ago, but I remember better the autumn of 1955 when I got back to England, after a year at Harvard where my research into poetry and patronage in the early seventeenth century seemed to be going precisely nowhere, to find a letter from Clifford Leech, then at Durham, asking me if I would edit *The Spanish Tragedy* for his new series of plays, soon to be called The Revels Plays. I felt a little like Hieronimo when the letter from Bel-imperia fell at his feet: a new direction had come into my life. I worked *con amore*, and my edition came out in 1959. I felt then that for the time being I didn't want to have any more to do with Kyd. But in the mid-1960s I was writing a little booklet on 'Early Elizabethan Tragedy' in a British Council series, and I took advantage of that to press the case for Kyd, at the same time putting him more in his historical context. Taking plays from Pickering's *Horestes* to the anonymous *Arden of Feversham*, I spoke of those comparatively rare plays which freed themselves from the moral clichés of the time, especially as regards divine guidance of human affairs. Kyd I paired with Marlowe, two men who were 'writing in one chamber', as writers 'of extraordinary originality'. Kyd, whom I then called, compared with Marlowe, a 'minor writer', had 'by a strange inspiration' produced 'something quite new'. Ignoring Marlowe's concern with the titanic individual, he concentrated in *The Spanish Tragedy* on 'the web of consequence' which Shakespeare was later to exploit in *Romeo and Juliet*: the interweaving of the passions, desires and plans of a number of individuals, the outcome of which had nothing to do with providence or divine guidance. In *The Spanish Tragedy*, our attention is centred (I then said) on Hieronimo's pain as he strives to clear a path for justice in a world too complex for anyone to understand, let alone control.

It was some years before I took up seriously the objection that the outcome of *The Spanish Tragedy* is not in the web of consequence I've been talking about but in the dictates of Destiny, as explained by the figure of Revenge, who is on the stage throughout the play. Both in my 1959 edition and in the British Council booklet it is implied that the whole apparatus of all-controlling Destiny is a farce, but it is only in my lecture of 1985, at Waterloo in Canada, that I tried to explain why.[1]

That lecture concentrated on the supernatural structures of *The Spanish Tragedy*. I emphasised the distance in time between the busy unavailing efforts of the human characters in the sixteenth-century Spain and Portugal, and the overarching supernatural control symbolised by the presence of Andrea's Ghost and the figure of Revenge. Andrea had been killed in the fictional sixteenth-century battle between Spain and Portugal, and his spirit had been transported back through the centuries to a carefully reconstructed Virgilian underworld. Those who judge the dead, Aeacus, Minos and Rhadamanth, could not agree whether Andrea should spend eternity with lovers or with martialists. So they sent him to Pluto, the king of the underworld, for a decision. His wife Proserpine intervenes and begs Pluto that the decision shall be hers. Pluto agrees and, after a certain amount of whispering, Andrea's Ghost is sent back, under the tutelage of Revenge, to witness the doings of the mortals he has left. Specifically, he is to see 'the author of thy death, / Don Balthazar the prince of Portingale, / Depriv'd of life by Bel-imperia' (I.i.87-9). Now, Andrea, who was killed by fortune of the wars and had never asked for revenge against his killer, Balthazar, shows great enthusiasm for this scheme, and is overjoyed at the end of the play to be reunited with Bel-imperia for eternity. It appears that the whole horrifying course of events, the murder of Horatio (Bel-imperia's new lover), the search by the father, Hieronimo, for the killer of his son, the extravagant schemes of Lorenzo to conceal the truth, Hieronimo's play and the murder of Lorenzo and Balthazar, the suicide of Bel-imperia, the grisly death of old Hieronimo, have been engineered to fulfil the whim of Proserpine that the death of Andrea should be avenged by the death of Balthazar. I emphasised that the decree of Proserpine was a mere whim. What is Andrea to her? The Ghost of Andrea is a little optimistic about his clandestine affair with Bel-imperia when he says that 'those infernal powers / [...] will not tolerate a lover's woe' (III.xv.37-8). Is the union in eternity of Andrea and his mistress worth the terrible route by which it is reached?

To balance these pagan infernal powers, who seem to have ultimate and absolute control, Kyd arranged a group of supernal powers, who are Christian. These powers are thanked in routine fashion by the Spanish king, when he learns of his military victory over the Portuguese: 'Then blest be heaven, and guider of the heavens, / From whose fair influence such justice flows' (I.ii.10–11). But Hieronimo, also believing that heaven supports justice, and seeking to know from there who killed his son, says: 'I find the place impregnable' (III.vi.17). Momentarily, Hieronimo appeals to the infernal gods for help, but there is no sign of assistance from Proserpine at Pluto's court (III. xiii.110, 120–1). Convinced that no gods of any kind are interested in helping him, Hieronimo resolves to pursue justice by himself and begins to make his plans. It is particularly interesting that it is just at this moment, when he overhears Bel-imperia castigating him for his inaction and he feels sure of her as an ally in his efforts, he says:

> Why then, I see that heaven applies our drift,
> And all the saints do sit soliciting
> For vengeance on those cursed murderers.
> (IV.i.32–4)

This late conviction, to which I shall return, seems sabotaged when Hieronimo's scheme goes wry with Bel-imperia's suicide, and his own gory death, dragging the unoffending Duke of Castile with him. At any rate, in my 1985 lecture, I was convinced that Kyd's play was, I quote myself, 'a denial of God's care for man',[2] and while it attributed the lethal cross-cancellation of human desires and intentions to Destiny, there was utter meaninglessness in the edicts of that destiny. I spent a good deal of time on Kyd's preoccupation with Seneca's tragedies (which, I argued, Kyd must have read in the original and not in the Christianised English versions available). In Seneca, I said, there was a 'dreadful logic' in the chain of crime from generation to generation. In Kyd, there was no such logic.[3] A careful and determined reading of Seneca might well have concluded that, among all the attempts of his characters to find reason for the awfulness he describes, 'no explaining voice is privileged: nothing is certain concerning the gods but their remoteness, indifference, absence'.[4] Such a reading might be based on the renowned conclusion of Seneca's *Medea*, when Jason shouts after the heroine, as she is borne away in her winged car, 'Testare nullos esse qua veheris, deos!' (V.1027).[5]

If, as I thought back in 1985, *The Spanish Tragedy* was a challenge to conventional ideas about the divine control of human affairs, Kyd's relationship with Marlowe may be seen in a different light. His denunciation of Marlowe may well have been dictated by fear, and was almost certainly the result of torture. The 'atheistical' disputations found among his papers, which he insisted were Marlowe's, might well have been his own. Utterly different in temperament though the two playwrights were, there may have been a real sympathy in their scepticism. And I noted then that there was a third dramatist whose tragedy seemed to take a view of human life not remotely compatible with the Christian view of providence, and that was Shakespeare in his *Titus Andronicus*.

My Waterloo lecture was given in the same year (1985) that saw the publication of my New Cambridge edition of *Hamlet*. In that edition, following a not particularly original course in a sea of guesses, I accepted the view that Shakespeare, around 1600, based his play *Hamlet* on an earlier play which might have been by Kyd. If Kyd wrote the *Ur-Hamlet*, that play probably preceded *The Spanish Tragedy*, and it introduced into the old story of Hamlet a ghost, who, we are told by Thomas Lodge in 1596, 'cried so miserally at ye Theator like anoister-wife, *Hamlet, reuenge*'.[6] I must admit I cherished the idea that at the height of his power Shakespeare was deeply influenced by twin revenge plays written by a dramatist whose view of life he had not despised in his younger days. When Shakespeare rewrote *Hamlet* he needed Kyd; both the *Ur-Hamlet* and *The Spanish Tragedy*. He borrowed from Kyd and he put him right.

He borrowed the ghost, and made that ghost the centre of his play. I have often thought that it was the existence of that ghost in the *Ur-Hamlet*, oyster-wife or not, that has made Shakespeare think of rewriting the play. After Stephen Greenblatt's book *Hamlet in Purgatory*, we can all see that forceful revival of the idea of Purgatory, in whose fires the Ghost of old Hamlet must spend most of his time, revives the link between the living and the dead which the Reformation, with its denial of Purgatory, had seriously harmed and perhaps severed. The use of the ghost does not provide much evidence about Shakespeare's own religious views. The ghost in *Hamlet* is a theatrical image. But that image is compounded of beliefs and ideas inherent in the forbidden doctrine of Purgatory, and Shakespeare's play needed the beliefs which the presence of the ghost conjured up. The presence in arms of the former king of Denmark keeps young Hamlet in touch with his father's values and everything he stood for. The ghost brings the past alive; not only the immediate past, with the circumstances of his wife's adultery and his own murder at Claudius's hand, but the longer past of Denmark wrapped up in the majesty of 'the King that's dead' (*Hamlet*, 1.1.39).[7] All these young Hamlet promises to honour and remember: not only what his ghostly father commissions him to do but also what his father stood for. It seems important that the idea of Purgatory, which brings most sharply into Hamlet's life not only the wishes of the dead but the world lived in by the dead, was by 1600, one might say, a dead letter.[8] This invocation of the past belongs to the past. The doctrine of Purgatory, as the anteroom of eternity where you wait while the crimes of nature are burned away, was a very late Catholic doctrine; it was abominated by proto-protestants for centuries, and, at the time that Shakespeare wrote his *Hamlet*, it had for decades been stamped out in England by the Reformation. Its revival, in the person of the Ghost on the battlements of Elsinore, seems a deliberate atavism.

In that atavism, there is a distinct parallel with *The Spanish Tragedy*, with its dispatch of Andrea from his death on the battlefield of a sixteenth-century Iberia to a Virgilian land of the dead, and the gloomy underground halls of Pluto. The glacial time-gulf between the frame of the story and the story itself, and particularly the casual intervention of Proserpine, seems to me to question the ideas of ultimate destiny at the very time that, with the presence on stage of the figure of Revenge and his constant insistence on the force of Destiny, Kyd calls attention to the continued presence of these ideas. Shakespeare's Ghost in his *Hamlet*, borrowed as I have suggested from Kyd, similarly represents both continuance and obsolescence; an out-of-date doctrine insists that the past is still alive.

Whatever the influence of Kyd there may be in Shakespeare's Ghost, there is no doubt about the parallels between the two dramatists in a major point of the plot in their most famous plays. In the soliloquy at the beginning of III.xiii of *The Spanish Tragedy*, when he enters with a book in his hand and starts with '*Vindicta mihi*', Hieronimo seems convinced that heaven in its own time will bring about the revenge for murder, but just as strongly he asserts his own responsibility for choosing the time and the means by which he himself will exact revenge. And he goes ahead with his plans for the climatic play.

In Shakespeare's play, although Hamlet has (unlike Hieronimo) not found heaven impregnable, he certainly enlarges and alters what seems to be heaven's orders. Most prominently, he passes up the opportunity of taking revenge on Claudius in the 'prayer' scene, and, going straight to his mother, defies the injunction to leave her to heaven, and he does his utmost to convert her. Later, after his return from his adventures at sea, he seems to renounce such individual responsibility when he says that '[w]hen our dear plots do pall', we should accept that '[t]here's a divinity that shapes our ends, / Rough-hew them how we will' (*Hamlet*, 5.2.9, 10–11). All the same, his later questions to Horatio stressed the role of individual decision and individual action once the conviction of divine guidance has been achieved: 'Does it not, think thee, stand me now upon – / [...] is't not perfect conscience / To quit him with this arm?' (*Hamlet*, 5.3.63, 67–8) He therefore accepts the challenge to the fencing match and so he enters the slaughterous confusion which ends the play.

Both Kyd's *The Spanish Tragedy* and Shakespeare's *Hamlet* have the same theme: the responsibility of the individual and the responsibility of the gods in carving out the future. The disastrous ending of both plays suggests that the future belongs neither to the individual nor to the gods. Yet the actual conclusions are so markedly different that we cannot help feeling that the later play, Shakespeare's *Hamlet*, is a comment on the earlier. I refer to the gloating of the Ghost of Andrea at the end of *The Spanish Tragedy*, and the absence of the Ghost of the old king at the end of *Hamlet*.[9]

'Ay, these were spectacles to please my soul' (IV.v.12). So speaks the Ghost of Andrea at the end of *The Spanish Tragedy*, having listed all those who have been killed, including the Duke of Castile, and Bel-imperia and Hieronimo killed by their own hands. But in *Hamlet* nothing follows the funeral procession; the Ghost, who enters in the first act of the play and reappears in the third, is never seen again. It is possible of course, that the Ghost was absent at the conclusion of the *Ur-Hamlet* but, whether Shakespeare is responsible or not for the failure of the Ghost to reappear, his absence is strikingly different from the endorsement of the decree of destiny provided by Andrea at the end of *The Spanish Tragedy*. Kyd surely made a mistake by bringing him on; Andrea's satisfaction at the workings of Destiny goes against the play. The failure of the Ghost of old Hamlet to express his approval or disapproval of the Prince's handling of his command, and the way Claudius died, and not only Claudius but Polonius, Gertrude and Ophelia, leaves the play in the uncertainty which rightly belongs to it, and which rightly belongs also to its predecessor.

The Kyd-trail proper in Shakespeare culminates in *Hamlet*. The Kydean inheritance, if it is only fitfully to be seen so openly in Shakespearean tragedy, was none the less deep and important. Kyd's legacy was less of a form of tragedy of the overweening individual than of the intersecting paths of desires and passions of relatively ordinary individuals; a sort of mutual cancellation or mutilation of intentions. Among the characters there is, in both dramatists, an overwhelming desire to believe in providence, leading to ideas of divine control and guidance of great ingenuity, especially when it comes to explaining the eventual benefits of adversity. These providential schemes may be ironised, sabotaged or even ridiculed. In the face of the apparent lack of transcendental support, the injured individual may be induced to force what he considers to be truth and justice on an unwilling social authority, but his determination ends, both in *Hamlet* and in *The Spanish Tragedy*, only in failure and disaster.

In Shakespearian tragedy as a whole, there is, apart from the Ghost in *Hamlet*, a remarkable absence of supernatural structures. The most obvious of such structures is of course the witches or Weird Sisters in *Macbeth*. They have nothing to do with Kyd. Indeed, *Macbeth* is an anti-Kydian play. Within their tragedies, there is in both Kyd and Shakespeare a latent Manichaeism. Society seems to be a contest between the well-intentioned and ill-intentioned. One is a good person or a bad person. Kyd's Lorenzo, superb villain, is succeeded by such outright villains as Iago and Edmund. As an explanation of why things go wrong in the world, the division into good people and bad people seems crude and facile. Perhaps Shakespeare's discomfort with this classification is shown in his preoccupations with people on the brink between the two, especially in *Macbeth*.

If *Macbeth* seems Manichaeistic, that may be because of the political prudence on Shakespeare's part: what is 'good', and what is a fortunate outcome, tend to be on the English side. But essentially the play is about the growth of evil, like some cancer, within goodness itself. The idea of evil as perverted good is very similar to the Christian idea of the fallen angels. Indistinguishability is the war-cry of the play of *Macbeth*:

> Angels are bright still, though the brightest fell.
> Though all things foul would wear the brows of grace,
> Yet grace must still look so.
>
> (*Macbeth*, 4.3.23–5)

The supernatural structure of the play that I only want to mention here is the provision of the Weird Sisters, the witches who know the future without causing it, and who use their knowledge in order to corrupt and to contaminate. They are utterly baffling. What is the relation of their knowledge to the decision of Banquo and Macbeth? All we know is that the latter two feel that they share their natural life with a supernatural life and that they are led in one direction or another by voices from another world, which they may obey or disregard. The Ghost of Banquo at the dinner reinforces this sense of living both inside and outside time, but it has no metaphysical implications. There is indeed a supernatural structure in *Macbeth*, but it leads nowhere.

It is in the slightly earlier play, *King Lear*, that there is more questioning by the characters about the ultimate control of human affairs, and in that play (which in my opinion Shakespeare never completed to his own satisfaction) there is no supernatural structure at all. But consider the role of Edgar in the play. Dispossessed by the lies and slanders of his half-brother, and hunted to the death by his gullible father, the Earl of Gloucester, who has believed those lies, he strips himself naked and takes on the identity of Poor Tom, one of those beggars who pretend to be escaped lunatics. In disguise of double pretence in 3.4, he convinces the king that he is in fact 'unaccommodated man' (98–9). 'Is man no more than this?' (95–6). Poor Tom invents his past: a servingman who has done 'the act of darkness' (82) with his mistress, one who has lived for sex, and finery, and wine, 'false of heart' and 'bloody of hand' (86). And now is a foul, ragged beggar, haunted and pursued by the foul fiend. In this guise he leads his blinded father, Gloucester, who wants only to end his life by throwing himself off the cliffs at Dover. So we come to the extraordinary farce of the pretended suicide everybody tried to explain. We understand that Edgar had begun to see his mission as that of a saviour of souls; he convinces his father that he (his father) has fallen off the cliffs and yet is still alive. Edgar disguised as Poor Tom now pretends to be a passer-by finding Gloucester at the foot of the cliff. 'Thy life's a miracle' (4.6.55) he says, and he goes on to pretend that he had seen Gloucester's former guide at the top of the cliff, a 'foul fiend' who had led Gloucester to end his life. And now he is saved. 'Therefore', says this mercurial Edgar to his blind father, '[t]hink that the clearest gods [...] / [...] have preserved thee' (72–4). And the bewildered Gloucester forswears despair: 'Henceforth I'll bear / Affliction till it do cry out itself / "Enough, enough," and die' (75–7). Fast-forward to Edgar's final change of disguise when he appears as a knight in armour to challenge his false half-brother Edward. He defeats him and speaks these astonishing words concerning his father's begetting of this illegitimate son:

> My name is Edgar, and thy father's son.
> The gods are just, and of our pleasant vices
> Make instruments to plague us.
> The dark and vicious place where thee he got
> Cost him his eyes.
>
> (*King Lear*, 5.3.168–72)

Shakespeare has made Edgar into a supernatural structure. Edgar has become a superb actor, appearing before his king, then his father, then his half-brother, and has convinced each of them of the way gods control the world. It is all made up, like his disguise. Here is a character who, like Hamlet, is an individual determined to put the world right, and who uses his gift as an actor to express the will of gods as he sees them. All this is scripted by Shakespeare, who does not expect us to believe that Edgar's self-righteous convictions are his own.

It is surely not a very long step from the creation of Edgar to the most elaborate of Shakespeare's supernatural structures which he presented in that extraordinary series of plays at the close of his career, including *Pericles*, *Cymbeline* and *The Tempest*. In *Cymbeline*, Jupiter, the 'king of gods', appears. He, Shakespeare's stage directions instruct in 5.5, '*descends*' to the stage '*sitting upon an eagle. He throws a thunderbolt*', then speaks to his audience, including the sleeping Posthumus:

> Be not with mortal accidents oppressed;
> No care of yours it is; you know 'tis ours.
> Whom best I love, I cross, to make my gift,
> The more delayed, delighted. Be content.
>
> (*Cymbeline*, 5.4.193–6)

In *The Tempest*, it is a mortal man, Prospero, cast up on an island, who has acquired magical powers, who sets up a structure in which the spirit Ariel, in the figure of a harpy, addresses the bad people as the voice of Providence itself. He begins: 'You are three men of sin, whom destiny – / That hath to instrument this lower world / And what is in't' (*The Tempest*, 3.3.53–5). Later in his speech, Ariel says: 'You fools! I and my fellows / Are ministers of fate' (3.3.60–1); afterwards, Prospero (the stage manager) congratulates Ariel on his performance: 'Bravely the figure of this harpy hast thou / Performed, my Ariel; a grace it had, devouring' (83–4).

The last plays of Shakespeare are dream plays, islands of improbable dreams made real by the potency of poetry and the skill of the actor, which, as they move remorselessly towards their happy conclusions, never reveal more clearly that the voice of God is the voice of the dramatist and the actor than when Prospero, offering '[s]ome vanity of mine art' (4.1.41), mimics the divine.

It is a long road from *The Spanish Tragedy* to *The Tempest*, from Proserpine to Prospero, but I believe it is a direct road. Kyd's scepticism lies in the preposterous idea of Destiny which rules in Pluto's caves. The idea of Destiny in *The Spanish Tragedy* is a blind to conceal what the play itself shows, that the future is brought about chiefly by the crossing intentions, desires and actions of individual human beings. Shakespeare's scepticism was nurtured by Kyd. There was an alarming turn in the road when Shakespeare's disbelief in the power of the theatre to enclose within a tragedy the full truth about human destiny was accompanied by an increase of the belief in the power of the theatre to please and console its audience. The latter belief inspires and explains the preposterous providential outcomes of his last plays. The supernatural structures in those last plays may seem to deny and oppose Kyd's scepticism. On the contrary, they support it. The road from Kyd's supernatural structures to those of Shakespeare's has curious bends, but it is in fact direct.

NOTES

1 See Edwards, 'Thrusting Elysium to Hell', pp. 117–32.
2 Edwards, 'Thrusting Elysium to Hell', p. 123.
3 Ibid., p. 119.
4 Ibid., p. 123.
5 'Bear witness, wherever you ride, that there are no gods!' My translation. *Medea, A Tragedy of Seneca*, ed. Charles Beck.
6 Lodge, *VVits miserie*, p. 56.
7 All quotations from plays by William Shakespeare in this book are from the second edition of *The Norton Shakespeare*, gen. ed. S. Greenblatt, and are referenced parenthetically in the text.
8 The continuance of the forbidden old religion and its doctrines in Elizabethan times is described in the early chapters of Richard Wilson's book *Secret Shakespeare*.
9 For more on this subject see my 'Shakespeare and Kyd'.

REFERENCES

Beck, C. (ed.), *Medea, A Tragedy of Seneca* (Cambridge, MA, and Boston: James Munroe, 1834).
Edwards, P., 'Shakespeare and Kyd', in Kenneth Muir, Jay Halio and D. J. Palmer *(eds), Shakespeare, Man of the Theater*: *Proceedings of the Second Congress of the International Shakespeare Association, 1981* (Newark, DE, London and Toronto: University of Delaware Press and Associated University Presses, 1983), pp. 148–54.
Edwards, P., 'Thrusting Elysium to Hell: The originality of *The Spanish Tragedy*', in A. L. Magnusson and C. E. Magee (eds), *The Elizabethan Theatre XI: Papers Given at the International Conference on Elizabethan Theatre Held at the University of Waterloo, Ontario, in July 1985* (Port Credit: P. D. Meany, 1990), pp. 117–32.
Lodge, T., *VVits miserie, and the vvorlds madnesse discouering the deuils incarnat of this age* (London: Printed by Adam Islip, 1596). http://eebo.chadwyck.com [last accessed 30 January 2014].
Shakespeare, W., *The Norton Shakespeare*, gen. ed. S. Greenblatt., 2nd edn (London: W. W. Norton, 2008).
Wilson, R., *Secret Shakespeare* (Manchester: Manchester University Press, 2004).

CHAPTER 2

Enacting revenge: the mingled yarn of Elizabethan tragedy
Jonathan Bate

According to George Puttenham's version of literary history, ancient poetry began with praise of the gods, then proceeded to reprehension of human abuses. The earliest poetry of rebuke was supposedly satire, followed by comedy, and only then tragedy.

For Puttenham, literary genre was a sociological matter. He supposed that primitive ('rude') cultures were essentially egalitarian. Early literary forms were therefore free from sharp social distinctions: men and women of all ranks may be mocked by satire and made to look foolish by comedy. But as civilisation advances, social hierarchies are established. A literary genre is then required specifically for the purpose of rebuking those who are born to, or who achieve, high estate, but whose behaviour is unworthy of their privileged status. The need to knock the mighty off their pedestal gives the new genre its structure: a great man, or occasionally woman, falls from high estate to low. Thus Puttenham writes, in a typically elaborate sentence in the fifteenth chapter of the first book of *The Art of English Poesy*:

> But after that some men among the moe [many] became mighty and famous in the world, soueraignetie and dominion hauing learned them all maner of lusts and licentiousnes of life, by which occasions also their high estates and felicities fell many times into most lowe and lamentable fortunes: whereas before in their great prosperities they were both feared and reuerenced in the highest degree, after their deaths when the posteritie stood no more in dread of them, their infamous life and tyrannies were layd open to all the world, their wickednes reproched, their follies and extreme insolencies derided, and their miserable ends painted out in playes and pageants, to shew the mutabilitie of fortune, and the iust punishment of God in reuenge of a vicious and euill life.[1]

He adds that, in order to walk tall in a manner appropriate to the great princes they were impersonating, the actors in plays of this kind wore leather buskins on their legs and high platform shoes on their feet. Since the buskins and shoes were supposedly made of goats' skin, and since the Greek for a goat is *tragos*, the plays were called *tragedies*.[2]

Puttenham would have read in Horace's *Ars poetica* that Thespis invented tragedy (hence 'thespian') and that Aeschylus was the first to teach the actors to talk big and wear high boots. The ultimate source for his key definition of tragedy as the fall of a person of high estate from good fortune to bad was the *Poetics* of Aristotle. Puttenham regarded Aristotle as the 'prince of philosophers', but his knowledge of the works seems to have been confined to Latin translations of the *Politics* and the *Ethics*. For most educated Elizabethans, Aristotle was a master of political theory and moral philosophy. He was not primarily a literary critic. The Elizabethan version of the *Poetics* was an indirect one.

The classical dramatist most frequently studied at school and university in Elizabethan England was Terence. Most editions of Terence's comedies included not only a prose account of his life but also an essay, ascribed to the fourth-century commentator Aelius Donatus, 'Concerning tragedy and comedy'. In it we find a rigid division of genres: comedies are concerned with private citizens and low life characters, tragedies with monarchs, rulers and heroes; comedies end in reversal for the better (recognition of children, happy marriage), tragedies in reversal for the worse (a mighty fall, a mournful death). As Thomas Heywood put it in part three of his *Apology for Actors* (1612), 'Comedies begin in trouble, and end in peace; Tragedies begin in calmes, and end in tempest'.[3]

This conception of tragedy was consistent with that of the Middle Ages. The absence of secular drama in Chaucer's England did not mean that there was no interest in tragedy. Tragedy may be thought of as a narrative structure rather than a dramatic event. There is a famous definition in the prologue to Chaucer's 'Monk's Tale':

> Tragedie is to seyn a certeyn storie,
> As olde bookes maken us memorie,
> Of hym that stood in greet prosperitee,
> And is yfallen out of heigh degree
> Into myserie, and endeth wrecchedly.[4]

In the high European art of the fourteenth century, tragedy and comedy were defined by their ending. Dante's poem went from Hell through Purgatory to Paradise. Its closing vision of redemption made it a *Divine Comedy*. Boccaccio's hugely influential *De casibus virorum illustrium* was a series of tales of the fall of illustrious men: both the title of the collection and the structure of each story were synonymous with tragedies. The *De casibus* tradition, in which Fortune turns her wheel and a great man tumbles from power, reached the Elizabethans via John Lydgate's *Fall of Princes* (founded on Boccaccio, written in the 1430s, and among the earliest English printed books) and the *Mirror for Magistrates*, in which 'illustrious men', mostly from English history, tell the stories of their own downfall:

> Loe! here (quoth Sorrowe) Princes of Renowne,
> That whilom late on top of Fortunes wheele
> Nowe layde full low, like wretches whurled downe,
> Euen with one frowne that stayede but with a smile,
> And nowe beholde the thinge that thou erewhile,
> Saw only in thought, and what thou now shalt heare
> Recompt the same to Kezar, Kinge, and Peere.[5]

Puttenham's view of tragedy as an admonitory mirror for princes and courtiers remains squarely in this tradition.

The distinctions traceable to Donatus are to be found everywhere in Elizabethan discussions of tragedy. 'The argument of Tragedies', wrote Stephen Gosson in his *Playes confuted in five actions* of 1582, 'is wrath, crueltie, incest, iniurie, murther eyther violent by sworde, or voluntary by poyson. The persons, Gods, Goddesses, furies, fiendes, Kinges, Quenes, and mightie men.'[6] By contrast, 'The ground worke of *Commedies*, is loue, cosenedge, flatterie, bawderie, slye conneighance of whordome. The persons, cookes, queanes, knaues, baudes, parasites, courtezannes, lecherouse olde men, amorous yong men.'[7] Gosson was poacher turned gamekeeper, a sometime playwright who joined the 'Puritan' attack on the stage. His enumeration of the typical content of tragedy and comedy is skewed in support of the argument that the Elizabethan playhouse was a 'school of abuse', a resort for wasters, troublemakers, pickpockets, whores and adulterers.

Gosson and his fellow polemicists were reach-me-down Platonists, crude recyclers of the ancient argument that plays are dangerous to the body-politic because by representing violence and transgression they destabilise propriety and stir up unhealthy emotions. The explicit objection is that, if commoners go to the playhouse and see stage persons breaking the moral law or taking justice into their own hands, they might be encouraged to do the same themselves. The implicit fear is that dramatic representations of the heinous deeds of divinities, monarchs, governors and legal officials (Gosson's 'juries') will diminish the authority of the real-life equivalents of such figures. If the king in the play marries his elder brother's widow and the avenging hero calls the union 'incestuous', what is to prevent such a judgement from leading to an awkward line of inquiry regarding not-so-distant history? Henry VIII married his elder brother's widow, Catherine of Aragon: was the founder of the Church of England therefore an 'incestuous, adulterate beast' (*Hamlet*, 1.5.42)?

It was in defence of the theatre, and in response to Plato's argument in the *Republic* that plays were dangerous and the state would be better off without them, that Aristotle wrote his *Poetics*. The defence was in a sense medicinal: by stirring up strong emotions in the controlled space of the theatre, the drama purges us of extremities and imbalances. Theatre in fact does society a service, providing containment rather than provocation. Thus Aristotle.

Sir Philip Sidney's *Apology for Poetry* was to Puritan anti-stage polemic as Aristotle's *Poetics* was to Platonic anti-theatrical prejudice. Sidney's retort to Gosson is that the properly structured tragedy, far from advocating wrath, cruelty, incest, injury and murder, will deliver a dire warning against the consequences of crime. The revenger gets his comeuppance, the usurper his just deserts. For Sidney, tragedy was a school not of abuse but of virtue. Where the moral philosopher will *tell* you about virtues, vices and passions in the abstract by means of arid classification, the tragic dramatist will *show* you them in action, so that 'we seem not to hear of them, but clearly to see through them'. The drama is an incomparable source of 'familiar insight' about human behaviour:

> Anger the *Stoicks* say, was a short maddesse, let but *Sophocles* bring you *Aiax* on a stage, killing and whipping Sheepe & Oxen, thinking them the Army of Greeks, with theyr Chieftaines *Agamemnon* and *Menelaus,* and tell me if you haue not a more familiar insight into anger, then finding in the Schoolemen his *Genius* and difference. See whether wisdome and temperance in Vlisses and Diomedes, valure *Achilles,* friendship in *Nisus,* and *Eurialus,* euen to an ignoraunt man, carry not an apparent shyning: and contrarily, the remorse of conscience in *Oedipus,* the soone repenting pride in *Agamemnon,* the selfe-deuouring crueltie in his Father *Atreus,* the violence of ambition in the two *Theban* brothers, the sowre-sweetnes of reuenge in *Medaea*.[8]

Sidney has intuited the integral relationship between 'virtues, vices, and passions' on the one hand, and dramatic structure on the other. The height of the hero's vertiginous fall is measured by the wise and good man's steadfast walk along the flat, straight road. The weft of tragedy is Aristotle's change from high estate to low: conscience catches up with Dr Faustus, Queen Tamora's cruelty in *Titus Andronicus* proves self-devouring (literally), revenge for Hieronimo in *The Spanish Tragedy* is sour-sweet. The warp is the constancy of the friend who remains loyal to the fallen hero, or the wise and temperate counsellor who sticks to his course even as his advice is neglected. Marcus Andronicus, for example, and Horatio in *Hamlet* are embodiments of friendship and temperance wrapped together.

For Sidney, the dramatist is superior to the philosopher because a story seen is more memorable than a moral told. And the theatre is superior to the history book because the dramatist can impose order on the chaos of events. Whilst the historian is 'captiued to the trueth of a foolish world' in which the wicked often thrive and the virtuous suffer, the dramatist can show 'virtue exalted and vice punished'. In real life, a tyrant may rule for years, but 'if euill men come to the stage, they euer goe out (as the Tragedie VVriter answered, to one that misliked the shew of such persons) so manacled, as they little animate folkes to followe them'.[9] Sidney is thinking of a famous defence of the tragedian's art reported in one of Plutarch's moral essays:

> For thus it is reported of *Euripides*, that upon a time some reviled *Ixion* & reproched him by the terms of Godlesse, Wicked & Accursed: he answered, True indeed quoth he, and therefore I would not suffer him to be brought from the Stage, before I had set him fast upon the wheele, & broken both his armes & legs.[10]

So might Christopher Marlowe have defended his representations of Tamburlaine the Great, Dr Faustus and Barabas, the rich Jew of Malta, all of whom end with a mighty fall.

Yet with Marlowe (as indeed with Euripides), one suspects that the defence would have been tongue-in-cheek. Sickness falls on Tamburlaine not when he commits one of his many un*christian* acts, such as ordering the slaying of the virgins of Damascus, but when he burns the book which men like Sidney would have regarded as the archetypal heterodox, pagan text – the Qur'an. The extolling of virtue and the punishment of vice provided neither the box-office spice nor the intellectual challenge for the tragedians of the late 1580s and 1590s. The typical English play of the earlier sixteenth century had been the 'interlude' in which an Everyman figure, an embodiment of 'Youth' or 'Worldly Man', would be tempted by a series of alluring emissaries of worldliness – a bearer of the gold of wealth and power, a portly glutton, a seductress oozing lechery – before being rescued from the clutches of these 'vices' by a pious, reasonable voice of 'conscience' or 'wise counsel'. The Elizabethan dramatists celebrated what the Puritan polemicists feared: that what is most memorable about these old plays is not the structure of redemption but the energies of the vice-figures. The audience cannot help but be disappointed at the moment when the Vice is driven out of the play, not least because his exit is the sign that the end of the entertainment is near.

As so often, one of the keys to late Elizabethan creative genius is its combination of native and classical inheritances. Hybridisation is apparent as early as 1567, when John Pyckering's *Horestes* brings 'The Vice' and 'Counsel' together with Clytemnestra and Orestes – and, for good measure, throws in some very English clowns, Hodge and Rusticus.[11] By the time we reach Marlowe and Shakespeare, the main character himself may be a historicised and individualised version of the Vice-figure – Barabas, for example, or Richard III. The Vice's self-conscious play-acting is thus grafted on to the ancient art of making theatre out of the *peripeteia* (reversal of fortune) and *anagnorisis* (self-recognition) of some hero from myth or history.

The problem with pedants and polemicists is that they like neat packages. Donatus parcels comedy and tragedy into different boxes. The Puritan pamphleteers regard dramatic characters as dangerous images of vice, so Sidney has to respond with an equally crude notion of heroic virtue. The dramatist knows, to the contrary, that in real life 'as Euripides saith, / It cannot be in everie point / That good and bad should be disjoint: / But in all actions we dayle see, / One with another medled will be'[12] – or, as Shakespeare's First Lord Dumain puts it, that 'The web of our life is of a mingled yarn, good and ill together' (*All's Well that Ends Well*, 4.3.69–70).

Readings of tragedy that follow from Donatus are simplifications of Aristotle's original treatment of the tragic fall. In the third chapter of the *Poetics*, Aristotle argued that it was not appropriate to represent an altogether virtuous man passing from good fortune to bad, because that would arouse only outrage, not the combination of pity and fear which are the emotions proper to the tragic response. Nor should one represent an altogether wicked man passing from good fortune to bad; there would be a certain satisfaction in his downfall, but neither pity, which we feel for someone who comes to grief without deserving it, nor fear, which we feel when we witness the sufferings of someone like us. It follows, says Aristotle, that the proper subject of tragedy is a person in-between: 'one who is not pre-eminent in moral virtue, who passes to bad fortune not through vice or wickedness, but because of some piece of ignorance [*hamartia*], and who is of high repute and great good fortune, like Oedipus and Thyestes and the splendid men of such families'.[13] For Aristotle, then, the cause of the tragic fall is very specifically *not* vice or wickedness. Oedipus is tragic not because of some moral failing but because he kills his father and marries his mother in ignorance of their identity. Theories of tragedy like Puttenham's embrace the Aristotelian structure – 'the mutability of fortune' – but justify it in the very terms which Aristotle said were *not* tragic: 'wickednes reproched' and 'the iust punishment of God in reuenge of a vicious and euill life'.[14]

Just as sixteenth-century tragic theory was frequently based on a moralistic misreading of Aristotle, so many twentieth-century readings of Elizabethan tragedy were based on a psychological misreading of Aristotle. Granted, Aristotle's theory was more psychological than moral. A principal emphasis in the *Poetics* is indeed the theatre audience's emotional response to tragedy: the play evokes strong feelings – pity, fear, wonder – in such a way that the intensification of emotion allows a release (*catharsis*) from it. But the interest here is the psychology of the audience. Aristotle does not explain the downfall of the tragic hero in psychological terms. Disaster follows from a mistaken action, a deed committed in ignorance of the fact that its consequences will be terrible. It does not follow from an inherent psychological 'flaw' in the hero's nature. For Aristotle, action determines character, not vice-versa. He recognised that drama is gripping when apparently small actions have large consequences. Nothing is more dramatic than a chain reaction. In Shakespeare's *Titus Andronicus*, the Romans perform their customary expiation of the spirits of those who have died in battle by sacrificing the highest-born male among their prisoners of war. Titus overrules Queen Tamora's supplication for her son's life. His ignorance of her cunning and her single-minded determination upon revenge costs his own daughter her chastity, two of his sons their heads and ultimately several others, including himself, their lives.

There is no warrant in either Aristotle or Elizabethan theory for the idea of the 'tragic flaw'. Aristotle's *hamartia* is an action, not a predisposition. Shakespeare's Romeo and Thomas Kyd's Hieronimo were two of the most highly praised creations of Elizabethan tragedy, yet neither has an obvious flaw. How can it be a flaw in Romeo's nature for him to love Juliet, or for Hieronimo to take it upon himself to hunt down his son's murderers once recourse to the proper authorities has failed? The tragedy of *Romeo and Juliet* is triggered not by a moral failing or psychological predisposition but by a tiny misadventure – a letter that does not get delivered.

The term 'Tragedy' as a generic description entered English usage with the Elizabethan translation of the Roman dramatist Seneca. In 1559 there was published *The sixt tragedie of the most graue and prudent author Lucius, Anneus, Seneca, entituled Troas with diuers and sundrye addicions to the same. Newly set forth in Englishe by Jasper Heywood student in Oxonforde*. A year later, *The seconde tragedie of*

Seneca entituled Thyestes was 'faithfully Englished', again by Jasper Heywood. Interestingly, the Stationers' Register entry referred to *Troas* as a 'treate' (i.e., treatise) rather than a tragedy; again, when *The lamentable Tragedy of Oedipus* [...] *out of Seneca* was published in 1563, it was entered in the Register as a 'lamentable history'. This suggests that 'tragedy' was not yet familiar descriptive shorthand for a kind of play. But by the end of the century, that was precisely what it was, as may be seen from Polonius's disquisition on the dramatic genres, in which Seneca is synonymous with a 'heavy' play (*Hamlet*, 2.2.382).

What is a Senecan tragedy like? It is structured in five acts, divided by a Chorus. The action is a reaction to a terrible event that has taken place in the past, of which we may be reminded by a ghost. The central character cannot easily be labelled either a hero or a villain. Usually he or she is called to revenge. But the drama takes place in his head, not on the stage. We hear a lot about blood and cruelty and sensational violence, but always at second hand. This is a drama to be heard or read more than to be seen. The principal interest is verbal – the rhetoric, the verbal figures, the *sententiae*, the set-piece descriptions of the 'Nuntius' (messenger). The play consists of a series of monologues of self-definition, in which the problem of evil is inextricable from the problem of knowledge. Once self-discovery is achieved, death is the only course. Seneca's philosophical essays are meditations on the art of quelling the passions through the power of reason. His tragedies show what happens when passion runs out of control.

The Elizabethan translations of the *Ten Tragedies* of Seneca were collected in a single volume in 1581. In the preface to that volume, Thomas Newton weighed the philosophising against the passion: 'grauity of Philosophicall sentences, more waightynes of sappy words, or greater authority of sound matter beateth down sinne, loose lyfe, dissolute dealinge, and vnbrydled sensuality'.[15] But this is a response to tragedy read, not tragedy seen. In the preface to Greene's *Menaphon*, Thomas Nashe noted that 'English *Seneca* read by Candle-light, yeelds many good sentences [...] and if you intreate him faire in a frosty morning, hee will affoord you whole Hamlets, I should say, handfuls of Tragicall speeches',[16] but he went on to suggest that, having bled Seneca dry for his language, playwrights working for the popular stage would need to look elsewhere – to lurid Italian novellas, for instance – for their dramatic action.

Seneca provided the professional dramatists with structures and *sententiae*. Kyd's *Spanish Tragedy* begins with a Ghost and a personification of Revenge, as *Thyestes* begins with a Ghost and a Fury advocating revenge; Shakespeare quotes a famous appeal to the gods from Seneca's *Hippolytus* (672) in its original Latin: '*Tam lentus audis scelera, tam lentus vides?*' ('are you so slow to hear and see crimes?') in his *Titus Andronicus* (4.1.81). The rhetoric of self-examination in the Elizabethan tragic soliloquy is learnt in part from Senecan man – but only in part, for its flexibility has more in common with the epistolary self-expression of Ovidian woman (the *Heroides*). At its core, popular tragedy was not Senecan. How could it be, when what was required for popularity was not philosophising but action, replete with spectacle and leavened by comedy?

For Sidney there was 'neither decencie, nor discretion', neither 'the admiration & commiseration' proper to tragedy nor the 'right sportfulnes' proper to comedy in the 'mungrell Tragy-comedie' of the contemporary drama. He looked down on the contemporary drama: 'all theyr Playes be neither right Tragedies, nor right Comedies: mingling Kings & Clownes'.[17] Sidney was writing in the early 1580s, perhaps thinking of works like *A Lamentable Tragedy mixed full of Pleasant Mirth, containing the Life of Cambises King of Persia* (1569–70?), 'The Tragecall comodye of Damonde and Pethyas' (Stationers' Register entry, 1571) and 'A new tragicall Comedie' of *Appius and Virginia* (1575). But there is no reason to suppose that Sidney would have thought any better of Kyd, Marlowe and Shakespeare, all notable minglers of king and clown. For Sidney, there was a single exception to the sorry norm. He had seen one play which was 'full of stately speeches, and well sounding Phrases, clym[b]ing to the height of *Seneca* his stile, and as full of notable moralitie, which it doth most delightfully teach; and so obtayne the very end of Poesie'[18] – though his praise was then qualified by the complaint that the play in question did not obey the classical unities of place and time.

The play was *The Tragedy of Gorboduc*, first performed on 6 January 1562 at the Inner Temple and repeated later the same month by royal command before the Queen's own presence at Whitehall. Its proximity to the era of Jasper Heywood's English Seneca is noteworthy. The joint authors, both students of the Inner Temple, were Thomas Norton and Thomas Sackville, both from well-to-do backgrounds (Sackville's father was a first cousin of Anne Boleyn). *Gorboduc* is often described as the first English tragedy. It is certainly the earliest surviving play for performance in the vernacular that resembles a classical tragedy, and the first to be written in the iambic pentameter blank verse that became the medium of the great tragedies of the 1590s and early 1600s. It was frequently revived at the Inner Temple, and was published in 1565 (reprinted c.1570), so was available for imitation. But it had little influence on the public stage.

English Senecan tragedy was written by elite amateur authors for elite courtly or academic audiences. It was something to be read in the closet or heard in a hall (often on the occasion of a banquet), as one would hear a lecture or attend a debate. It was above all concerned with wise policy. Classical tragedy is more concerned with how people react to terrible events than with the events themselves. Revenge is the archetypal theme of tragedy because it is the most drastic reaction to an earlier action. In *Gorboduc*, which is divided into a classical five acts, bloody deeds are symbolically anticipated in a dumb show before each act, then narratorially reconstructed in messenger speeches towards the end of the acts. A moralising Chorus then signals the act closure. The debates that form the bulk of the play are witnessings of the space between – the sowing of the dangerous seed and the reaping of the bloody whirlwind. Tragedy is what happens in the 'interim'. The various counsellors represent externalisations of the choices available to the main characters, and in this sense they are structurally analogous to the vice and virtue figures of the morality tradition. The function of the characters is to convey different positions in the political debate; the human interest of dramatic interaction is merely a consequence of this. The soliloquy as a vehicle of character development is absent.

In the public drama of the 1590s, tragedy is still located in the 'interim', but both the sowing of the seed and the reaping of the whirlwind are seen before our eyes, and the choices facing the protagonists are explored more inwardly, typically through soliloquy. The psychological dimension of the political becomes as important as the political itself. Thus Brutus's version of the 'interim':

> Between the acting of a dreadful thing
> And the first motion, all the interim is
> Like a phantasma or a hideous dream:
> The genius and the mortal instruments
> Are then in counsel, and the state of man,
> Like to a little kingdom, suffers then
> The nature of an insurrection.
>
> (*Julius Caesar*, 2.1.63–9)

Julius Caesar is a dramatisation of the most famous political assassination in history, yet at this moment insurrection is merely a metaphor for the mental turbulence of the individual on a sleepless night before a momentous day.

The professional dramatists of the next generation capitalised on the potential for audience-pleasing spectacle provided by tableaux such as this. George Peele's *The Battle of Alcazar* (c.1589) is a revenge drama in which the action is driven by possibly the first of the Machiavellian Moors of the English drama, 'Muly Mahamet', spiritual father of Aaron in Shakespeare's *Titus Andronicus* and Eleazar in *Lust's Dominion* (c.1600, probably by Thomas Dekker and others). It is also a play which incorporates dumb shows – of *'Three ghosts crying Vindicta* [revenge]', of a bloody banquet, a blazing star and so on – in the prologues to four of its five acts. Once the dumb show had become a still popular but now old-fashioned device, the challenge was to do something new with it. Marlowe and Shakespeare had the answer: to incorporate it in the action of the play itself, rather than keep it apart in the act-divisions. Hamlet stages his own play, complete with dumb show; in *Titus Andronicus*, instead of avenging Furies coming forth from under the stage as though out of hell, we have a character pretending to be Revenge (Tamora in 5.2), and in *Tamburlaine the Great*, instead of mythical kings and queens drawing the chariots of the Furies, we have the conquered kings from within the play drawing the chariot of Tamburlaine himself. In *Gorboduc*, mythological figures are introduced as symbolic representations of ideas (political division, vengeance, unnatural murder) of which the characters are also symbolic representations. In *Tamburlaine* and *Titus*, the characters develop an imaginative life of their own: they take mythic identity upon themselves, making claims which rebound ironically against them: Tamburlaine rises like a god, but falls like Phaethon; Tamora becomes a victim of revenge as well as a perpetrator of it.

The Spanish Tragedy of Thomas Kyd (late 1580s) simultaneously set the pattern for late Elizabethan revenge drama and raised theatrical self-consciousness to a new level of sophistication. Kyd was the first to deploy the device of the 'frame' – an induction, chorus or series of prologues surrounding the action – to its full potential of multivalency and irony. Hieronimo's masque of English conquests is the first surviving instance of a character playing the role of Master of the Revels, and his play in sundry languages is the seminal example of revenge performed through dramatic performance. More broadly, the play is thoroughly suffused with an interest in the resources and semiotic potentialities of theatre (there is, for instance, a profusion of wittily deployed props: box, dagger, rope, book, napkin, pen).

The frame device – we are to imagine the whole action as a performance summoned by Revenge for the edification of the Ghost of Don Andrea – is not without precedent. *The Rare Triumphs of Love and Fortune*, dating from the early 1580s, is framed by a controversy between Venus and Fortune, carried on apart from the characters in the play until the final act, when the two goddesses descend from the 'above' area and influence the action directly. In *The Spanish Tragedy*, on the other hand, the frame is kept rigorously apart from the main action, Revenge and the Ghost functioning as a non-intervening 'Chorus'. Kyd has skilfully combined two Senecan devices: the figure from beyond the grave who initiates the action (most relevantly, the ghost of Tantalus driven on by a Fury at the beginning of the *Thyestes*) and the Chorus that divides the acts and comments on the action. As spectators, Revenge and the Ghost must in some sense function as representatives of the theatre audience. They are not, however, the 'ideal spectators' that A. W. von Schlegel took the chorus of Greek tragedy to be, for they embody the ethic of revenge which the play investigates critically. The audience goes to the theatre having been taught by church and law that revenge is wrong, yet the first encounter they witness is one in which not merely the ethos but the person of Revenge is in charge. By the end of the play, Revenge now performed, the two members of the onstage (or above-stage) audience are well satisfied; their more numerous counterparts in the auditorium will, however, be less certain.

From his debate with himself in III.xiii (book in hand, to revenge or not to revenge, that is the question) to his final acts (foreclosures of communication and revelation – tongue bitten out, penknife used to bring death, not to facilitate writing), Hieronimo is a figure who presents the audience with questions, not answers. Even after the full details of his plot have been explained, he insists that something is being held back: 'But never shalt thou force me to reveal / The thing which I have vow'd inviolate' (IV.iv.187–8). As with Iago's 'Demand me nothing. What you know, you know. / From this time forth I never will speak word' (*Othello*, 5.2.309–10), there is an uncomfortable sense that the end has not revealed all. Andrea is confident that Hieronimo is off to the Elysian Fields, but the offstage audience may not be so sure: one may very well imagine his arrival in Avernus being greeted by precisely the kind of disputation about his disposal between the three judges of the underworld as that concerning Don Andrea with which the play began. The frame sets up a value-structure that is complicated and questioned by the protagonist's anguished quest for justice in the main action.

When Hieronimo stages the tragedy of Soliman and Perseda (which was expanded into a full-length tragedy in its own right),[19] he uses the extraordinary device of having it performed with one character speaking in Latin, another in Greek, a third in Italian and the fourth in French. He deliberately rejects the languages of both his onstage audience (who are Spanish and Portuguese) and his offstage one (the English men and women in the theatre). By writing in a language that no one understands, Kyd makes room for complete concentration on the action. Such concentration is needed because of the dazzling complexity of layers of illusion: in playing the murderer Hieronimo actually commits the murder; stage-daggers actually take the lives of Lorenzo, Balthazar and Bel-imperia. But the moment one says this, one recognises that that is how it looks to the onstage audience, whereas the offstage audience knows perfectly well that Hieronimo, or rather Edward Alleyn or whoever is taking the lead, is only playing the murderer. Then again, since the offstage audience is in a similar position to the onstage audience, in so far as it is baffled by the play of sundry languages, perhaps the knowledge that it is only a play has become an *im*perfect knowledge. As with Hermione's statue in Shakespeare's *The Winter's Tale*, but far more troublingly, the interplay of art and life has become blurred.

That blurring is all-important because it forces the critical gaze to turn from art to life. Hieronimo's playing, central to which is his assumption of the role of madman, has created a kind of total theatre, in which every object, word and action becomes potentially illusory. 'See here my show, look on this spectacle' (IV.iv.89), says mirror on mirror mirrored is all the show. Attention is drawn to the tools of the poetic dramatist's craft – tongue, pen, penknife – but then they are instantly transformed from instruments for the creation of art to instruments for the destruction of life. Earlier, proleptically, there has been a tearing of paper, the artist's other instrument. But the papers in question have been not plays but legal documents presented to Hieronimo in his capacity as Knight Marshal: a declaration of debt, an 'action of the case' requiring a special writ, and an '*ejectione firmae* by a lease' (III.xiii.61–2). In Kyd's total theatre, the law becomes a text, something as vulnerable as an author's foul papers. As the artist is deconstructed by his own instruments, so the law is deconstructed by being reduced to a series of props that are displayed and then evacuated of meaningful content. At one moment there is an onstage execution, but at another the law's final instrument, the hangman's rope, appears not on the gallows but in Hieronimo's hand, from which it is then flung away; as for the law's most merciful instrument, the pardon, it is apparently kept ceremoniously in a box. But the box is never opened and, besides, we know it is empty. Hieronimo, the man of law, fulfils his role as bringer of justice not in legislation or litigation but when he knocks up a curtain.

The public drama progressed by means of bold experimentation and self-conscious playing of this kind. Because of their dazzling theatricality the tragedies of Kyd, Marlowe, Shakespeare and Marston have remained alive in later centuries. Senecan drama, on the other hand, has died with the death of the classics. Even in the sixteenth century, it was largely confined to the media of the elite: performances in the Inns of Court and at court, Latin plays at university, closet drama.

The most distinguished tragedies for reading, or 'closet dramas', of the period emerged from the Pembroke circle in the 1590s. The Countess of Pembroke herself translated the *Marc Antoine* of the French neoclassical dramatist Robert Garnier. The Sidney circle, with their strong commitment to Protestant virtue, were deeply committed to an image of Elizabeth as noble Roman, not sensuous Cleopatra. Samuel Daniel's *Cleopatra* (published 1594), a sequel to his patroness's play, is a further exploration of the potential of erotic passion to bring down a royal line. Fulke Greville, also a member of the Sidney circle, destroyed his own *Antony and Cleopatra* for fear that its representation of a queen and a great soldier 'forsaking Empire to follow sensuality' might be 'construed, or strained to a personating of vices in the present Governors, and government'. On 'seeing the like instance not poetically, but really fashioned in the Earle of *Essex* then falling; and ever till then worthily beloved, both of *Queen,* and people', Greville's own 'second thoughts' were 'to bee carefull'.[20] The need for caution is well demonstrated by the fate of Daniel's second Senecan tragedy, *Philotas*, which concerned a notable soldier and a conspiracy against Alexander the Great: it was written for private performance some years before the fall of Essex, but then staged by the Queen's Revels after the fall, and misconstrued as an allegory of the Essex plot, causing Daniel to be called before the Privy Council to defend himself.[21]

Greville's most celebrated lines of verse occur in one of the choruses in *Mustapha*, one of his two surviving Senecan tragedies (published in 1609, with a date of composition more likely to be early Jacobean than late Elizabethan):

> O wearisome condition of humanity,
> Borne vnder one law, to an other bound,
> Vainely be got, and yet forbidden vanity,
> Created sicke, commanded to be sound:
> What meaneth Nature by these diuers lawes?
>
> ('Chorus Sacerdotum')[22]

The paradox compounded here offers a distinctively Protestant, even Calvinist, version of tragedy: we are begotten and born, we decay and die, under the rule of the body, yet spiritually we are bound to a law which requires the mortification of bodily desire. The sentiment belongs in a closet drama because the paradox can be resolved only through an individual act of faith that is dependent on the work of the private closet: examination of conscience, meditation upon biblical texts and disciplined prayer.

When the paradox of humankind's bodily and spiritual duality is explored on the public stage, it must be enacted visually rather than stated rhetorically as it is by Greville. The two most powerful examples are Marlowe's *Faustus* and Shakespeare's *Hamlet*. Hamlet himself speaks of the duality:

> What a piece of work is a man! How noble in reason, how infinite in faculty, in form and moving how express and admirable, in action how like an angel, in apprehension how like a god – the beauty of the world, the paragon of animals! And yet to me what is this quintessence of dust?
> (*Hamlet*, 2.2.293–8)

Hamlet's public image is that of the versatile 'Renaissance man' who is at once soldier, scholar and courtier. Privately, he struggles to hold together the many pieces of the jigsaw of human being: he finds it difficult to move from 'apprehension' to 'action'. Soliloquising on what Brutus called the 'interim', and in reflecting upon his father's untimely murder and his mother's hasty remarriage, he is unable to sustain his belief in humankind's beauty and admirability. It is only when he faces up to the graveyard and the skull that he is able to accept the mortification of the body, the implication of the words of the funeral service which will be evoked by the entrance, as Hamlet throws down the jester's decayed head, of the cortège of Ophelia: 'we therefore commit [her] body to the ground, earth to earth, ashes to ashes, dust to dust, in sure and certaine hope of resurrection to eternall life, throughe our Lord Jesuse Christe, who shal change our vile body, that it may be lyke to his glorious body, accordyng to the mightie working whereby he is hable to subdue all thinges to himselfe'.[23]

Hamlet is obsessed by the division between words – the medium of noble reasoning, the faculty of admirable expression – and matter, the substance of the body and of action. The play begins from something insubstantial: a moral imperative, a paternal injunction from beyond the grave. The first question to be resolved is whether the Ghost has substance. Hamlet's tragic dilemma is to proceed to something substantial, an act of revenge, without himself becoming the beast which he takes Claudius to be. The dilemma is dramatised by the duality between soliloquy (words, the self) and action (deeds, engagement with others). It is compounded by the play's restless self-consciousness: Lucianus in *The Mousetrap* has no difficulty in proceeding from words to action, but his identity as a player raises the possibility that to perform the action demanded may be to act a performance. Hamlet has an existential problem: he wishes to be himself rather than a role which one might play (the Revenger), but for much of the play he cannot reconcile his wish with the knowledge that to be human means to have a set of social relations (which are especially constrained if one is a prince) and a body that is both desiring (like his mother's) and mortal (like his father's).

Literary genre is a means of structuring experience. As the title of Dante's great poem reminds us, the structure of Christianity is essentially that of comedy: it looks forward to the day of resurrection, when, as 'The Ordre for the Burial of the Deade' puts it, 'our vile body' is sloughed off and we become like to the 'glorious' (eternal, pure, spiritual) body of Jesus Christ. Elizabethan tragedies usually end with piles of bodies being carted off for burial. Elizabethan audiences would be bound to ask themselves which souls among the dead persons of the drama are imagined to be saved. Hamlet and Laertes exchange forgiveness, Laertes dying on a prayer that on the day of judgement he should not be held to account for Hamlet's death nor Hamlet for his and his father's. Ophelia is not mentioned here, for hers – as we learn from the gravediggers' debate about burial rites – was a doubtful case, since suicide meant damnation whereas accidental death left open the possibility of salvation. In his 'To be, or not to be' soliloquy, Hamlet has worried about the hereafter; in his dying speeches, he is more concerned with the manner in which his history is recorded on earth. The audience cannot know his ultimate destination, just as they cannot know their own. In the Protestant worldpicture 'a noble heart' – Horatio's final judgement on his friend – does not guarantee salvation. 'Goodnight, sweet prince, / And flights of angels sing thee to thy rest' (*Hamlet*, 5.2.302–3) is the expression of a hope, not the statement of a fact.

NOTES

1 Puttenham, *The arte of English poesie*, pp. 26–7.
2 Puttenham admits that there were alternative explanations for the denomination: perhaps something to do with the sacrifice of a goat, or the goat was the prize given to the best player.
3 Heywood, 'Of actors and The true vse of their quality', p. 48.
4 Chaucer, *The Canterbury Tales*, lines 1973–7.
5 Sackville, 'Induction', fol. 138.
6 Gosson, *Playes confuted in fiue actions*, p. 49.

7 Ibid., pp. 49–50.
8 Sidney, *An apologie for poetrie*, pp. 24–5.
9 Ibid., pp. 30–1.
10 Plutarch, 'How a young man ought to heare Poets', pp. 24–5.
11 Pickering's source of material regarding Orestes' revenge on Clytemnestra for the murder of Agamemnon was not Greek tragedy or Seneca, but Caxton's *Recuyell of the Historye of Troye* (1468–71), translated from the French Troy narrative of Raoul Le Fèvre, itself partly deriving from a Sicilian's judge's Latin translation of an earlier French work): the appropriation of classical myth into the vernacular traditions meant that hybridisation had a long history before the Elizabethans.
12 Euripides quoted in Plutarch, 'How a young man ought to heare Poets', p. 33.
13 Aristotle, *Poetics*, 1453a, p. 66.
14 Puttenham, *The arte of English poesie*, p. 27.
15 *Seneca his tenne tragedies*, pp. 2–3.
16 Nashe, 'To the Gentlemen Students', p. 5.
17 Sidney, *An apologie for poetrie*, p. 71.
18 Ibid., p. 68.
19 The play was entered in the Stationers' Register in 1592, printed 1599, and is sometimes attributed to Kyd himself.
20 Greville, *The life of the renowned Sr Philip Sidney*, pp. 178–9.
21 See Tipton, 'Caught between "Virtue" and "Memorie"'.
22 Greville, *The Tragedy of Mustapha*, p. 8.
23 'The Ordre for the Burial of the Deade', in *The booke of common prayer*, p. 274.

REFERENCES

Aristotle, *Poetics*, trans. M. E. Hubbard, in *Classical Literary Criticism* (Oxford: Oxford University Press, 1972).
Chaucer, G., *The Canterbury Tales* (London: Penguin Books, 2005).
Daniel, S., *Delia and Rosamond augmented Cleopatra* (London: By James Roberts and Edward Allde for Simon Waterson, 1594). http://eebo.chadwyck.com [last accessed 30 January 2014].
Daniel, S., *The tragedie of Philotas* (London: Printed by Melch. Bradwood for Edw. Blount, 1607). http://eebo.chadwyck.com [last accessed 30 January 2014].
Daniel, S., *The ciuile wars betweene the howses of Lancaster and Yorke corrected and continued by Samuel Daniel* (London: By [Humphrey Lownes for] Simon Watersonne, 1609). http://eebo.chadwyck.com [last accessed 30 January 2014].
Gosson, S., *Playes confuted in fiue actions* (London: Imprinted for Thomas Gosson, 1582). http://eebo.chadwyck.com [last accessed 30 January 2014].
Greville, F., *The Tragedy of Mustapha* (London: Printed [by John Windet] for Nathaniel Butter, 1609). http://eebo.chadwyck.com [last accessed 30 January 2014].

Greville, F., *The life of the renowned Sr Philip Sidney. Written by Sir Fulke Grevil Knight, Lord Brook, a servant to Queen Elizabeth, and his companion & friend.* (London: Printed for Henry Seile, 1651). http://eebo.chadwyck.com [last accessed March 2015].

Heywood, T., 'Of actors and The true vse of their quality', in *An apology for actors. Containing three briefe treatises* (London: Printed by Nicholas Okes, 1612), pp. 48–52. http://eebo.chadwyck.com [last accessed March 2015].

Nashe, T., 'To the Gentlemen Students', in Robert Greene, *Menaphon* (London: Printed by Valentine Simmes for Nicholas Ling., 1599), pp. 1–13. http://eebo.chadwyck.com [last accessed 30 January 2014].

Plutarch, 'How a young man ought to heare Poets: and how he may take profit by reading Poems', in *The philosophie, commonlie called, the morals vvritten by the learned philosopher Plutarch of Chaeronea*, trans. Philemon Holland (London: Printed by Arnold Hatfield, 1603), pp. 17–50. http://eebo.chadwyck.com [last accessed 30 January 2014].

Puttenham, G., *The arte of English poesie* (London: Printed by Richard Field, 1589). http://eebo.chadwyck.com [last accessed 30 January 2014].

Sackville, T., 'Induction', in *The last part of the Mirour for magistrates* (London: Printed by Thomas Marsh, 1578). Fols 130–9. http://eebo.chadwyck.com [last accessed 30 January 2014].

Sackville, T. and T. Norton, *Gorboduc; or Ferrex and Porrex*, ed. I. B. Cauthen (London: Edward Arnold, 1970).

Seneca, *The sixt tragedie of the most graue and prudent author Lucius, Anneus, Seneca, entituled Troas with diuers and sundrye addicions to the same. Newly set forth in Englishe by Jasper Heywood student in Oxonforde* (London: In Fletestrete within Temple barre, by Richard Tottyll, 1559). http://eebo.chadwyck.com [last accessed 30 January 2014].

Seneca, *The seconde tragedie of Seneca entituled Thyestes faithfully Englished by Iasper Heywood fellowe of Alsolne College in Oxforde* (London: In Fletestrete in the hous late Thomas Berthelettes, 1560). http://eebo.chadwyck.com [last accessed 30 January 2014].

Seneca his tenne tragedies, translated into Englysh (London: Imprinted by Thomas Marsh, 1581). http://eebo.chadwyck.com [last accessed March 2015].

Sidney, P., *An apologie for poetrie* (London: Printed [by James Roberts] for Henry Olney, 1595). http://eebo.chadwyck.com [last accessed 30 January 2014].

'The Ordre for the Burial of the Deade', in *The booke of common prayer, and adminystracion of the sacramentes, and other rytes, and ceremonies in the Churche of Englande* (Londini: in officina Edovardi Whitchurche, 1552). http://eebo.chadwyck.com [last accessed 30 January 2014].

Tipton, A., 'Caught between "Virtue" and "Memorie": Providential and political historiography in Samuel Daniel's *The Civil Wars*', *Huntington Library Quarterly* 61:3/4 (1998): 325–41.

CHAPTER 3

Vindicating revenge

Evghenii Musica

The word 'revenge' is said so quickly, it almost seems as if it could not contain more than one root concept and feeling. And so people are still trying to find this root [...] as if all words were not pockets into which now this and now that has been put, and now many things at once!
                                                              Friedrich Nietzsche[1]

It is hard to argue with Nietzsche: despite countless attempts at familiarising ourselves with revenge, we, 'people', are invariably baffled by it. Whether it is the subject of an analytic inquiry, debate or artistic representation, and, particularly, if it is an act to be executed, suffered or investigated, revenge remains particularly unsettling.

Yet, because of its ambiguity, revenge has not lost any of its attraction. That 'people are still trying' to get at its 'root' has been obvious not only in Nietzsche's *Human, All Too Human* but long before and after its publication. What has also been obvious is that revenge's aporetic status, transcending time and cultural differences, is an expression of the more fundamental question of justice, for which we have so far been unable to find a universally satisfying answer. What light can Elizabethan revenge tragedy and Thomas Kyd's *The Spanish Tragedy* in particular shed for us today on the problematic relationship between the two?

The standard approach of civilised modernity to the relationship between revenge and justice conceives of the former as an imperfect means to achieve the latter. Revenge is an individualistic, uncontrollable, malignant and archaic exception while the modern courts of law are universal, well-governed, impartial and, thus, much closer to the idea of justice. Revenge, from this point of view, is a regrettable aberration caused either by a lack of civilisation or by a significant regression from it. The value of Elizabethan revenge tragedy and Thomas Kyd's *The Spanish Tragedy* in particular is in their unique ability to expose universality assumed by law and civilisation at the break of modernity as completely illusory and, thus, as the true problem pertaining to the notion of justice.

This problem does not amount to a simple misperception of one truth as universal instead of another. Facing it in *Human, All Too Human*, Nietzsche shows little patience with 'people' fumbling for answers to universal questions altogether while neglecting their immediate necessities – the 'despised closest things', the 'elementary laws of the body'.[2] Far from banishing universality, however, this focus on the immediate, personal and exceptional, advocated by Nietzsche and evident in tragic theatre, inevitably uncovers the universal – and, particularly, the question of justice – at the very centre of the immediate necessities. There is a moment when every human being becomes aware that satisfaction of even the most elementary, physical need must be legitimated by the surrounding social network, if not by some higher powers. This is what is certainly implied in the famous '*cogito, ergo sum*' formula, for example: it is not just the endowment of the human being with reason but also the opportunity and *right* to exist physically that make the manifestation of reason possible. Thus the distinction between the physical and metaphysical needs, the exceptional and universal, is quickly blurred, all the more so because even the particular ways in which we follow our physical needs are determined as much by their metaphysical circumstances as they are by their material nature.

Nevertheless, precisely because the notion of justice represents an attempt to legitimate life (i.e., articulate and confer the right to exist), insisting, at the same time, on life's absolute value, it remains abstract and paradoxical despite its deep implication in all the most straightforward aspects of existence. Revenge seems to be a natural solution to this paradox, as it prefers to deal in radically concrete, mutual absolutes: 'eye for an eye', etc. However, on a closer look, it seems only the most extreme expression of the paradox in question, for, if we do agree on the absolute value of (individual) life, then we should also agree that this life is irreplaceable in principle and that the 'eye for an eye' rule of judgement is absurd. Although the best justice systems, ancient or modern, have always endeavoured to offer more sophisticated alternatives to this rule, they have remained mired in the initial paradox of having to legitimate something that should, *a priori*, have an absolute value and, therefore, be inviolable. As a result, they are perpetually haunted by the ghost of revenge that seems to be responsible for all the true, radical and fateful decisions. In the early twenty-first century, this topic is as burning as it has ever been, and Thomas Kyd's *The Spanish Tragedy*, with its sophisticated intertextuality – involving the unresolved clashes between life and death, crime and punishment, war and peace, fiction and reality, natural and supernatural – proves extremely relevant.

This relevance is certainly not purely thematic. Rather, it starts with the very form of the play which radically metaphorises justice as theatre and theatre as justice. It is true that both drama and revenge tragedy in particular have, from their ancient roots, tended in this direction. As we know, the ancient Greek theatre was not a purely aesthetic phenomenon but an institution that was inalienable from the intensely litigious life of the polis, and *The Oresteia* of Aeschylus, the classic and revenge tragedy *par excellence*, is a dramatisation of justice as a truly cosmic phenomenon ranging from personal revenge to a trial by jury predicated on the divine as much as on the human character.

One of the earliest attempts at tragedy in English, John Pickering's *History of Horestes* (1567), marks a moment of return to the same plot with its translation of the classical source into a version of the medieval morality play that strives to follow the same progression from crime through revenge to its complex implications. Even though Aeschylus's and Pickering's works are not comparable, the juxtaposition of both in relation to Kyd's later dramaturgical innovations clearly demonstrates that Aeschylus, despite uncovering the irresolvable deadlock of the 'eye for an eye' rule across generations in a combination of uniquely polyvalent verbal and visual imagery (the beacon, the prophecies, the purple carpet, the net, the invisible and visible Erinyes), stops short of erasing the distinction between justice as political rule and theatrical performance. In his case (and, necessarily to a much more limited degree, in Pickering's adaptation of the plot), theatrical presentation of a socio-ethical deadlock works only to enhance the urgency of its problematics and of the proposed solution, namely the necessity to transform the Erinyes ('the angry ones') and the narrow absolutism of revenge that they represent into the Eumenides ('the kindly ones') who will support the democratic trial by jury as the foundation of justice. As many critics have noted, the striking conversion of the Erinyes into Eumenides that does take place in the end of Aeschylus's trilogy seems to resolve all of the vengeful tension of the preceding conflict only in theory or, indeed, theatre. It is precisely this scepticism as to the viability of the conflict solution in a revenge tragedy that the theatre of Thomas Kyd builds on. This theatre does not want to afford the audience the option of stepping outside the theatrical experience in order to evaluate the difference between theatre and justice in reality.

We may see this already in Kyd's choice of the plot in *The Spanish Tragedy*. Unlike the traditional, clearly signposted returns to the classical sources of which Pickering's *Horestes* is a prime example, Kyd chooses to create an original plot that seems to speak directly to the urgent political issues of the day *and* the fashionable interest in classical literature. However, as the wide range of in-depth research has shown, the relation of the play to the contemporary English–Spanish conflict and the classical texts on which Kyd relies is deeply problematic. The 'Spain' and 'Portingale' of *The Spanish Tragedy* are represented very schematically, and Kyd's Virgil and Seneca, instead of supplying a recognisable plot outline, are only borrowed from in an episodic and often puzzling fashion, which resembles more a modern pastiche than a faithful adaptation. Thus, Kyd's audience quickly realises that there is no straightforward way to relate the complex action of the play to any particular source or historical event: it is only by engaging with its bewildering complexity that the way to the historical world can be negotiated.

This task, however, is complicated not just by Kyd's freedom with the sources but, as it was suggested above, by his striking use of the dramatic form. First and foremost, it is evident in the ingenious structure of the conflict that consists of multiple dramatic frames positioned on different levels along two axes. There is the vertical axis which presents the outer frame with the Ghost of Andrea and the figure of Revenge; the main frame with Hieronimo and the other living characters; and the inner frame of the play-within-the-play, *Soliman and Perseda*. Then there is the horizontal axis within the main frame with the relatively parallel revenge plot of the Portuguese court and the noticeably parallel existence of the various segments within the Spanish court vis-à-vis each other (Hieronimo's family and the King's entourage). By arranging the revenge action into such an intricate dramatic structure, Kyd doubles the difficulty of his theme with an extreme emphasis on its theatricality. Thus, it is only logical that revenge is presented not just as a morally ambivalent and legally problematic act but also as a character in his own play.

This is not so innocent an innovation because it does not refer only to a personified theme, as happens in the morality play, but directly to the authorship and meaning of the action. Revenge's outwardly choric role – 'Here sit we down to see the mystery, / And serve for Chorus in this tragedy' (I.i.90–1) – is ironic, given the fact that he sleeps through, at least, Act III. This is certainly because he is the only character on stage who knows in advance how the play is going to end. Moreover, he knows it not just because of some prophetic insight unavailable to mortals but because, as he reassures Andrea at the end of Act I:

> ere we go from hence,
> I'll turn their friendship into fell despite,
> Their love to mortal hate, their day to night,
> Their hope into despair, their peace to war,
> Their joys to pain, their bliss to misery.
>
> (I.v.5–9)³

This refers to the amicable resolution of the Spanish–Portuguese conflict at the beginning of the play which cost Andrea his life and landed his vanquisher, Balthazar the Portuguese prince, in a very cosy imprisonment. Then, after Revenge is roused from his sleep at the end of Act III by an angry Ghost of Andrea, who has been watching in dismay how Balthazar and his Spanish host Lorenzo succeed in their ruinous intrigues against everyone whom Andrea loved and honoured, Revenge gives another reassurance: 'though I sleep, / Yet is my mood soliciting their souls' (III.xv.19–20), referring to the characters in the main action. Finally, at the end of Act IV, Revenge closes the play's action with the most ominous conclusion:

> Then haste we down to meet thy friends and foes,
> To place thy friends in ease, the rest in woes:
> For here though death hath end their misery,
> I'll there begin their endless tragedy.
>
> (IV.v.45–8)

The audience has thus no choice but to conclude that Revenge stands in a direct authorial relationship to the action contained within the plot's main frame.

Nevertheless, Kyd's design is even more intricate. Because he chooses to introduce the Ghost of Andrea and Revenge in a separate and, as it were, timeless action frame with no visible connection to the temporal world, Kyd endows Revenge's authority with such deterministic connotations that seem to reduce the temporal world indeed to a 'mystery' that is only dramatising his 'mood'. Yet we should not forget that Revenge is himself a character in the play and that, in particular, he must be, according to Andrea's opening speech, the executor of 'doom' (I.i.79) that Proserpine specifically chooses for Andrea. In order to understand more precisely the peculiarity of Revenge's position, we should look at Andrea's relationship to the plot.

He opens the play by appearing on stage (presumably in its upper section signifying afterlife), silently accompanied by Revenge. He briefs us on the fact that he is a ghost and on the circumstances of his death 'in the late conflict with Portingale' where his 'valour drew [him] into danger's mouth, / Till life to death made passage through [his] wounds' (I.i.15–17). Later, we gather more from the General in the main plot, to which we, Andrea's Ghost and Revenge are an audience: 'in that conflict was Andrea slain – / Brave man at arms, but weak to Balthazar', the 'Portingales' young prince' (I.ii.71–2, 68). There is no mention of injustice pertaining to the manner of his death either in Andrea's own speech or in the General's. Moreover, Andrea's account of his affair with the Spanish King's niece, Bel-imperia, his death in battle, his journey through the underworld and his presumable return to the temporal world of Spain are presented as a matter both of fact and of bafflement. He appears awed not only by the sheer experience of the world of the dead but particularly by his 'doom' to return and watch what happens in his former world after his death.

As many have noted, Andrea's defeat by Balthazar could hardly be a reasonable pretext for a vengeful return from the underworld: Balthazar was only doing his best to defend himself against a fierce enemy in battle. What is also striking about Andrea's 'doom' is that the regular three judges of the underworld, Minos, Aeacus and Rhadamanth, are in disagreement over it. It is not clear why Andrea could not, for example, divide his time between the 'bounds' of dead 'martialists' and 'lovers' (I.i.61–2) just as he did during his life in Spain – especially given the fact that he finds these bounds located next to each other in the underworld.

Andrea's reception by Pluto and Proserpine, the king and queen of the underworld, is even more enigmatic: after looking at his 'passport', 'fair Proserpine began to smile, / And begg'd that only she might give [his] doom. / Pluto was pleas'd and seal'd it with a kiss' (I.i.77–80). This can only suggest that the royal couple have just stumbled upon a possibility to undo the amicable resolution of the conflict between 'Spain' and 'Portingale' in a very amusing way without providing a shred of justification: as Lorenzo, the scheming nephew of the Spanish king, puts it in reference to his plots, '*E quel che voglio io, nessun lo sa, / Intendo io: quel mi basterà.* [And what I want, no one knows; I understand, and that's enough for me]' (III.iv.87–8).[4] Proserpine happens to know just the right professional, Revenge, to trust with the job, and she certainly shows her royal gratitude to Andrea by letting him enjoy the show instead of sending him back to the underworld's dreary pursuits. In comparison, Lorenzo and Balthazar's reprehensible decision to revenge themselves upon Horatio only because Bel-imperia happens to prefer him to the captured prince does look more justified – each of them has at least a semblance of a motive.

The juxtaposition of Pluto and Proserpine's treatment of Andrea with Lorenzo and Balthazar's treatment of Horatio, Andrea's close friend and son of the magistrate Hieronimo, the central character of the main plot, reveals that Revenge's 'mood' in this play 'solicits' not only the souls of mortals but also, and more crucially, the rulers of the underworld. The only conclusion that we can draw from these observations is that, with Kyd, Revenge turns out to be not so much the executor of a particular 'doom' as the embodiment of justice in principle. There seems to be simply no viable alternative to his influence either in this world or the next. An extraordinary corroboration to this conclusion can be found in Horatio's account of Andrea's death. According to it, Balthazar would have never brought Andrea down single-handedly:

> But wrathful Nemesis, that wicked power,
> Envying at Andrea's praise and worth,
> Cut short his life to end his praise and worth.
> She, she herself, disguis'd in armour's mask
> (As Pallas was before proud Pergamus),
> Brought in a fresh supply of halberdiers,
> Which paunch'd his horse and ding'd him to the ground.
> *Then* young Don Balthazar with ruthless rage,
> Taking advantage of his foe's distress,
> Did finish what his halberdiers begun,
> And left not till Andrea's life was done.
>
> (I.iv.16–26)[5]

If Horatio's imaginative vision here is to be trusted and if Nemesis and Revenge are to be considered avatars of the same power, then Revenge really *is* the author of *The Spanish Tragedy* in the sense that Andrea's death in that battle is the *sine qua non* of the entertainment for Pluto and Proserpine, *as well as* for Andrea's Ghost (and for us, the audience).

Such an interpretation of the above-quoted passage may be far-fetched, but it cannot be too far from the reality of the plot where Revenge is the Alpha and Omega of the action. Even Bel-imperia gives way to her 'second love' for Horatio in order to 'further' her 'revenge' against Balthazar, the murderer of her first love Andrea. (I.iv.66)

Nevertheless, it can certainly be argued that Hieronimo, who represents the earthly justice at the Spanish court, does present a viable alternative to Revenge's omnipotence and, thus, the real dramatic centre of the plot. First of all, as the respected Knight Marshal of Spain, he is motivated by the explicit letter of the law and not the entertainment value of the punishment. His treatment of Pedringano (Lorenzo's hired killer) is exemplary: Hieronimo's judgement is purely retributive, but he is only punishing the unabashed murderer of (as far as he knows) an innocent man (who happens to be another one of Lorenzo's hired killers). As much as he is distraught by the inability to find his son's murderers, it takes a complicated series of clues to reveal to him their identities. By contrast, if he were indeed anything like Revenge in character, he would have started directly by hatching a plot to drown the whole world in blood, for that way he would have certainly killed all the birds with one stone – that is, eliminated the culprits and, together with them, the very world that gave rise to them.

Instead, as many have again noted, during most of the action Hieronimo is concerned not only, and, perhaps, not so much with revenge but with remembrance of his son and the impossibility of bringing him back and undoing the violence done to him. The powerful role of the props in this play – Horatio's body, the arbour where he was slain and hanged, the bloody handkerchief, the scarf, the letters – is to register this painful ambivalence of Hieronimo's memory. To be sure, Hieronimo (unlike his more famous successor on the tragic stage, Hamlet) never quite forgets about the revenge itself and makes a determined progress towards the staging of his play-trap, *Soliman and Perseda*, in which all of his son's murderers are killed. However, to his credit, he remains humane enough to be regretful of Bel-imperia's unnecessary suicide in the process. This is certainly in contrast to the Ghost of Andrea who, in his last appearance, concludes that *all* the deaths he witnessed in the main plot, including Bel-imperia's and even that of Horatio's mother Isabella, distraught by the brutal murder of her son, were, in the end, indeed, 'spectacles to please [his] soul' (IV.v.12).

Nevertheless, for all the poignant humanity of his search for justice, Hieronimo's potential to counterbalance Revenge's point of view and impact on the action is certainly very limited. First of all, there is the irony of the fact that Hieronimo, a court marshal, should be counterbalancing the judges of the underworld and Revenge himself. Given the identity of the retributive justice that they all represent, they should be working together as two branches – physical and metaphysical – of the same executive institution. Yet they are at cross purposes, for, as the only high power present in Kyd's plot, the underworld is certainly directly implicated in the murder of Hieronimo's son. Working towards *Soliman and Perseda*, Hieronimo is thus ironically furthering their agenda, which consists in the identification of justice with entertainment violence – namely, with an 'endless tragedy', as Revenge puts it in the last words of the play (IV.v.48).

The point of deeper irony here is certainly that Hieronimo is not only a Knight Marshal but a known amateur dramatist himself. He certainly shows a sharp appreciation of the court's theatricality when he decides to kill the murderers of his son, once he has ascertained their identities, by means of a play. This is a worthy *revanche* against those who have been trying to manipulate him by playing roles of benevolent superiors. It is also, thus, as others have argued, an effective deconstruction of the theatricality of the law itself which, as Hieronimo discovers, is at best an empty performance of rules which cannot bring back lost lives and, at its worst, an empty performance that can be used to disguise any amount of malignancy. It is already evident in the case of Pedringano's trial, which covertly serves not only Lorenzo's interests of covering up his murder of Horatio but also, ultimately, Revenge's design. The law here is that empty box – or, indeed, Nietzsche's empty 'pocket' of a word – that Lorenzo's 'boy' is holding up, in III.v, while the absurdly hopeful Pedringano is quipping away the last moments of his life at the trial because he thinks that this box contains his royal pardon.

Despite the seemingly liberating political message that such a deconstruction of the law sends to the audience, Kyd's play leaves little ground for optimism precisely because he presents this deconstruction as an intrinsic part of the fascinating entertainment that the infernal powers prepared for themselves. Their dominance in both temporal and timeless worlds remains unchallenged. Kyd's radical deconstruction of the law as cruel, Revenge-driven theatre thus does not imply that, once we become aware of it, we may be able to switch to a different paradigm where, ideally, revenge would entail not the habitual multiplication of crime but the impossible act of total remembrance – that is, an actual physical and moral restoration of the lost, unique and inviolable lives of victims and perpetrators to the pristine state – and, thus, the act of total justice. Instead, Kyd's deconstruction, ending with Revenge's ominous promise of an 'endless tragedy', constitutes an act of total theatre where, even though we may be aware of the fact that we are engaged in a play, we can never know exactly how, which makes our 'tragedy' indeed endless.

At this point, it is worth reminding ourselves again that we are only the audience and *The Spanish Tragedy*, as well as countless other revenge tragedies, is only a figment of human imagination. However, this only shifts the problem without resolving it. Retribution and, more often than not, indiscriminate vengefulness are still an age-proven model of our relationship to the world. In this context, any vindication of revenge – and Revenge in *The Spanish Tragedy* – must indeed remain only 'all too human'.

NOTES

1 Nietzsche, *Human, All Too Human*, p. 159.
2 Ibid., p. 303.
3 My italics.
4 Edwards, note 87–8, p. 62.
5 My italics.

REFERENCES

Nietzsche, F., *Human, All Too Human*, trans. R. J. Hollingdale (Cambridge: Cambridge University Press, 1996).

CHAPTER 4

Gendering revenge in *The Spanish Tragedy* feminine fury and the contagiousness of theatrical passion

Kristine Steenbergh

'For what's a play without a woman in it?' (IV.i.97), asks Hieronimo when the revenge plot of *The Spanish Tragedy* starts to crystallise. Following this cue, interpretations of the play from a gender perspective have tended to focus on its female characters. Since Bel-imperia is the driving force behind the revenge plot, Alison Findlay has convincingly argued that revenge is represented as feminine: '*The Spanish Tragedy* dramatizes the gendered shift from masculine justice to feminine revenge.'[1] According to Findlay, in depicting retribution as feminine the revenge genre taps into fundamental fears about women, fears concerned with their maternal power and agency.[2] The representation of revenge as feminine in the play can also be read, however, in another context than that of ideas about women in the period. As Joan Scott has argued, gendered representations need not always be directly related to power relations between the sexes.[3] This chapter will explore how one of the first revenge tragedies to be performed on the commercial stage employs gender strategies to problematise the theatrical performance of vengefulness.

GENDERBENDING AND REVENGE

The Spanish Tragedy's problematisation of revenge tragedy's move to the commercial theatre is highlighted by a reversal of gender patterns. In *The Spanish Tragedy*, Bel-imperia is represented as a patient and rational avenger, whereas Hieronimo is infected by feminine fury. Women in revenge tragedy tend to fall into two categories, writes Janet Clare in her book on the genre. Firstly, since blood revenge is traditionally a male duty, women's role in revenge is to remain essentially passive.[4] Isabella belongs to this category: she is driven to madness because she has to rely on her husband to take revenge for the death of her son. When she sees her son's ghost beckoning for revenge, the only thing she feels she can do is to curse and attack the tree in which her son was hanged. Eventually she commits suicide. Women of the second category, who do transgress into the male territory of revenge, are represented as out of control and deviant.[5] In *The Spanish Tragedy*, the character of Bel-imperia is clearly an exception to this rule. She is one of the driving forces behind the revenge plot: she decides to use her love for Horatio to further her revenge on the murderers of Don Andrea; writes a letter in her own blood to incite Hieronimo to revenge; and when that has no effect, she lectures him on the necessity to take action:

> For here I swear in sight of heaven and earth,
> Shouldst thou neglect the love thou shouldst retain
> And give it over and devise no more,
> Myself should send their hateful souls to hell,
> That wrought his downfall with extremest death.
>
> (IV.i.25–9)

Finally, Bel-imperia does indeed avenge her lovers' deaths when she kills Balthazar in the climactic play-within-the-play. Despite her major role in the revenge plot, she is never depicted as deviant or out of control. Lorenzo may claim that 'women oft are humorous' (I.iv.105) but his sister does not display any character traits of the overly emotional woman. Balthazar has noticed that 'her reason masters his desire' (II.i.22) and Bel-imperia enjoins herself: 'Well, force perforce, I must constrain myself / To patience' (III.ix.12–13). As Janet Clare writes, she 'retains her wits in a way that Hieronimo does not'.[6] Indeed, it is Hieronimo, rather than Bel-imperia, who is depicted as mad and out of control because of his devotion to the feminine fury of vindictiveness.

Seneca and feminine vindictiveness

In *The Spanish Tragedy*, the supreme judge of Spain abandons faith in the legal system and takes private revenge for the murder of his son. This shift from law to revenge is marked as a transition from the masculine to the feminine gender through the imitation of a female character from Seneca's tragedies. In the scene traditionally identified as the turning point in Hieronimo's trajectory from law to vengeance, he ponders the possibility of revenge while carrying a volume of Seneca's tragedies in his hand:[7]

> *Vindicta mihi!*
> Ay, heaven will be reveng'd of every ill,

Nor will they suffer murder unrepaid:
Then stay, Hieronimo, attend their will,
For mortal men may not appoint their time.
Per scelus semper tutum est sceleribus iter.
Strike, and strike home, where wrong is offer'd thee;
For evils unto ills conductors be,
And death's the worst of resolution: [...]
And to conclude, I will revenge his death!

(III.xiii.1-9, 20)

Critics have been puzzled by the use of lines from Seneca in this soliloquy.[8] The expression *'vindicta mihi'* ('revenge is mine') suggests that the desperate father has decided to appropriate the right to revenge. Frederick Boas glosses the words as deriving from Seneca's *Octavia*, where they are indeed used in this sense.[9] As a biblical passage, however, God's words 'vengeance is mine' serve to mark revenge as a divine prerogative, thus prohibiting its appropriation by an individual.[10] Hieronimo indeed interprets the quotation in this biblical sense when he adds that 'heaven will be reveng'd of every ill' and 'mortal men may not appoint their time' (III.xiii.2, 5). The soliloquy soon leaves behind this biblical prohibition of revenge, however, and unequivocally turns to Seneca's tragedies. The shift from patriarchal legal authority to feminine passionate vindictiveness is emphasised by contrasting the Bible with a quotation from a furiously vengeful female character. Hieronimo reads from the book in his hand: *'per scelus semper tutum est sceleribus iter'*. These words, an (incorrect) quotation of Clytemnestra's words in Seneca's tragedy *Agamemnon* (line 115) could be translated as 'the safe way for crime is through further crimes'.[11] They mark the moment when Clytemnestra devotes herself fully to her passions. Her desire to take revenge on her husband is driven by her illicit love for Aegisthus, her fears for Agamemnon's reprisal and her jealousy of Agamemnon's mistress Cassandra, as well as her anger over Agamemnon's sacrifice of their daughter Iphigenia. In the sixteenth-century English translation her passions are rendered as intensely physical phenomena:

> So grievous is my careful case which plungeth me so sore,
> That deale I cannot with delay, nor linger any more.
> The flashing flames and furious force of fiery fervent heate,
> Outraging in my boyling brest, my burning bones doth beate:
> It suckes the sappy marrow out the juice it does convay,
> It frets, it teares, it rents, it gnaws, my guttes and gall away.
> Now feble feare stil egges mee on (with dolor beyng prest)
> And cankred hate with thwacking thumpes doth bounce upon my brest.[12]

Like Stephen Greenblatt, we might ask what happens when a text is taken out of one context and appropriated by another: '[w]hose interests are served by the borrowing? And is there a larger cultural text produced by the exchange?'[13] Clytemnestra's words can be said to have made more than one move in early modern culture: they were translated from the Latin, adapted into neo-Senecan tragedies in the Inns of Court and then found their way on to the commercial stage. An analysis of the travels of this borrowed phrase from a vindictive female character reveals the uses to which feminine fury has been put in these different institutional contexts.

One of the main channels through which the works of Seneca were fed into early modern culture was the dramatic tradition of the Inns of Court, London's law school. It was in this institutional context that the first translations and adaptations of Seneca's tragedies in early modern England were written and performed. In 1581, Thomas Newton published a volume of ten tragedies in English, most of which had been translated during the 1560s.[14] Jessica Winston has shown the extent to which these translators were connected to, and even members of, the Inns of Court.[15] Adaptations of Seneca's tragedies were also performed in the great halls of the Inns during festivities. Among these tragedies are *Gorboduc, or Ferrex and Porrex* (1562), written by Inner Temple members Thomas Norton and Thomas Sackville, and *The Misfortunes of Arthur* (1588), a collaborative product of members of Gray's Inn including the future prosecutor of the Star Chamber, Francis Bacon. In both *Gorboduc* and *The Misfortunes of Arthur*, the Inns of Court playwrights draw on Seneca's tragedies to represent private revenge as a feminine vice. They appropriate the vindictive rhetoric of female characters such as Medea and Clytemnestra, and merge these Senecan representations of feminine fury with characters from English national history, such as Guinevere (based on Clytemnestra) and Queen Videna (based on Medea). Not only do elements from these characters' lives resemble those of their classical counterparts, they also often cite Medea's and Clytemnestra's words from the Latin plays.

The sudden popularity of revenge tragedies in the commercial theatres has often been related to the English state's attempts to eradicate traditions of revenge in society. As Deborah Willis writes, '[r]evenge plays became popular in England at a time when Protestant reformers and state authorities were energetically denouncing the private revenges of aristocratic clans and "brawling" at all social levels, while seeking to expand a centralized legal system'.[16] The fact that the roots of English revenge tragedy lie in an institution located at the centre of this expanding centralised legal system is therefore extremely significant, and has not been sufficiently examined. The Inns of Court trained students in the legal profession, providing the professionals necessary to sustain the growing legal system. Lincoln's Inn, Gray's Inn, the Middle Temple and the Inner Temple functioned as the main gateways to a career in common law and also trained many of the country's future governors and administrators.[17] These Inns had a vested interest in subduing the practice of private revenge among the aristocracy.

The Inns of Court plays consistently relate women's vindictiveness to internecine murders and the outbreak of civil war in England. In *Gorboduc*, Queen Videna's fatal revenge on her own son is paralleled to the outbreak of a destructive civil war reminiscent of the Wars of the Roses. In *The Misfortunes of Arthur*, Queen Videna's vindictiveness towards her husband finds continuance in the rebellion of King Arthur's son, which similarly results in a civil war. Thus, these Inns of Court tragedies forged an association in the political unconscious between private revenge, feminine fury and civil war. In these plays, performed in one of the central institutions of the law, revenge is represented not as an instrument of male aristocratic honour but as an uncontrolled feminine passion that undermines the stability of the state. The translators and adaptors of Senecan tragedy thus used a gendered strategy to invest their work with a warning about the volatile nature of vindictiveness. By introducing this discourse of revenge and vindictive fury into early modern culture, however, the Inns created possibilities of appropriation that lay outside their control.

READING PIECEMEAL

Some feared that the introduction of Senecan tragedy into English culture might cause immorality. In his dedication of the volume of ten translated tragedies (1581), Thomas Newton writes that:

> it is by some squeymish Areopagites surmyzed, that the readinge of these Tragedies, being enterlarded with many Phrases and sentences, literally tending [...] sometyme to the mayntenaunce of cruelty, now and then to the approbation of incontinencie, and here and there to the ratification of tyranny, cannot be digested without great daunger of infection.[18]

The term 'Areopagite' locates these critics in the legal sphere, since it refers to a member of the court of Areopagus: a hill in Athens where the highest judicial court of the city held its sessions. Some members of the legal circuit, then, worried that phrases and sentences from Seneca taken out of their context might lead to cruelty, a lack of self-restraint or tyranny, which in the 1580s could mean 'violent or lawless action'.[19] The passage casts this danger in expressly physical terms. The work of Seneca is 'interlarded' with these sentences, as if it were a meal with streaks of dangerous fat in it – a meal that cannot be 'digested' without danger of 'infection'.

Hieronimo, in citing Clytemnestra, eats only the fat of Seneca's works and is in serious risk of indigestion. His method of reading was not uncommon in the Renaissance, however. Kevin Sharpe studied the reading habits of Sir William Drake and concluded that early modern reading was an active, non-linear process, in which readers collected fragments of the texts they read in a commonplace book under subject headings of their own devising.[20] Indeed, Drake himself formulates this idea in his notes, using a similar metaphor of digestion:

> The meat which we have taken, so long as it swimmeth whole in our stomachs, is a burden, but when it changeth from that which it was, then at length it turns into strength and nourishment. The same let us do in our reading books. Let us not suffer these things to remain entire which we have gathered from various authors for they will not then be ours, but let us endeavour to digest and concoct them – otherwise they will fill the memory and leave the understanding void and empty.[21]

Thomas Newton's solution to the danger of infection, that one need only 'mark and consider the circumstances, why, where and by what manner of persons such sentences are pronounced',[22] will not work in the face of these eclectic early modern reading habits which refuse to swallow a volume in its entirety, but select phrases to be used for the reader's own purposes.

Whereas the Inns of Court employed Seneca's revenge tragedies to represent private, feminine revenge as passionate, uncontrollable and therefore to be avoided, Hieronimo explicitly does not use his collection of Seneca's tragedies as a reminder of the dangers of vindictiveness. *The Spanish Tragedy* does not adopt the moralistic plot of the Inns of Court plays, but uses only those elements suitable for its own purposes.[23] Clytemnestra's lines serve to counter a biblical prohibition of private revenge, presenting Christian and classical images of retribution as conflicting rather than mutually reinforcing.

Hieronimo reads Seneca piecemeal and uses Clytemnestra's words for his own purpose. Indeed, he interprets them as a call to revenge: 'Strike, strike home, where wrong is offer'd thee' (III.xiii.7). Scott McMillin has argued that this passage has 'nothing to do with revenge, and wrenching [it] to prove the case for vengeance seems to be a piece of desperate logic'.[24] I would argue, however, that it is

Hieronimo who wrenches the passage, in accordance with the early modern reading habits described above. He uses the passage to reach his own conclusion – 'I will revenge his death' (III.xiii.20) – but also to transport himself into the state of mind required to perform the act of revenge. In order to act, the avenger must pass beyond the rational world: passion must consume his entire being.[25] The quoted phrase helps Hieronimo to leave behind the masculine law and to become a passionate, feminine avenger. Reading in the early modern period was thought to have immediate physical effects and could incite intense passions.[26] Reading from Seneca's plays, indeed, has such an effect on the Knight Marshal. Although he decided to be wise in his revenge, '[d]issembling quiet in unquietness' (III.xiii.30) and – like Bel-imperia – enjoined 'heart to patience, and [his] hands to rest' (III.xiii.42), his desire for revenge overturns this rational resolve. He announces he will go to the underworld 'in this passion' to get 'a troop of Furies and tormenting hags' (III.xiii.109, 112).

In using the words of a female avenger to incite his own vindictiveness, Hieronimo sets a tradition in early modern revenge tragedy.[27] When Shakespeare's Titus Andronicus changes from a Roman general into a passionate private avenger, he compares himself to Progne, a character from Ovid's *Metamorphoses*. He tells Tamora's sons: 'For worse than Philomel you used my daughter, / And worse than Progne I will be revenged' (5.2.193–4). In *Antonio's Revenge* (1600), Marston's avenger imitates Hieronimo when he enters with a book in his hand. From it, Antonio reads Seneca's *De providentia*, which tells him stoically to endure with fortitude, to control his passions with reason.[28] He also cites a passage from Seneca's *Medea* which enjoins precisely the contrary: Medea mocks her nurse's counsel of patience, speaking of a grief so overwhelming that it cannot tolerate rational advice.[29] Antonio's reaction copies Medea's:

ALBERTO: Nay, sweet, be comforted, take counsel and—
ANTONIO: Alberto, peace! That grief is wanton-sick
          Whose stomach can digest and brook the diet
          Of stale ill-relished counsel. Pigmy cares
          Can shelter under patience' shield, but giant griefs
          Will burst all cover.
                              (*Antonio's Revenge*, II.iii.2–6)

Stressing the uncontrollability as well as the bodily nature of passion, this quotation of the lines of a vindictive female character from classical tragedy marks the moment at which the protagonist gives way to his voracious desire for revenge. In Shakespeare's *Hamlet*, the performance of Hecuba's grief (who was known in early modern England for the combination of passionate grief and triumphant revenge in the Latin and Greek literary tradition) is one of the spurs to revenge.[30] In these examples, as in *The Spanish Tragedy*, classical feminine vindictiveness serves as an inspiration and a model for the protagonists. Like the invocation of the Furies, the performance of the words of female avengers prepares the protagonists for their vindictive acts, making them lose their sense of self as well as their reason.[31] The feminine fury of Seneca's women is indeed, as the men of law in Newton's dedication feared, greatly contagious.

PERFORMING FEMININE FURY

Thomas Nashe famously remarked upon the way in which the commercial stage ransacked the English translations of Seneca for its own purposes: 'English *Seneca* read by candlelight yields many good sentences, as *blood is a beggar*, and so forth. And if you entreat him fair in a frosty morning, he will afford you whole *Hamlet*s, I should say handfuls of tragical speeches.'[32] Again, it is the borrowing of isolated sentences and rhetorical tricks that invites censure. Kyd's *The Spanish Tragedy* shows itself to be very much aware of the dangers of appropriating the Senecan tradition for the commercial stage. As the first surviving revenge tragedy to be performed in the commercial theatres,[33] *The Spanish Tragedy* problematises the performance of feminine vindictive passion outside its original context of the English legal institutions of the Inns of Court.

If the reading of individual lines from Seneca was cause for anxiety with representatives of the law, the performance of elements from his plays out of context probably was even more so. Tanya Pollard has argued that the heated debates about the theatre in early modern England centred on the power of the theatre to bring about both physical and mental change. 'Literary language, especially when spoken aloud, was understood to be directly linked with the imagination and to have special rhetorical properties, taking on a synesthetic power to transform the body', she writes.[34] The performance of feminine fury could, thus, spill over into reality, creating material effects both in the actor and the spectator.

In *The Spanish Tragedy*, Hieronimo attempts to put Balthazar's mind at rest by reminding him of the classical precedents for the acting of tragedies: 'Why, Nero thought it no disparagement, / And kings and emperors have ta'en delight / To make experience of their wits in plays!' (IV.i.87–9). That the acting of Roman 'kings and emperors' need not be reassuring is signalled by Thomas Heywood in his *An Apology for Actors*. Although postdating the play by more than two decades, Heywood's defence of the theatre recounts an anecdote about an acting emperor that might have been known to the audience of *The Spanish Tragedy*. He relates how a Roman emperor once played the role of Hercules in Seneca's *Hercules Furens*. During the performance, he became so engrossed in his part, that Hercules's fury overwhelmed his reason:

> Being in the depth of a passion, one of his seruants (as his part then fell out) presenting *Lychas* [the tyrant] [...] [Caesar] in the middest of his torture and fury [...] although he was, as our Tragedians use, but seemingly to kill him by some false imagined wound, yet was *Caesar* so extremely carried away with the violence of *Hercules*, to which he had fashioned all his active spirits, that he slew him dead at his foot, & after swung him *terq; quaterq;* (as the Poet sayes) about his head.[35]

The emperor is so carried away by the anger he impersonates that he kills in reality where he should only have pretended to murder. Interestingly, in Seneca's *Hercules Furens* – the play which is probably being performed in this anecdote – the eponymous hero similarly kills people unintentionally in a fury. Driven to madness by the vindictive goddess Juno, Hercules thinks he is fighting the tyrant Lychas when he mistakenly kills his own family. As in Seneca's play, the transgression of the boundaries of fiction is here caused by passion: Caesar had 'fashioned all his active spirits' to the performance of Hercules's anger. His body was so engrossed in the role of the furious classical hero that his mind was 'extremely carried away' with the illusion.

Passion is at the heart of early modern theories of acting. In order to move his audience, the actor needs to experience the desired passion himself and then send it out into the theatre. 'Thus we moue, because by the passion thus we are mooued, and as it has wrought in vs, so it ought to worke in you' is what Thomas Wright imagines an actor saying to his audience.[36] The danger, however, is that the performed passion takes over the actor's body and mind, and makes him lose control. The actor 'toys with enormous forces that he can evoke quickly but not easily subdue. For this reason imagination was both powerful and dangerous. [It] fuels the most excessively violent passions, the ones actors are, by nature of dramatic literature, most frequently called upon to depict.'[37]

Hieronimo's mad fury, incited by his quotation of Clytemnestra, leads to similar confusions of fiction and reality. The Additions of 1602 in particular stress Hieronimo's madness and the fluid boundaries between fiction and reality. In the added Painter's scene, the

Knight Marshal instructs the Painter to depict the moment at which he finds his son's body in the arbour. He tells him:

> Let the clouds scowl, make the moon dark, the stars extinct, the winds blowing, the bells tolling, the owl shrieking, the toads croaking, the minutes jarring, and the clock striking twelve. [...] There you may show a passion, there you may show a passion. [...] Make me curse, make me rave, make me cry, make me mad, make me well again, make me curse hell, invocate heaven, and in the end, leave me in a trance – and so forth. ('Painter scene', 147–61)[38]

Hieronimo asks the Painter to recreate the moment of discovery on that tragic night. The atmosphere of scowling clouds and croaking toads is intended to feed Hieronimo's passion: he wishes to be depicted as cursing, raving and crying to reach a state of suspension, a trance in which he is both mad and 'well again' – the proper mood to perform deeds of revenge. The requested painting, like the quotation of Clytemnestra's words, brings Hieronimo into a state of passion: the painting is a '*memento vindictae*, whose purpose is to incite the viewer to action'.[39] By bringing him back to the moment of the discovery of his son's murder, the painting gives Hieronimo the energy to perform revenge: like theatre, a painting can evoke vindictive passion in its viewers. When the Painter asks him how this will end, Hieronimo orders him: 'bring me to one of the murderers, were he as strong as Hector, thus would I tear and drag him up and down' ('Painter scene', 167–9). As the stage direction suggests, he attacks the Painter as he speaks these words, bringing the proposed image to life by acting it out. As after his quotation of Clytemnestra, when Hieronimo rages 'Then will I rent and tear them thus and thus' (III.xiii.122), the conditional and the actual, the artistic fictional rendering and reality, are blurred by vindictive fury.

The 1615 edition, subtitled 'Hieronimo is mad againe', carries an engraving which reproduces the described painting on its title page, once more blurring the boundaries between illusion and reality. Thus, the quarto edition presents its readers with the painting commissioned by Hieronimo to remind him of his duty to avenge the death of his son. Like him, they can recreate the moment of discovery and experience the Knight Marshal's passions.

VINDICTIVE FURY IN THE COMMERCIAL THEATRE

The performance of vindictive passion on the stage, like the engraving, was thought to affect the audience. Hieronimo's performance of feminine fury could not only affect the actor performing his role, it could also infect the audience. In the plays of the Inns of Court, this potential of infection was contained by a moralistic plot, as Thomas Newton advocates in his Introduction. On the commercial stage, elements of the Inns of Court plays are used outside of their original context. Like Hieronimo's piecemeal reading of Seneca's works, *The Spanish Tragedy* as a whole appropriates those elements from the Inns of Court tradition it can use for its own purposes.

The Spanish Tragedy makes explicit reference to the origins of the genre of revenge tragedy in legal institutions: before he became Knight Marshal of Spain, Hieronimo was once a student of law in Toledo.[40] He resembles the men of the Inns of Court: as Spain's Knight Marshal, he occupies an important position in the rising professional class. Katharine Eisaman Maus sees 'allegorised in the struggle between Lorenzo and Hieronimo the conflict between an old-fashioned aristocratic esteem for inherited status and a new emphasis on the intellectual and practical accomplishments demanded by the recently centralised Tudor bureaucracy'.[41] The Knight Marshal's social position thus echoes that of the Inns of Court men rather than that of the feuding aristocrats they sought to control.

At the Toledo legal faculty, a tradition of writing and performing plays similar to that of the Inns of Court apparently existed, because Hieronimo confesses that 'When in Toledo there I studied, / It was my chance to write a tragedy' (IV.i.77–8).[42] Like the tragedies of the London schools of law, the play was performed within this legal institution, by and before law students: 'It was determined to have been acted / By gentlemen and scholars too, / Such as could tell what to speak' (IV.i.101–3). Also like the Inns of Court plays, Hieronimo's tragedy combined the theme of revenge with native history. The subject matter of *Soliman and Perseda* was found in '[t]he chronicles of Spain' (IV.i.108). Moreover, like the tragedies of the Inns of Court, the play features a woman who takes revenge. That is where the comparison stops, however. Instead of imprinting on its audience the destructive nature of private retribution, the play is itself the vehicle of revenge in *The Spanish Tragedy*. Transplanted from its legal context, the play Hieronimo wrote when he was training in the law has come to serve the purpose of private vengeance.[43]

In the play-within-the play, as in the tragedy as a whole, the gender roles of the Inns of Court plays are reversed. Perseda stabs Balthazar/ Soliman out of revenge for his murder of her beloved Erasto, but does so in a way that cautiously remains within feminine gender boundaries. She acknowledges that she should obey the authority of the tyrant, yet stabs him with the following words: '*And to thy power Perseda doth obey: / But were she able, thus she would revenge / Thy treacheries on* thee, ignoble prince' (IV.iv.64–6). Her use of the subjunctive indicates that Perseda is aware of the limits of her power, but also signals the blurring of performance and reality that characterises *Soliman and Perseda*.[44] The suggestion seems to be that, once the revenge tragedy is taken out of its legal context and is no longer performed before an audience of judges and law students, the performance of revenge threatens to bleed into real life.

In the case of the murdered Roman servant discussed above, Heywood attempts to contain the blurring of performance and life by adding that emperors habitually used convicted criminals to play the role of their victims. These tragedies were therefore 'naturally performed' – the killings were expressions of the authority of the emperor.[45] Early modern revenge tragedy had no such institutional framework to fall back on, however, and early modern anti-theatrical authors worried about this. I. G., for example, objects that theatres, in appropriating the genre of revenge tragedy, also seize the authority to judge: 'Players assume an unlawfull office to themselues,' he writes. The theatre, in his view, transgresses on the authority of the church as well as the law: 'God only gave authority of publique instruction and correction [...] to his Ecclesiasticall Ministers, and temporal Magistrates: he never instituted a third authority of Players'.[46] Like the private avengers that feature on their stages, the theatres cross the line between public and private justice in their representation of right and wrong. For whereas a court of law can engage its authority to ensure good behaviour, the stage has no means to control its audience: 'Players haue no authority in their enterludes: they haue no law to cause men to fly that which is euill and to follow that which is good'.[47]

An important factor in these concerns over the performance of revenge is the composition of the audiences in the commercial theatres. Whereas the Inns of Court performed their plays for the higher classes and the educated – judges, government officials, Elizabeth's court – the commercial theatres staged their plays for anyone who could afford the entrance fee. The mixed composition of these audiences was a cause for concern:

> At Stage Plaies [...] the worste sorte of people haue the hearing of it, which in respecte of there ignorance, of there ficklenes, and of there furie, are not to bee committed in place of iudgement. A Judge must be graue, sober, discrete, wise, well exercised in cases of gouernement. Which qualities are neuer founde in the baser sort.[48]

The lower classes were thought incapable of judging a play on the basis of reason. The discourse of passionate femininity generated

Like Hieronimo who thinks he sees his son in an old man in court and asks him '[a]rt thou come, Horatio, from the depth, / To ask for justice in this upper earth?' (III.xiii.133–4), the gentlewoman in Brathwait's anecdote thinks she sees Hieronimo before her, and is driven to madness by her identification with him. Brathwait relates this gentlewoman's madness once again to the question of 'the lawfulnesse of Stage-playes': contagious feminine fury is seen as a reason to doubt the legality of the commercial theatres.

CONCLUSION

The Spanish Tragedy engages with the Inns of Court tradition of neo-Senecan revenge tragedy and its representation of feminine vindictive fury. A volume of Seneca's plays is carried on to the stage and Hieronimo explicitly mentions that he wrote his climactic play-within-the-play as a student of law in Toledo, in similar circumstances in which the Inns of Court plays were written. As some members of the legal profession feared, phrases from Seneca's plays could be quoted out of context to achieve an effect opposite to the intentions of their translators and adaptors in the Inns of Court. Hieronimo lets the Senecan rhetoric of a female character work in him to inspire the fury that he needs to commit wild justice. The image of feminine, passionate revenge that the Inns of Court sought to propagate as a counter-discourse to the masculine representations of the duty of revenge among the aristocracy is troubled in *The Spanish Tragedy*, where a male judge cites a female vindictive character, and a female avenger behaves in a masculine, controlled and rational manner.

The oldest surviving revenge tragedy performed on the public stage problematises the move of the genre from the legal institutions into the public arena. The vindictive feminine fury shaped in Inns of Court tragedies with the purpose to support the expanding legal system leaks into the commercial theatre and there 'infects' the lower classes and female members of the audience. Such anti-theatrical ideas were to haunt the performance of vindictive passion in the commercial theatres until they were, ironically, closed by the outbreak of a nationwide civil war – the very thing the Inns of Court saw as the inevitable outcome of feminine vindictive fury in their Senecan tragedies.

NOTES

1. Findlay, *Feminist Perspective*, p. 57.
2. Ibid., p. 49.
3. Scott, 'Gender'.
4. Clare, *Revenge Tragedies*, p. 115.
5. Ibid., p. 118.
6. Ibid., p. 120.
7. See Erne, *Beyond*, pp. 109–10.
8. See McMillin, 'Book of Seneca', p. 201.
9. Boas, *Works*, p. 408. For an overview of other Senecan elements in the play, see Kyd, *Spanish Tragedy*, ed. Boas, p. xvii; Erne, *Beyond*, pp. 67 and 80; and Clare, *Revenge tragedies*, p. 26.
10. The words derive from Romans 12:19.
11. My translation.
12. Newton, ed., *Seneca*, vol. 2, p. 107.
13. Greenblatt, *Shakespearean Negotiations*, p. 95.
14. The authors and the translations collected in *Seneca His Tenne Tragedies* are: Jasper Heywood, *Troas* [*i.e.* Troades] (1559), *Thyestes* (1560) and *Hercules Furens* (1561); Alexander Neville, *Œdipus* (1563); Thomas Nuce, *Octavia* (1566); John Studley, *Agamemnon* (1566), *Medea* (1566), *Hercules Œtæus* (1566) and *Hippolytus* [*i.e.* Phaedra] (1567); Thomas Newton, *Thebais* [*i.e.* Phœnissæ] (1581).
15. See Winston, 'Seneca in early Elizabethan England', p. 33.
16. Willis, 'Gnawing vulture', p. 23. For a contrary view, see Steven Mullaney, who argues that Elizabethan society was 'most emphatically not a revenge culture in any sociologically defensible sense of the phrase', in 'Affective technologies', p. 83.
17. Prest, *Inns of Court*, p. 39. See also Raffield, *Images and Cultures of Law*, p. 66.
18. Newton, ed., *Seneca*, vol. 1, pp. 4–5.
19. *OED* tyranny, *n.* 3b.
20. See Sharpe, *Reading Revolutions*, passim.
21. Drake quoted in Sharpe, *Reading Revolutions*, p. 182. Sharpe notes that Ben Jonson used the same metaphor (182, n. 95).
22. Newton, *Seneca*, vol. 1, p. 5.
23. William West in 'Confusions' has read *The Spanish Tragedy* as signalling a new protocol of dramaturgy in which meaning is not contained by the plot structure, but confusion is actively cultivated.
24. McMillin, 'Book of Seneca', p. 202.
25. Hallett and Hallett, *Revenger's Madness*, p. 62.
26. Craik, *Reading Sensations*, passim.
27. Lynn Enterline in *Shakespeare's Schoolroom* argues that such metatheatrical moments in which male characters imitate the emotions of classical female characters derive from and react to the authors' experiences in grammar school.

28 Marston, *Antonio's Revenge*, II.iii.45.
29 Seneca, *Medea*, lines 155–6: '*Levis est dolor qui capere consilium potest / et clepere sese; magna non latitant mala*' ('Light is the grief which can take counsel and hide itself; great ills lie not in hiding', Miller, *Seneca's Tragedies*, vol. 1, p. 241).
30 Pollard, 'What's Hecuba to Shakespeare', p. 1064 and *passim*.
31 McMillin, 'The Book of Seneca', argues that the Senecan quotations in Hieronimo's soliloquy all refer to this idea of losing oneself in revenge. See also Findlay, who views this loss of the masculine self from a psychoanalytic perspective (*Feminist Perspective*, pp. 61–3).
32 Greene, *Menaphon*, pp. 85–6. Nashe implicates Thomas Kyd in this practice of lending sentences and speeches from the English translations of Seneca when he accuses 'noverints' of this practice of borrowing.
33 See Erne, *Beyond*, pp. 95–6.
34 Pollard, *Drugs and Theater*, p. 16. On the effects of performed emotion on an audience, see also Roach, *Player's Passion*, pp. 23–57; Smith, 'E/loco/com/motion'; Rowe, 'Minds in company'; Mullaney, 'Affective technologies'.
35 Heywood, *Apology*, sig. E3v. Heywood proceeds to cite lines IV.i.87–9 from Kyd's *The Spanish Tragedy* as evidence. The phrase, in full 'terque et quaterque', translates as 'again and again'.
36 Wright, *Passions*, sig. M8v.
37 Roach, *Player's Passion*, p. 47.
38 *Fourth Addition* (between III.xii and III.xiii, pp. 132–3).
39 Tassi, 'Player's Passion', p. 91.
40 For the role of Spanish universities in the growing Spanish legal system, see Kagan, *Students and Society*, esp. p. 70.
41 Maus, 'Machiavel's Revenge', p. 91.
42 See Shapiro, who also states that Hieronimo's play becomes subversive in its new context ('Tragedies naturally performed', p. 101), and Erne, who thinks this argument is dubious because Hieronimo is probably inventing this story of the origins of his play (*Beyond The Spanish Tragedy*, p. 114, n. 29). Whether Hieronimo invents it or not, the play's supposed origins in a legal institution are brought to the fore in the play, and therefore must be part of its analysis.
43 Maus writes that Hieronimo 'infiltrates' the genre of the court masque 'in order to turn it against itself' (Maus, 'Machiavel's Revenge', p. 100). I would suggest that, similarly, he uses the dramatic tradition of revenge tragedy of the Inns of Court in order to turn it against itself.
44 See also Findlay, *Feminist Perspective*, pp. 59–60.
45 Heywood, *Apology*, sig. E3v.
46 I. G., *A Refutation*, sig. H2r.
47 Ibid.
48 Ibid., sig. C8v.
49 Wright, *Passions*, sig. M7v.
50 William Prynne, *Histrio-mastix* (London, 1633 [1632]), sigs Xxx3r–v.

51 Brathwait, *English Gentleman*, p. 195.
52 Gurr, *Playgoing*, p. 168.
53 See Erne, *Beyond*, pp. 67–8.
54 Shapiro, 'Tragedies naturally performed', pp. 107, 109.
55 May, *The Heir*, quoted in Tassi, 'Player's passion', p. 81. I am indebted to Tassi's article for bringing this quotation to my attention.

REFERENCES

Boas, F. S. (ed.), *The Works of Thomas Kyd* (Oxford: Clarendon Press, [1901] 1962).
Brathwait, R., *The English Gentleman* (Amsterdam: Theatrum Orbis Terrarum, [1630] 1975).
Clare, J., *Revenge Tragedies of the Renaissance* (Tavistock: Northcote House Publishers, 2006).
Craik, K., *Reading Sensations in Early Modern England* (Basingstoke: Palgrave Macmillan, 2007).
Enterline, L., *Shakespeare's Schoolroom: Rhetoric, Discipline, Emotion* (Philadelphia: University of Pennsylvania Press, 2012), especially chapter 5.
Erne, L., *Beyond the Spanish Tragedy: A Study of the Works of Thomas Kyd* (Manchester: Manchester University Press, 2001).
Findlay, A., *A Feminist Perspective on Renaissance Drama* (Oxford: Blackwell, 1999).
G., I., *A Refutation of the Apology for Actors* [1615], in *'An Apology for Actors' by Thomas Heywood; 'A Refutation of "The Apology for Actors" by I. G.'* (New York and London: Garland Publishing, 1973).
Greenblatt, S., *Shakespearean Negotiations* (Oxford: Oxford University Press, 1988).
Greene, R., *Menaphon*, ed. Brenda Cantar (Ottawa: Dovehouse Editions, [1589] 1996).
Gurr, Andrew, *Playgoing in Shakespeare's London* (Cambridge: Cambridge University Press, 2004).
Hallett C. and E. Hallett, *The Revenger's Madness: A Study of Revenge Tragedy Motifs* (Lincoln, NE: University of Nebraska Press, 1980).
Heywood, T., *An Apology for Actors*, 1612, STC 13309.
Kagan, R. L., *Students and Society in Early Modern Spain* (Baltimore: Johns Hopkins University Press, 1974).
Marston, J., *Antonio's Revenge*, ed. W. R. Gair (Manchester and Baltimore: Manchester University Press and Johns Hopkins University Press, 1978).
Maus, K. Eisaman, 'The Spanish Tragedy, or, The Machiavel's Revenge', in S. Simkin (ed.), *Revenge Tragedy* (Basingstoke: Palgrave Macmillan, 2001), pp. 88–106.
McMillin, S., 'The Book of Seneca in *The Spanish Tragedy*', *Studies in English Literature, 1500–1900* 14:2 (1974): 201–8.
Miller, F. J., trans., *Seneca's Tragedies*, 2 vols (London: William Heinemann; Cambridge, MA: Harvard University Press, 1938).

Mullaney, S., 'Affective technologies: Toward an emotional logic of the Elizabethan stage', in M. Floyd-Wilson and G. A. Sullivan, Jr (eds), *Environment and Embodiment in Early Modern England* (Basingstoke: Palgrave Macmillan, 2007), 71–89.
Newton, T., (ed.), *Seneca His Tenne Tragedies* [1581] (London: Constable; New York: Alfred A. Knopf, 1927).
Pollard, T., *Drugs and Theater in Early Modern England* (Oxford: Oxford University Press, 2005).
Pollard, T., 'What's Hecuba to Shakespeare', *Renaissance Quarterly* 65:4 (2012): 1060–93.
Prest, W. R., *The Inns of Court under Elizabeth I and the Early Stuarts 1590–1640* (London: Longman, 1972).
Prynne, M., *Histrio-mastix. The players scourge, or, actors tragaedie, divided into two parts. By William Prynne, an vtter-barrester of Lincolnes Inne* (London: Printed by E[dward] A[llde, Augustine Mathewes, Thomas Cotes] and W[illiam] I[ones] for Michael Sparke, 1633 [1632]).
Raffield, P., *Images and Cultures of Law in Early Modern England: Justice and Political Power, 1558–1660* (Cambridge: Cambridge University Press, 2004).
Roach, J. R., *The Player's Passion: Studies in the Science of Acting* (Ann Arbor: University of Michigan Press, 1993).
Rowe, K., 'Minds in company: Shakespearean tragic emotions', in *A Companion to Shakespeare's Works, vol. 1: The Tragedies* (Oxford: Blackwell, 2003), pp. 47–72.
Scott, J. W., 'Gender: A useful category of historical analysis', *The American Historical Review* 91:5 (1986): 1053–75.
Shapiro, J., 'Tragedies naturally performed: Kyd's representation of violence, *The Spanish Tragedy* (1587)', in D. S. Kastan and P. Stallybrass (eds), *Staging the Renaissance* (London: Routledge, 1991).
Sharpe, K., *Reading Revolutions: The Politics of Reading in Early Modern England* (New Haven, CT: Yale University Press, 2000).
Smith, B. R., 'E/loco/com/motion', in P. Holland and S. Orgel (eds), *From Script to Stage in Early Modern England* (Basingstoke: Palgrave Macmillan, 2004), pp. 131–50.
Steenbergh, K., 'Wild justice: The dynamics of gender and revenge in early modern English drama', PhD dissertation, Utrecht University, 2007.
Tassi, M. A., 'The Player's Passion and the Elizabethan painting trope: A study of the Painter Addition to Kyd's *The Spanish Tragedy*', *Explorations in Renaissance Culture* 26:1 (2000): 73–100.
West, W. N., '"But this will be a mere confusion": Real and represented confusions on the Elizabethan stage', *Theatre Journal* 60:2 (2008): 217–33.
Willis, D., 'The gnawing vulture: Revenge, trauma theory and *Titus Andronicus*', *Shakespeare Quarterly* 53:1 (2002): 21–51.
Winston, J., 'Seneca in early Elizabethan England', *Renaissance Quarterly* 59:1 (2006): 29–58.
Wright, T., *The Passions of the Minde in Generall*, 1604, STC 26040.

PART II

The Spanish Tragedy in print

CHAPTER 5

'Undoing Kyd':
The texts of *The Spanish Tragedy*

Simon Barker

This chapter arises from the work Hilary Hinds and I undertook in preparing the text of *The Spanish Tragedy* for our jointly edited book, *The Routledge Anthology of Renaissance Drama*.¹ Later I shall address some of the challenges and difficulties of editing Kyd's play for an anthology of the kind that we assembled, so it is worthwhile making some opening remarks about how the project came into being and the general conditions and methods that applied to its production. These point to an important factor of our work on *The Spanish Tragedy*, one that makes me doubt my credibility in terms of being included in the present volume alongside such eminent Kyd scholars. The fact is that our edition of *The Spanish Tragedy* came about not by our own desire to present yet another edition of this particular play to the world but by a kind of ballot arranged by our publishers.

I should explain that *The Routledge Anthology of Renaissance Drama* was a publishing venture based on economic hardship. I hasten to add that the hardship to which I refer was not our own (as editors), but that of our students. We had both lamented the paucity of serviceable and attractively priced anthologies of Renaissance drama. Before meeting Hilary Hinds (we were appointed within months of each other to what is now the University of Gloucestershire) I had at an earlier institution found myself having to ask students to purchase several volumes of non-Shakespearian early modern drama. These plays were to be studied alongside Shakespeare texts on one unit, and form the basis of a more specialised non-Shakespearian optional unit elsewhere. This was in the last years of the twentieth century when universities began to change the constituency of their students, the numbers on courses, their funding regimes (particularly for libraries); and it was when we heard the first rumblings of the idea of students as our 'customers'. It was, of course, before the internet took hold, a phenomenon which has undoubtedly addressed some of the problems we then faced with the availability of texts, since the most obscure early modern play can often now be accessed with a couple of clicks.

Faced with the choice between asking students to spend their money on several individual volumes, despite the attractiveness of these with their comprehensive introductions and full editorial and bibliographical apparatuses, I searched for a long time for a usable anthology, eventually coming across M. L. Wine's *Drama of the English Renaissance*, which contained many of the plays that ended up in our anthology, including *The Spanish Tragedy*.[2] But this volume, edited in 1969, proved hard to come by, having to be imported from the USA, and had so little in the way of scholarly apparatus that it was the antithesis of the separate edited texts that our students were constrained to buy. Hilary Hinds and I thus embarked on a project that addressed students' pockets as well as their intellectual requirements in the field of non-Shakespearian late Tudor and early Stuart drama. The idea was to find some 'middle way' between a simple compendium of raw texts and the literally more weighty versions that students had hitherto to obtain. Our publishers inevitably framed what we considered a gap in students' needs as a 'gap in the market', giving some support to T. H. Howard Hill's gloomy remarks on developments in the field of non-Shakespearian editing:[3]

> The elevation of standards of execution and expectation for scholarly editions is accompanied by the reluctance of publishers to support scholarly enterprises from which the expectation of profit is small. Although editions of early plays other than Shakespeare's are not now regarded as commercial prospects and the costs of their preparation have been transferred from publishers to academically supported scholars, the texts of scholarly editions have increased in complexity. Despite what benefits computers may have brought to photocomposition, production costs are high. But the market for scholarly editions is small, largely confined to universities. There is consequently an urgent need for editors to devise acceptable means to accommodate scholarly standards to the discipline of the marketplace.[4]

Our helpful and enthusiastic publishers were far from the cool-eyed profit-orientated creatures Howard Hill conjures; Routledge, through Talia Rodgers and Liz Thompson, supported the project both in spirit and financially. Yet financial constraints there had to be, thinking again about our students' pockets, and these did affect editorial decisions along the way.

In negotiation with Routledge it was decided that the content of the volume would be determined by a species of questionnaire issued by the publisher to the academics on their contact lists in universities in Britain and Ireland, the USA, Canada and further afield. A description of the project was issued along with a request for selections of individual plays that these colleagues would most like to see in such a volume. I recall Talia Rodgers describing the complex matrix of responses as 'mind-boggling' with respect to the diversity of texts mentioned, but also in terms of the individual rationales that usually accompanied the incoming lists. Once digested, however, the survey seemed a revealing document in itself, happily mixing genres, and covering the period (with Thomas Kyd at the beginning and John Ford towards its end), but excluding some of the better known plays of the period in what seemed a surprising way. In the end, the anthology featured the following plays:

Thomas Kyd, *The Spanish Tragedy*
Anon., *Arden of Faversham*
Christopher Marlowe, *Edward II*
Thomas Heywood, *A Woman Killed with Kindness*
Elizabeth Cary, *The Tragedy of Mariam*
Ben Jonson, *The Masque of Blackness*
Francis Beaumont, *The Knight of the Burning Pestle*
Ben Jonson, *Epicoene, or the Silent Woman*
Thomas Middleton and Thomas Dekker, *The Roaring Girl*
Thomas Middleton and William Rowley, *The Changeling*
John Ford, *'Tis Pity She's a Whore*

Whilst it is tempting to see the result as some kind of conspiracy between Jonson and Middleton scholars to secure a place for their men, the list is of interest for these diverse rationales. Many of those involved seemed to want to promote plays with a particular concern with gender and the domestic: powerful dramas to do with sexuality and power. *The Tragedy of Mariam*, one of the most anthologised and re-edited texts of the last decade, is an unsurprising presence; but the absence of, say, *Doctor Faustus* or *The Duchess of Malfi* is rather more arresting. The respondents had made the point that these plays were so readily available second-hand that to include them in the proposed anthology would have been a waste of space. Thus, by a curious process that involved a long tradition of syllabus planning, earlier aesthetic judgements, publishers' lists, students' impoverishment and performance, *The Routledge Anthology of Renaissance Drama* came to include works that were sometimes at the edge of the canon but central to many teachers' interests.

The Spanish Tragedy, however, and for whatever reason, proved a recurring choice for those responding to the questionnaire. Back in the early days of the century, it would seem that this preference presaged the resurgence of interest in the work of Thomas Kyd, exemplified by the very successful conference held at the University of Warwick, the emergence of the present volume and new individual editions of *The Spanish Tragedy*. Some of our respondents drew attention to a clear paradox concerned with the relationship of Kyd to Shakespeare's work in general and *Hamlet* in particular. Not forgetting speculation over the *Ur-Hamlet*, the play is often cited as a kind of forerunner to *Hamlet*, and in that relationship lies both its importance and its marginality. Students are sometimes surprised to discover what they see as traces of Shakespeare's play in this earlier one (rather than vice-versa), thus maintaining the hold Shakespeare has on their imagination as an original mind. Attempts to dislodge this hierarchy by indicating complex borrowings between Renaissance writers of all kinds, not to mention the direct borrowings Shakespeare makes from Christopher Marlowe, are of little avail. *The Spanish Tragedy* is therefore at once elevated as a kind of source for Shakespeare, but simultaneously demoted as a poor effort, which clearly needed Shakespeare's improvements. Having said this, students do respond well to *The Spanish Tragedy* and, as editors of an anthology that has been reprinted many times and is enjoying increasing sales, those responding to the Routledge questionnaire were wise in recommending its inclusion in the volume.

Students enjoy reading the play for many reasons but these undoubtedly include its quasi-Gothic atmosphere, the grim humour, the unsubtle violence and the accessibility of Kyd's verse when compared with other plays of the period. It also appeals because of the way in which it makes such full use of the range of theatrical devices and staging opportunities available in the Elizabethan popular theatre. It is a play that requires the reader to 'block' the imagined action carefully throughout, not least because of the continual presence – somewhere or other – of Revenge and the Ghost of Andrea; our footnote described the effect of this presence thus:

> The audience is told in advance the substance of the drama to come, importantly affecting its response to and judgement of the unfolding events. Revenge and Don Andrea remain on view throughout the play, often in a location somehow 'between' the action and the audience (downstage or in a gallery), their presence almost mediating the developing action upon which they comment as a chorus.[5]

The Spanish Tragedy requires the reader to disengage from the familiar narrative codes of the modern world at a number of different levels. It is not unusual to find students dependent upon preconceptions of early modern drama (and particularly Shakespeare) that are based on linear plots of revelation and character that *The Spanish Tragedy* simply defies. The audience, like Revenge and Don Andrea, await not the naming of the guilty but their disclosure and punishment – although the play does benefit from sufficient suspense and surprise to make its plot appealingly unpredictable at many points.

There are two other areas that make the play important for contemporary students. One concerns the sheer range of ethical problems and contradictions that the play foregrounds, and these are set in the context of a theological collision between the brilliantly visual classical underworld to which Don Andrea has been led and the Christian world of Thomas Kyd, one which was itself in violent crisis over matters of authority and justice. What the modern world has sometimes spoken of as 'grand narratives' (belief in the late medieval church, the divine person of the monarch and the singularity of European and near Eastern culture) are under scrutiny in *The Spanish Tragedy* and the evolving dramatic genres that it stood at the head of, the genres which the anthology tried to represent. It is not unusual to find some students in seminars seeing a resonance in a modern world where there is sometimes little faith in the instruments of government or faith, and still less in the potential of political movements that will answer Hieronimo's central dilemma: how does a good person find justice in a bad world?

The other aspect of *The Spanish Tragedy* that made it a suitable text to open the sequence of plays that made up the anthology is that it introduces so many concerns that are to be found in the later plays. Although never formally discussed by Hilary Hinds and myself as its editors (as far as I can recall) there is a general sense, and occasionally a concrete reminder in the overall editorial apparatus of the volume, that the reader should have read the plays as a sequence. This is probably not the way in which the anthology is actually used in the classroom, but it is a fact that many editorial decisions were based upon an understanding that a reader of the later plays, such as *The Changeling* and *'Tis Pity She's a Whore*, would have already learned much from reading *The Spanish Tragedy* and its notes of explanation, just as they should have gained something from the introduction to the volume and the accompanying Chronology of English Culture and Society 1558–1642.[6]

The volume's introduction gave a broad account of the scope and extent of the subject matter of late Elizabethan and early seventeenth-century drama with an emphasis upon the theatre as one institution among many that were either rapidly evolving or had their entire origins in the period. In this way, readers were reminded that although the Elizabethan public playhouse was an innovation, some of its mechanics and concerns were drawn from classical and medieval forms of dramatic representation. Similarly, 'institutions' such as the family, the state and the church were described as in flux (transformed from earlier models), yet recognisable as the precursors of the world of the early twenty-first century. Examples were given from the plays and other written texts to support this institutional context, and the emphasis was upon the context of ideas in the period, played out on the stage with the theatre as a kind of moral, political and psychological laboratory for the testing of various alternatives. An attempt was made to describe the plays as exciting and difficult, rather than to soothe the reader with idealist claptrap about the historical period being a Golden Age of literature. There was little editorial comment on the aesthetic appeal of the group of plays being introduced other than this sheer acknowledgement of their eloquence as vehicles for the ideas of the time, although an enthusiasm for this idea itself pays tribute to the craft of the playwright and his or her work. We were very aware, as editors, of the weight of our responsibility in producing such a framing introduction and in particular the inevitable pitfall of a kind of 'History of the (early modern) World'; and yet editors, and there are some, who bypass 'the world' on their way down a narrow path of textual niceties do little service to playwrights who clearly bore that world on their shoulders. That said, we were anxious not to give the impression that textual variants, compositors' errors, source materials, glossaries and editorial decisions were to be overlooked. Neither did we want our interpretation of the plays – hinted at in the overall introduction and the subsequent introductions to individual plays – should stand alone without giving the reader an account of the vast quantity of high-quality interpretative and contextual material available to date. Although it was immediately *out-of-date*, we offered our readers our recommendations for further reading under the following headings and subheadings:

Drama Criticism
    Drama and society
    Genre studies
    Gender, sexuality and the body
    Drama and the early modern 'other'
    Surveys and essay collections
    Histories of drama and the theatre

Histories: Social, Political and Cultural
  Surveys
  Social status
  Family and marriage
  Gender relations, sexuality and the body
  Travel, colonialism and the early modern 'other'
  Religion and the church
  Politics, monarchy and government
  Sourcebooks
Journals
Websites

The volume also had its own website, to which I shall return later as it became important with respect to one very major editorial decision that was made about *The Spanish Tragedy*. In terms of further reading, context and help the book spoke of its website thus:

> This anthology has its own website. It includes a range of early modern documents selected for their relevance to the plays included in the volume. There are, for example, source texts for some of the plays, accounts of early modern theatres and play-goers, and examples of some of the attacks on and defences of the theatres made at the time. The site also provides links which will help readers undertaking further research into the drama of the English Renaissance. Visit The Renaissance Anthology of Renaissance Drama website at www.Routledge.com./textbooks/0415187346.[7]

The website therefore functions as a gateway through which the reader can pass in order to access a significant realm of electronic research materials and journals, as well as (inevitably) other volumes of interest published by Routledge, which they may wish to buy. Although there has been some updating of links and other adjustments, the website requires revision, in readiness for a new edition.

If in the course of the editorial process we received generous and enthusiastic support from colleagues at Routledge, there was also a constant (but friendly) tension about the volume's length. It would have been entirely possible, in exchange for lengthening it, to have sacrificed some of the volume's material quality by having it printed on lighter paper. Equally, we could have reduced the number of plays, but not the overall word-count, allowing a much longer introduction and more in the book of the kind of material that was banished to the website. At stake then, in the triangulation between cost (and therefore purchase price) and length and quality – since the bare text of the plays remained fairly static – was the amount of editorial support we could include in terms of the overall introduction and chronology, the introductions to the individual plays and, most crucially, the footnotes. The 'exception to the rule', in terms of the relatively static nature of the word-count of the texts was, of course, *The Spanish Tragedy* – and the 'Additions' loomed over the editorial procedure for this particular play.

The original concept for the volume's main introduction became a victim of the process of weighing length against costs, eventually becoming a mere shadow of what had been envisaged. Even more so, in balancing the book against 'the books' we were as economical as possible with the introductory material for each of the eleven plays. For each text the reader would find a kind of mini-essay followed by a 'textual note' and an indication of 'further reading', including other editions (single and anthologized) and 'critical and contextual reading'. We tried to range across alternative editions so that readers could themselves, as we had done, look at the history of the editing process. In the case of *The Spanish Tragedy* we cited *The Works of Thomas Kyd* edited by F. S. Boas in 1901, and seven other editions, including that edited by Arthur F. Kinney in his *Renaissance Drama: An Anthology of Plays and Entertainments* of 1999.[8] Similarly, we wanted to offer the reader as full a range as possible of critical and contextual reading, although the emphasis was squarely on that produced in the second half of the twentieth century. We had hoped to annotate these lists in order to steer readers to each critic's main concerns or theoretical position – but such detail would have again used space. Instead we tried to give a flavour of the kind of critical response that each play had attracted in the individual introductions. Having set the scene for *The Spanish Tragedy* by reference to its relationship with Shakespeare, Seneca, Machiavelli, Pope Pius V, Queen Elizabeth of England and the relationship between her government and Spain, it seemed worthwhile to bring in the critics in the form of Andrew Mousley and Catherine Belsey, quoting each on matters of justice, divinity and subjectivity.[9] These few pages of introductory material concluded with a list of 'works of related interest'. Looking back, this seems to be in the case of *The Spanish Tragedy* a simple list of the fourteen bloodiest revenge plays of the period.

With regard to the text itself we were charged with presenting a readable version of the play based on the octavo-in-fours edition believed to date from 1592 (the single copy of which is housed by the British Library in London). Like most editors, we referred to this as 'Q' in the footnotes. We paid attention to the further nine editions between 1594 and 1633, with special attention paid to the 1602 copy and its 'Additions', taking note of the corrections and variants that have influenced other editors. Given the constraints imposed, it quickly became clear that there would be too little space in the volume to record every single instance of variation (let alone earlier editors' decisions about them), so we confined ourselves to the more important moments when what we considered serious interpretations of meaning were at stake. One advantage of working with Hilary Hinds is her prodigious memory for these evolving 'rules' at these times of rapid decision-making – and later in responding to the creative rules of our own compositors at The Running Head.[10]

Michael Hunter has remarked in his book *Editing Early Modern Texts* that:

> [An] editor is trying to reconstruct the intentions of the author whose text is being presented. She or he is, or should be, trying to do justice to the text's history. And he or she is attempting to provide a text that will be useful to potential readers, or offering materials that should enable users to adapt a text to their own requirements or to construct a new version of their own (this arises particularly in relation to electronic editions).[11]

Whatever view we might take on such a surprisingly old-fashioned notion as 'the intentions of the author' (in Kyd's case a 'phone call' to check them would be extremely long distance), there is an argument in the editing process for making the reader aware of the author's other works. There has been considerable scholarly debate about the provenance of *Soliman and Perseda*, just as there has been about the date of the first performance or composition of *The Spanish Tragedy*: but these discussions are remarkably fruitful in our understanding of both texts. My experience of editing *The Spanish Tragedy* was that I found myself entranced by the *presence* of the later work in the earlier one, despite the fact that it had not yet been written. We set the first performance of *The Spanish Tragedy* at 1585, which was probably too bold, too early and based on evidence that was too thin; but all earlier editors agree that the play was written before the Spanish Armada in 1588. However, a play in which the protagonist (Hieronimo) and others experience such agonies of injustice that proceed from anti-chivalric behaviour on the battlefield is of interest in relation to *Soliman and Perseda*, which I am convinced was written by Kyd and about which we can be clearer in terms of its date. In *Soliman and Perseda*, Kyd distils the business of war, showing that the *only* victor in any battle is Death. The play is, of course, a 1591 elaboration of the play-within-the-play that features in *The Spanish Tragedy*, but in many ways it is a powerful kind of 'addition' to the play in terms of the ideological approach to warfare that existed at the time Kyd was thinking about issues of chivalry. Debating the outcome of a complex and bloody conflict between Christian and Muslim, the figures of Death, Fortune and Love assess their comparative strengths and weaknesses in terms of their influence over human activity. Death weighs his own part and, rightly in the context of the play, proclaims victory:

> By wasting all I conquer all the world:
> And now, to end our difference at last,
> In this last act note but the deeds of Death.
> Where is Erastus now, but in my triumph?
> Where are the murtherers, but in my triumph?
> Where's judge and witness, but in my triumph?
> Where's false Lucina, but in my triumph?
> Where's Basilisco, but in my triumph?
> Where's faithful Piston, but in my triumph?
> Where's valiant Brusor, but in my triumph?
> Their loves and fortune ended with their lives,
> And they must wait upon the car of death.
> Pack, Love and Fortune! Play in comedies:
> For powerful death best fitteth tragedies.[12]

Kyd goes on to assert that Death will triumph over all those who participate in wars *except* those who are friends of Elizabeth. The play is, despite this loyal but somewhat weak caveat, a compellingly graphic representation of the outcome of war. It complements *The Spanish Tragedy* itself and stands in stark opposition to the energies of the military theorists of the time who became increasingly bellicose in the years following the Armada scare.[13] It may sound as humanist as Hunter's assertion over the 'intentions of the author', but there may well be a case for a responsible editor to set a work in the context of the ideological narrative of the author's known canon; and this was a responsibility that could not really be fulfilled in the anthology as it emerged.

If *Soliman and Perseda* can be seen in this way as a kind of extension of *The Spanish Tragedy*, a kind of additional element, that reflects upon Kyd's evolving thoughts upon the play, then there are also the five more literal 'Additions' that have occupied scholars for some time. The authorship and intent of the five Additions to *The Spanish Tragedy* are disputed by scholars. Few agree that they greatly contribute to the play, although the Third Addition is of interest for the style of its rhetoric and the Fourth Addition is a good example of the Elizabethan vogue for scenes of madness. These scenes were probably the result of revising or refreshing this popular play. We recommended to students the full discussion of the fragments that can be found in Philip

Edwards's Revels edition of *The Spanish Tragedy*. Although we were aware that many earlier individual editions of the play had included the 'Additions', usually as a kind of appendix, we were not aware of the greater importance attached to them by recent critics. In *The Routledge Anthology of Renaissance Drama*, then, the 'Additions' fell easy victim to the overall economy of scale that informed the volume at every point of its production. They were not ignored, but banished to the website where students could and do consult them, and are able to reinsert them in the appropriate places in the main text. Having said that, I would still rather students read *Soliman and Perseda* in conjunction with *The Spanish Tragedy* than the 'Additions'.

Thus we ended up with a paper core text and internet contexts and Additions. This seemed a hierarchy that was not to last – and the possibilities of the internet are such that editors in the future might well be able to fulfil the high ideals set out by Michael Hunter. Early modern texts have had a very unstable history in print. Kyd is a good example of a writer who has been 'done' by a literary establishment at pains to diminish his voice by comparison with Shakespeare – a voice that we found radical and disturbing when viewed alongside *Soliman and Perseda*. What future editors might attempt is an 'undoing' of Kyd in the manner I have here described; and it is pleasing to see new attention being given to this important playwright.

Working on *The Spanish Tragedy* in particular and *The Routledge Anthology of Renaissance Drama* was a tremendous opportunity to explore editorial work in a period of important changes for this kind of scholarly activity. Wondering why there had been so few anthologies of this kind in the past, the people at Routledge suggested that nobody had had the audacity to attempt to decide (with or without a survey) on which plays should be included in such a volume: a form of 'canon creation'. While we worked on the Routledge book, Arthur Kinney was at work on a similar but even more audacious project, *Renaissance Drama: An Anthology of Plays and Entertainments* for Blackwell.[14] This bigger, bolder project emerged not long before our volume was completed but in time to serve as a check on our work. So we owe a debt to Kinney and are pleased to see that his volume has been reissued and enlarged. Like our own, it was aimed at students and general readers with a love for the period and its plays.[15]

NOTES

1 Barker and Hinds (eds), *The Routledge Anthology*.
2 Wine, *Drama of the English Renaissance*.
3 I suspected that our own students, when faced with purchasing the published volume, also saw the project more in these terms, imagining Hilary and myself funding exotic holidays on the proceeds.
4 Howard-Hill, 'English Renaissance: non-Shakespearean drama', pp. 244–5.
5 Barker and Hinds (eds), *The Routledge Anthology*, p. 39.
6 The chronology took time, and the responsibility for the managing of history (and was it English or British history?) in this fashion was a considerable one. A debt emerged to our colleague, the late Peter Widdowson, who was simultaneously working on his own formidable *Palgrave Guide to English Literature and Its Contexts, 1500–2000* (2004), a work in timeline form containing individual entries on history, politics, culture and literature for every year since 1500.
7 Barker and Hinds (eds), *The Routledge Anthology*, p. 20.
8 The other five editions listed, in alphabetical order, are: Philip Edwards (ed.) *The Spanish Tragedy*, The Revels Series (London: Methuen, 1959); Bertram Joseph (ed.), *The Spanish Tragedy*, The New Mermaids (London: Ernest Benn, 1964); Emma Smith (ed.), *The Spanish Tragedie*, Renaissance Dramatists Series (Harmondsworth: Penguin, 1998); A. K. McIlwraith (ed.), *Five Elizabethan Tragedies*, The World's Classics Series (Oxford: Oxford University Press, 1938); and J. R. Mulryne (ed.), *The Spanish Tragedy*, The New Mermaids (London: A. & C. Black, 1989).
9 Mousley, *Renaissance Drama and Contemporary Literary Theory*, and Belsey, *The Subject of Tragedy*.
10 Carole Drummond and David Williams at The Running Head company in Cambridge performed consistent wonders with typesetting, pagination and, most daunting of all, line-numbering.
11 Hunter, *Editing Early Modern Texts*, p. 58.
12 Kyd, *Soliman and Perseda*, pp. 373–4.
13 See Barker, *War and Nation*, for a discussion of these theorists in relation to the drama of the period.
14 See Kinney, *Renaissance Drama*.
15 The blurb for the book on Amazon notes: 'This pioneering collection of non-Shakespearean Renaissance drama has now been updated to include more early material, plus Mary Sidney's *The Tragedy of Antony*, John Marston's *The Malcontent* and Ben Jonson's *Masque of Queens*. Second edition of this pioneering collection of works of non-Shakespearean Renaissance drama. This book: covers the full sweep of dramatic performances, including State progresses and Court masques; contains material useful for courses on women playwrights or women in Renaissance drama, including Middleton's *A Chaste Maid in Cheapside*, Webster's *The Duchess of Malfi* and Thomas Middleton and William Rowley's *The Changeling*; includes

plays and pageants not anthologized elsewhere, such as the coronation entries of Elizabeth I and Queen Anne, and Thomas Heywood's *A Woman Killed with Kindness*. For the second edition more early material has been added, such as *Noah* and *The Second Shepherd's Play*.'

REFERENCES

Barker, S., *War and Nation in the Theatre of Shakespeare and His Contemporaries* (Edinburgh: Edinburgh University Press, 2007).
Barker, S. and H. Hinds (eds), *The Routledge Anthology of Renaissance Drama* (London and New York: Routledge, 2003).
Belsey, C., *The Subject of Tragedy* (London: Methuen, 1985).
Boas, F. S. (ed.), *Works of Thomas Kyd* (Oxford: Clarendon Press, 1901).
Howard-Hill, T. H., 'English Renaissance: Non-Shakespearean drama', in D. G. Greetham (ed.), *Scholarly Editing: A Guide to Research* (New York: Modern Language Association of America, 1995), pp. 234–6.
Hunter, M., *Editing Early Modern Texts: An Introduction to Principles and Practice* (Basingstoke: Palgrave Macmillan, 2007).
Joseph, B. (ed.), *The Spanish Tragedy*, The New Mermaids (London: Ernest Benn, 1964).
Kinney, A. F. (ed.), *Renaissance Drama: An Anthology of Plays and Entertainments*, new extended edn (Oxford: Blackwell, 2004).
Kyd, T., *Soliman and Perseda* [1591], in W. Carew Hazlitt (ed.), *Dodsley's Old English Plays*, vol. V (London: Reeves and Turner, 1874).
McIlwaith, A. K. (ed.), *Five Elizabethan Tragedies*, The World's Classics Series (Oxford: Oxford University Press, 1998).
Mousley, A., *Renaissance Drama and Contemporary Literary Theory* (Basingstoke: Macmillan, 2000).
Mulryne, J. R. (ed.), *The Spanish Tragedy*, The New Mermaids (London: A. & C. Black, 1989).
Smith, E. (ed.), *The Spanish Tragedie*, Renaissance Dramatists Series (Harmondsworth: Penguin, 1998).
Widdowson, P. (ed.), *The Palgrave Guide to English Literature and Its Contexts, 1500–2000* (Basingstoke: Palgrave, 2004).
Wine, M. L. (ed.), *Drama of the English Renaissance*, Modern Library College Editions (New York: Random House, 1969).

CHAPTER 6

Editing *The Spanish Tragedy* in the early twenty-first century
Jesús Tronch

This chapter discusses the options, premises and conditions of editing *The Spanish Tragedy* as considered at the time of my participation in the 2006 workshop held at the University of Warwick on Kyd and the most famous play attributed to him.[1] I will focus on assessing what a new edition may now contribute to, by addressing the three constituent elements of the title of my chapter. Firstly, *editing* as opposed to *not editing*, which may be understood as simply deciding not to edit for reasons explained below, or as *unediting*, the editorial stance associated with Randall McLeod and Leah Marcus inviting the interpretation of Renaissance texts as they are, without modern editorial interventions in spelling and typography. Secondly, editing *The Spanish Tragedy* as compared to editing other plays, and mainly to editing Shakespeare. And thirdly, editing this play *in the early twenty-first century* as set against the past, against previous editions, such as those by Edwards, Cairncross, Mulryne or Smith.

Considering whether to edit or not to edit (and this is not a joke on Hamlet's famous line) is not an idle question. In his classical editorial manual, Martin West exhorts editors to ask themselves: 'is your edition really necessary?'[2] West advised that 'a new edition can only be justified if it represents a marked advance on its predecessors in some respect, whether in the fullness, accuracy or clarity with which the evidence for the text is presented, or in the judiciousness with which it is used in constituting the text'.[3] So, the question whether *The Spanish Tragedy* needs to be re-edited must be addressed. If we take *editing* in the broad sense of updating scholarship, the answer is 'yes', there's room for new, updated annotations and introduction. If we focus on the narrow sense of textual editing, of handling the arrangement of words, punctuation and typographical signs that embody the play's text, we then need to consider it carefully. In confronting *the* early twenty-first century with the past, one can observe that from the late 1950s to the 1980s there have been changes in editorial theory, in Shakespearian and early modern drama textual scholarship, that invite a fresh consideration of the texts from different premises. Editorial theory now puts an emphasis on the social dimension of texts, not exclusively on authors' intentions. Post-structuralist thinking has dethroned the assumption that texts are stable, that there is a single, determinable text. It also has diminished the editors' confidence in the conventional authorial goal, and has opened the doors to notions of text dissolved into textuality, and to greater respect for the integrity of the early textual forms of works as well as greater attention to their textual multiplicity.

The editorial options for an editor in the early twenty-first century are: (1) facsimiles, (2) literal transcriptions, (3) editions restoring the author's intentions (whether original, intermediate or final intentions), (4) editions reconstructing the texts of 'works viewed as collaborative (social) products', that is, reconstructing the 'publishers', directors' or others' texts', or the 'texts made available to readers at given times'.[4] To this, we could add varieties of presentation and media that allow for several further combinations: (5) multi-textual editions (usually parallel texts, but also multi-reading texts),[5] and (6) electronic or hypertextual editions.

The choice among these options is determined by negotiations among the intended readership, the editor's purpose and the publisher's conditions. In my case, I will entertain editorial possibilities of *The Spanish Tragedy* for the Arden Early Modern Drama series, an editorial task I share with my friend and colleague Clara Calvo, from the University of Murcia. This series subscribes to the conventional modern-spelling, single-text, critical edition, with specific book dimensions and readership, in competition with other series such as Revels (Edwards, Bevington) and New Mermaids (Mulryne). This leaves out options 5 (multi-textual, and electronic editions), and 1 and 2 (the non-critical editions materialised in facsimiles and literal transcriptions, and favoured by the *unediting* programme of McLeod and Marcus), and allows for two options: (3) authorially intended texts and (4) editions reconstructing publishers', directors' or historical readers' texts. Option 3 has been followed, and judiciously so, in previous critical editions such as Edwards (1959), Mulryne (1989), and Maus (1995). So, if our edition has to represent a 'marked advance on its predecessors', either we strive to improve in 'fullness, accuracy or clarity with which the evidence for the text is presented'[6] or we attempt the more socially and historically concerned editorial objective of option 4. In this chapter, I will examine the problems involved in the latter option, an objective that is not ruled out in the Guidelines of the Arden Early Modern Drama series.[7] And since the evidence for the text(s) of *The Spanish Tragedy* comprises a series of printings from 1592 in which the publishers' reconstructed texts may be seen to coincide with the texts made available to late sixteenth-century and early seventeenth-century readers, I will summarily refer to this objective as the publisher's intentions or the publisher's text.

COPY-TEXT: Q_1 OR Q_4?

Whether establishing the author's text or the publisher's text, a further option involves the choice, if appropriate, of one of the early documents as base text (or copy-text) for any edition, including ours. With the exception of Smith's, previous critical editions use the earliest surviving text, the undated quarto 'piratically' published by Edward White and printed by Edward Allde in 1592 (STC 15086, henceforth Q1).[8] We could justify a new edition of *The Spanish Tragedy* by offering a modern-spelling, critical text based on the 1602 quarto (STC 15089, henceforth Q4), specially for the interest in the so-called five 'Additions'.[9] Smith based her edition on Q4 but hers is an old-spelling text. Moreover, it retains so many inadequate readings that it seems to lie mid-way between a documentary transcript and a very conservative critical edition.

Besides this dissatisfaction with Smith's edition, a number of scholars have made explicit to Clara Calvo and myself their interest in – and reasons for – an edition of *The Spanish Tragedy* based on Q4. In essence, their reasons focus on the importance of Hieronimo's madness developed in the 'Additions' and on the reception of this version of the play. Also, there are socio-historical grounds for using Q4 as base text since it is the version of *The Spanish Tragedy* known to readers between 1602 and 1773: all the quartos in the seventeenth century offered the 'full' text of *The Spanish Tragedy*, as did Dodsley's 1744 edition, until Hawkins (1773) placed the 'Additions' in footnotes. Even later editions by Reed (1780), Scott (1810) and Collier (1825) continued to privilege the 'Additions' by printing them in the main text, albeit italicised, and by demoting to footnotes the fragments unique to Q1 that are replaced in the second and fifth 'Additions'.

I will then examine the practical results of editing *The Spanish Tragedy* using Q4 as base text and seeking to reconstruct its publishers' intentions. In order to do so, I will closely look at Q4 with a view to assessing its contribution to the history of the play's 'text'. Q4 was published by Thomas Pavier and printed by William White, who had already printed the previous quarto in 1599 (Q3). Pavier acquired publishing rights over *The Spanish Tragedy* on 14 August 1600.[10] With the exception of the 'Additions', Q4 seems to have been largely copied from Q3. In its turn, Q3 is a reprint of the 1594 quarto (Q2), which, in its turn, is a reprint of the earliest 'illegal' quarto of 1592. As usual, each subsequent reprint corrects some errors but preserves others and commits new ones. There are thirty-five errors in common to the four quartos, ten in fragments in Latin, six in Italian and nineteen in English, four of which are names of mythological characters that might have been unfamiliar to compositors.

With respect to the earliest text, Q4 has about 245 substantive variants.[11] Of these, some 110 (excluding the five 'Additions') are readings that first appear in Q4. The rest are inherited from Q2 and/or Q3, as for instance: 'And Murderers ^{Q1}grone^{Q1} ^{Q4}greeue^{Q4} with ^{Q1}neuer killing^{Q1} ^{Q4}euerkilling^{Q4} woundes' (A3^r 6; I.i.69). Some sixteen of these inherited variants correct Q1 errors, while the remaining 120 variants are unwarranted innovations in Q2 and Q3 that Q4 perpetuates, including erroneous readings, as for instance: 'Mingled with weapons and ^{Q1}vnboweld^{Q1} ^{Q4}vnbowed^{Q4} steedes' (A4^r 18; I.ii.62).

I will now focus on the variants peculiar to Q4 in order to check whether they derive from some authority (as the 'Additions' certainly do). A figure of 110 readings unique to Q4 stands slightly above the 95 variants first appearing in Q2 without any authority. Q4 produces some twenty errors of its own, as for example:

Vil. Rent with remembrance of so foule a deed,
   My ^{Q1}guiltie^{Q1} ^{Q4}guiltelesse^{Q4} soule submits me to thy doome:
                                    (E1^v 18–19; III.i.92–3)

Five variants simply involve matters of spelling, as in 'They ^{Q1}reeke^{Q1} ^{Q4}reake ^{Q4} no lawes that meditate reuenge' (B2^v 28; I.iii.48); and some twenty-five variants a grammatical change without substantial semantic difference, as for instance: 'What meanes this warning of this ^{Q1}trumpets sound^{Q1} ^{Q4}Trumpet sound^{Q4}?' (A4^v 24; I.ii.101). All these may easily be compositorial innovations.

A further twenty-three variants invite us to infer a policy of regularisation and modernisation of morphology and grammar ('you' becomes 'ye' in II.iv.54, III.xi.6 and III.xiv.10; 'Portingall' and 'Portingale' in I.iv.111 and 119 are respectively changed to 'Portugall' and 'Portugal', which became standard). These could be compositorial in origin, perhaps following instructions by the printer or publisher. In II.v.64, 'Isabel' is regularised to the most frequent from 'Isabella' and therefore 'let us' in the same line seems to have been changed into 'let's' in order to re-balance the metre.

The rest of the unique to Q4 variants involve a substantial discrepancy in meaning. Five or six are trivialisations or simplifications (as in 'more fewell to ^{Q_1}your^{Q_1} ^{Q_4}the^{Q_4} fire', at G2^v 31; III.x.74), probably accidental, while six variants actually correct errors in Q1 (they are now accepted by most editors taking Q1 as copy-text, such as the transposition of lines at IV.i.185–6, and the addition of a needed speech prefix for Lorenzo at III.ii.98). The latter suggest an alertness to the text unlikely in compositors.[12] Thirteen variants in the dialogue present a more significant lexical difference, as in 'The ^{Q_1}sweet^{Q_1} ^{Q_4}swift^{Q_4} reuenge of thy *Horatio*' (H2^v 28; III.xiii.107), and could be the work of either a compositor or an 'editor'.[13] In any case, all these significant variants in Q4 can be made without reference to an authority.

Yet this inference is not so evident in the case of stage directions and speech prefixes. Noticeably, Q4 has fourteen significant innovations in these elements.[14] Three added stage directions in IV.i simply make explicit a possible action implied in the dialogue: '*They breake in, and hold* Hieronimo' (L4^v 7; IV.iv.156), '*He bites out his tongue*' (M1^r 32; IV.iv.191) and '*Exeunt*' just before the final ceremonial exit of the play's main plot (M1^v 32; IV.iv.217). Two more added stage directions in II.i indicate action and gesture that are not immediately inferred from the dialogue: '*Draw his sword*' (C3^r 25; II.i.67) and '*Offer to kill him*' (C3^r 35; II.i.77). And significantly, Q4 omits the speech prefixes for Bel-imperia's letter in the middle of Hieronimo's famous soliloquy 'O eyes, no eyes …' in III.ii. These innovations are in line with a deliberate, but not wholly consistent, policy to improve stage directions and to regularise speech prefixes.

Given this analysis, Q4 seems to have been printed from an exemplar of Q3 with some sporadic editing that modernises some forms, smoothes grammar, emends some errors but perpetuates others, inserts markings referring to the 'added' manuscript material and pays special attention to the stage directions (and perhaps speech prefixes) in this consulted manuscript.

If we are to restore the publisher's intentions with respect to the text now present in Q4, we can aim to reconstruct that marked copy of Q3. To that end, we need to emend Q4's obvious errors and those readings suspected of being compositorial innovations, and to retain regularisations and modernisations (assuming that the publisher intended them), the improvements of stage directions and speech prefixes, the five 'new' stage directions, and, of course, the 'Additions'. As expected, it is difficult to discern whether some variants were compositorial errors (e.g, 'sweet/swift' in III.xiii.107) and whether some sophistications and slight grammatical changes were deliberate or accidental. Yet another difficulty arises when we consider more important variants such as 'And Murderers ^{Q_1}grone^{Q_1} ^{Q_4}greeue^{Q_4} with ^{Q_1}neuer killing^{Q_1} ^{Q_4}euerkilling^{Q_4} woundes' (I.i.69), which we know originated in Q2 or in Q3: had the Q4 publisher Thomas Pavier known that Q4 contained some 120 mistakes made by the compositors of Q3 and Q2, would he have accepted them in his edition?

If we assume a positive answer, then we proceed to edit Q4 as outlined above, and the result would be a very conservative edition of Q4 that at least would be more adequate than Smith's unsatisfactory text. But we may as well ask ourselves whether our present-day readers would be interested in a new critical edition that, *we know*, would contain some 120 readings that are errors of transmission made by compositors, readings that are neither the author's nor the reviser's lexical changes.

If we assume that Pavier would *not* want a text perpetuating unwarranted errors, we would have to correct those 120 readings inherited from Q2 and Q3 by going back to Q1, and the resulting edited Q4 would be, with exceptions, *almost identical* to an edited Q1.[15] These exceptions are: the 'Additions', three variants in stage directions and speech prefixes,[16] thirteen significant variants in the dialogue and some twenty insubstantial sophistications, such as 'you/ye' (II.iv.54), which we assume were part of the publisher's editorial policy of regularisation and modernisation. Among these exceptions, only the 'Additions' are as significant as to shape Q4 into a markedly different version of the play.

However, if the result of editing a Q4-based *The Spanish Tragedy* (because we are mainly interested in the 'Additions' and *not* in the 'you/ye' sophistications and thirteen significant variants that do not develop Hieronimo's madness) is an edited Q4 *almost identical* to an edited Q1, it is a more sensible method for us to edit *The Spanish Tragedy* by using Q1 as base text and incorporating the 'added' Q4 material in it.

This position does not *a priori* lead to a new and original edition to offer our readers. Some 'marked advance' could then be achieved by (1) considering editing Q1 with a view to restoring its publisher's text and (2) incorporating the 'added' Q4 material in a new and original way. Such a Q1-based edition can be equally defended on socio-historical grounds. *The Spanish Tragedy* is a seminal play in the history of English tragedy, and this role is certainly assigned to the earliest version (the pre-*Hamlet* version, as Clara Calvo defined it at the 2006 *Doing Kyd* workshop) that we can approximate by editing Q1. If we are also interested in the Q4-only material that is really significant to this (perhaps post-*Hamlet*) version, we can also serve this interest by easily accommodating this material (the 'Additions', five variants in stage directions and speech prefixes) in a Q1-based edition.

ACCOMMODATING THE 'ADDITIONS'

Apart from simply omitting the 'Additions' altogether, as do Ross (1968), Kinney (1999), Bevington and Rasmussen (2002), and Barker and Hinds (2003),[17] three different treatments can be observed: appendix, footnotes and in-text insertion. McIlwraith (1937), Edwards (1959), Mulryne (1989), Tydeman (1992), Maus (1995) and Bevington (1996) relegate the 'Additions' to an appendix. Pursuing as they are the author's text, they discard what does not belong to Kyd (as some editors of *Macbeth* did with the Middleton scenes). Interested as we are in the 'Additions', the appendix solution is clearly awkward.

Footnotes, used by Hawkins (1883) and Manly (1897), have the 'Additions' closer to the main text, but present problems. In Hawkins's edition, the Fourth Addition runs for seven pages with only two or

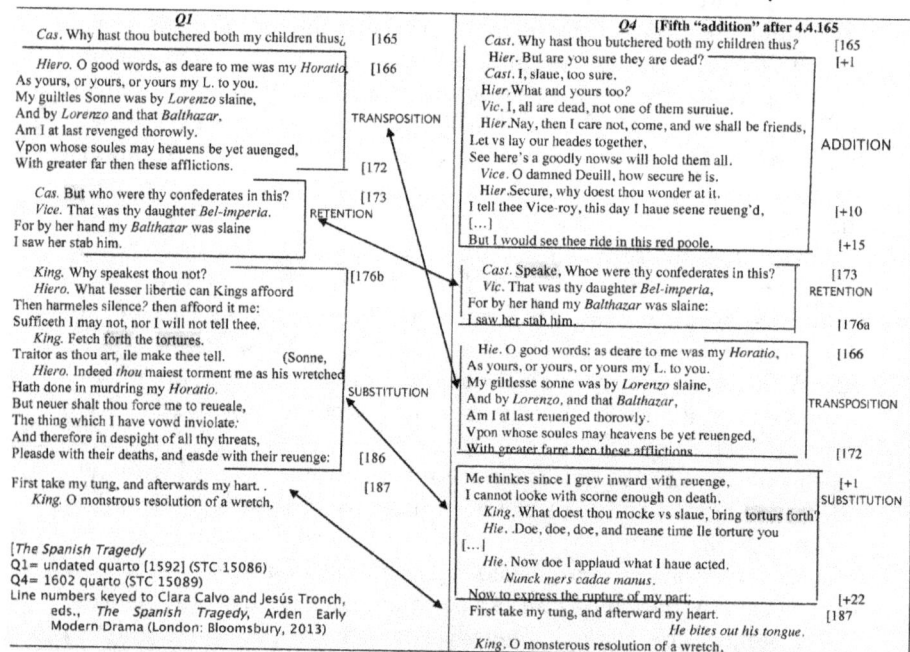

Figure 6.1 The fifth 'Addition' in Q1 and Q4 – parallel text.

three lines of the main Q1 text on most pages. Apart from this typographical awkwardness, footnotes diminish the importance we aim to confer on the 'Additions'. To print them in the main body of the text and mark them off typographically is the best solution, but again the complexity of the second and fifth Additions, which contain substitutions, is a challenge. Especially problematic is the fifth 'Addition' in IV.iv, shown in Figure 6.1, with Q1 and Q4 in parallel.

At a closer examination, the fifth 'Addition' consists of: an addition of fifteen lines ('But are you sure they are dead? / [...] / But I would see thee ride in this red poole'), followed by a transposition of four Q1 lines ('Speake, Who were thy confederates in this? / [...] / I saw her stab him' 176–9a), with initial 'Speake' replacing Q1 initial 'But' (176), a retention of seven Q1 lines ('O good words: as dear to me was my *Horatio* / [...] / With greater farre then these afflictions' 168–75) and, finally, a substitution of Q4 twenty-two lines ('Me thinkes since I grew inward with reuenge / [...] / Now to express the rupture of my part') for twelve Q1 lines ('Why speakest thou not? / [...] / Pleasde with their death, and easde with their reuenge' 179b–90), although retaining the King's order 'Fetch forth the tortures' in Q1 (IV.iv.183) as 'bring torturs forth' after 'What doest thou mocke vs slaue'.

Schick (1898), followed by Craik (1974), resorted to both in-text insertion and footnotes. The fifteen Q4 lines that are really an addition ('But are you sure [...] this red poole') are printed in italics and between square brackets; then follows the text in Q1 'O good words [...] afterwards my heart' with a footnote – which Schick, but not Craik, keys to 'Why speak'st thou not?' – explaining the substitution of 'Methinks, since I grew inward with revenge [...] rupture of my part' and the transposition of lines 190–3 before line 182, and then printing the Q4 substitution in italics. This system demands considerable attention on the part of the reader to visualise the divergences clearly.

Hazlitt substitutes the whole fifth 'Addition', marked off by square brackets,[18] for Q1's lines 168–79a, that is, for those lines that the Q4 passage retains although in transposed order, and continues with Q1's 'Why speakest thou not?' (IV.iv.179b), to which he keys the footnote: 'i.e., In reply to the question as to his confederates'. Matthews and Lieder (1924) simply bracket the whole 'Addition' and place it after 'First take my tung, and afterwards my heart' (IV.iv.191). The effect is that readers have no idea as to how Q1 actually prints this section. In order to alert readers to this complex discrepancy, other editions, such as Boas (1901), Thorndike (1910), Prouty (1951) and Cairncross (1967), include an editorial instruction in the main text. This is a step towards immediacy but not towards clarification. For instance,

Boas prints the Q4 fragment in a smaller font after Q1's IV.iv.191 and heads the fragment with the following obtrusive instruction, printed in small capital letters and between the angular brackets he uses for editorial additions: '<FIFTH PASSAGE OF ADDITIONS, REPLACING 168-90, BUT INCORPORATING, IN TRANSPOSED ORDER, 168–78 (... STAB HIM) AND 190 OF ORIGINAL TEXT>'.[19] Neilson (1911) and Brooke and Paradise (1933) bracket the whole Q4 fragment in the main text, and provide the instruction in a footnote that reads 'Fifth passage of additions, replacing ll. 171–94'. However, these editorial directions do not clarify to readers that lines 175–78 are placed before 168–74 ('O good words [...] stab him'). In all these cases, the edited texts repeat, both in the Q1-based main text and in the Q4-only fragment, the retained lines ('O good words [...] these afflictions' 168–75) and the transposed lines ('Speake, Who were thy confederates [...] saw her stab him' 176–9a).

It would be more helpful if readers could discern both the Q1 version and the Q4 alternative. For that purpose, we would need to mark off not only what is peculiar to Q4 but also what is unique to the Q1 version, those Q1 lines and speech prefixes that are mutually exclusive with respect to Q4. For precedents of this double typographical distinction, we can look at Bernice W. Kliman's enfolded *Hamlet*, which uses curly brackets for the Second Quarto-only readings, and pointed brackets for Folio-only variants,[20] and at R. A. Foakes's Arden edition of *King Lear*, which uses superscript letters Q and F to frame words and passages found only in the Quarto and in the Folio respectively.[21] These minimal typographical signs can effectively avoid the obtrusiveness of the editorial directions. Besides, the Q4-related text can be further distinguished by using a sans-serif font, as Jonathan Bate does in his Arden edition of *Titus Andronicus* with Act 3 scene 2, absent in Q1 (his copy-text) and taken from F1. In his edition of *The House that Jack Built*, Fotheringham uses superscript letters M and S to frame words, phrases and lines found only in the Melbourne and the Sydney versions of the play respectively; besides, he prints all the Sydney-only material in a sans-serif font, and, for larger blocks of variant material, he draws a vertical line down both margins, headed by 'M only' and 'S only' in the right margin 'at the start of the block and on any following pages'.[22]

The following two excerpts represent how the second and fifth 'Additions' could appear, in modernised spelling and punctuation, with the use of superscripts Q1 and Q4, and a sans-serif font for the Q4-only passages:

LORENZO
   Why so, Hieronimo? Use me.   65
Q^1 HIERONIMO
   Oh no, my lord, I dare not, it must not be.
   I humbly thank your lordship.$^{Q^1}$
Q^4 HIERONIMO   Who, you, my lord?   +1
   I reserve our favour for a greater honour.
   This is a very toy, my lord, a toy.
LORENZO
   All's one, Hieronimo, acquaint me with it.
HIERONIMO I'faith, my lord, 'tis an idle thing, I must   +5
   confess. I ha' been too slack, too tardy, too remiss unto your
   honour.
LORENZO How now, Hieronimo?
HIERONIMO
   In troth, my lord, it is a thing of nothing,
   The murder of a son, or so: +10
   A thing of nothing, my lord.^{Q4}
LORENZO   Why then, farewell.   67
HIERONIMO
   My grief no heart, my thoughts no tongue, can tell.   *Exit.*
                       [III.ii.65 – Second 'Addition']

For the fifth 'Addition', the following excerpt seeks not to repeat the retained lines ('O good words [...] these afflictions' 168–75), but it is inevitable to do so with the transposed lines ('But who were thy confederates [...] saw her stab him' 176–9ₐ):

CASTILE
   Why hast thou butchered both my children thus?   167
Q^4 HIERONIMO
   But are you sure they are dead?
CASTILE   Ay, slave, too sure.   +1
HIERONIMO
   What, and yours too?
VICEROY
   Ay, all are dead, not one of them survive.
HIERONIMO
   Nay, then I care not. Come, and we shall be friends;
   Let us lay our heads together.   +5
   See, here's a goodly noose will hold them all.
VICEROY
   O damned devil, how secure he is!
HIERONIMO
   Secure? Why doest thou wonder at it?
   I tell thee, Viceroy, this day I have seen revenge,

And in that sight am grown a prouder monarch +10
Than ever sat under the crown of Spain.
Had I as many lives as there be stars,
As many heavens to go to as those lives,
I'd give them all, ay, and my soul to boot,
But I would see thee ride in this red pool. +15
CASTILE
Speak! Who were thy confederates in this?
VICEROY
That was thy daughter Bel-imperia,
For by her hand my Balthazar was slain.
I saw her stab him. Q4
HIERONIMO
Oh, good words,
As dear to me was my Horatio, 170
As yours, or yours, or yours. my lord, to you.
My guiltless son was by Lorenzo slain,
And by Lorenzo and that Balthazar
Am I at last revenged thoroughly,
Upon whose souls may heavens be yet avenged 175
With greater far than these afflictions.
Q1 CASTILE
But who were thy confederates in this?
VICEROY
That was thy daughter Bel-imperia,
For by her hand my Balthazar was slain.
I saw her stab him.
KING   Why speakest thou not? 180
HIERONIMO
What lesser liberty can kings afford
Than harmeless silence? Then afford it me:
Sufficeth I may not, nor I will not tell thee.
KING
Fetch forth the tortures.
Traitor as thou art, I'll make thee tell.
HIERONIMO   Indeed 185
Thou mayst torment me as his wretched son
Hath done in murdering my Horatio.
But never shalt thou force me to reveal
The thing which I have vowed inviolate.
And therefore, in despite of all thy threats, 190
Pleased with their deaths, and eased with their revenge, Q1
Q4 Methinks since I grew inward with revenge, +1
I cannot look with scorn enough on death.
KING
What, doest thou mock us, slave? Bring tortures forth.

HIERONIMO
Do, do, do, and meantime I'll torture you.
You had a son, as I take it, and your son   +5
Should ha' been married to your daughter. Ha, was't not so?
You had a son too; he was my liege's nephew.
He was proud and politic, had he lived,
He might a' come to wear the crown of Spain,
I think twas so. 'Twas I that killed him.   +10
Look you this same hand, 'twas it that stabbed
His heart. Do you see this hand?
For one Horatio, if you ever knew him,
A youth, one that they hanged up in his father's garden;
One that did force your valiant son to yield,   +15
While your more valiant son did take him prisoner.
VICEROY
Be deaf, my senses, I can hear no more.
KING
Fall heaven, and cover us with thy sad ruins.
CASTILE
Roll all the world within thy pitchy cloud.
HIERONIMO
Now do I applaud what I have acted.   +20
Nunc iners cadat manus.
Now to express the rupture of my part,^Q4
First take my tongue, and afterwards my heart.
  [*He bites out his tongue.*]
KING
O monstrous resolution of a wretch!
                              [IV.iv.167 – Fifth 'Addition']

RECONSTRUCTING Q1'S PUBLISHER'S TEXT

For a final comment on editing a publisher-oriented edition based on Q1, I would like to go back to the opposition between *The Spanish Tragedy* and Shakespeare editions.

If *The Spanish Tragedy* were a play by Shakespeare, we would ground our decisions on a sophisticated textual analysis determining how the printing process affected the text (compositors' proclivity to certain kinds of errors and of spellings, problems of cast-off copy, etc.). But *The Spanish Tragedy* is not by Shakespeare. This means that there has not been much attention paid to compositorial analysis, except by Arthur Freeman in his 1969 article on the printing of Q1, and by Paul Werstine in his analysis of the performance of William White's compositors in Q3 and two other reprints produced around

1599. Freeman concluded that Q1 was printed seriatim, that 'a single compositor was employed at any one time throughout the setting' and that a different, second compositor took over the setting of the text from G4^r onward.[23] Yet Freeman did not identify these compositors' working habits in relation to other printings by Edward Allde. Further compositorial analyses remain to be done.[24]

As a conscientious textual editor, I would have to carry out this research, but as an editor in 2006, I have not – at least, not yet. The reason simply lies in the fact that today there is not much emphasis on or interest in compositor studies. As a senior textual scholar told me, unless it were one of the passions of my life, investing time in determining particular compositors and their printing habits would not be worthwhile, advising me to focus on the publisher instead. So our edition of *The Spanish Tragedy* in the early twenty-first century involves preparing a Q1-based edition without the helpful knowledge of compositors' working habits that Shakespearian editors have at their disposal. In this respect, a Kydian editor's judgement is comparatively less informed, with fewer bibliographical arguments for suspecting readings in the early texts and consequently for correcting these presumed errors. Yet less informed does not necessarily mean under-informed, since, apart from detecting and emending errors on the basis of language, idiom and dramatic context, Kydian editors can rely on textual criteria inferred from Elizabethan printing in general, and, in particular, from Kyd's handwritten letters, a reliable evidence for knowing authorial handwriting features that Shakespeare editors lack.

If *The Spanish Tragedy* were a play by Shakespeare and were to be edited by Shakespearean editors who have lately been – generally – more inclined to editorial conservatism, an edition of the play in the early twenty-first century would probably be conservative too. As Proudfoot observed in 2002 with respect to Shakespeare editing, 'it is fashionable to distrust editorial alteration in the editing of texts',[25] to reconsider 'traditional editorial interventions' and to reject them 'when the reading of an early edition is reasonably defensible'.[26] This editorial tendency can be seen not only in editions of specific plays (David Scott Kastan's *Henry IV Part One* for Arden, or the Arden 3 *Hamlet* edited by Ann Thompson and Neil Taylor)[27] but also in whole series such as the recent Pelican Shakespeare under the general editorship of Stephen Orgel and A. R. Braunmuller, and in *The RSC Shakespeare Complete Works* edited by Jonathan Bate and Eric Rasmussen.[28] Moreover, given the options of aiming either at authorial intentions or at the publisher's text, a conservative editing is *a priori* closer to the latter, as a number of non-authorial readings would be retained on the assumption that they were changes welcomed by the publisher.

I have entertained a conservative edition of *The Spanish Tragedy* seeking to reconstruct the text of the Q1 publisher (or the text made available to readers in Q1), and I have realised that the resulting edition is not very different from an author-focused edition, such as those by Edwards or Mulryne. Between my drafted publisher-oriented edition and Edwards's there are only ten differences: four substantive readings in the dialogue, four differences in modernisation and two in stage directions – excluding four discrepancies in significant punctuation. Would, then, this new edition of *The Spanish Tragedy* be justified? For comparison, out of a range of 120 possibilities of variance, Mulryne differs from Edwards in six (two substantive readings in the dialogue, two modernisations and two stage directions). The reasons for this ironic or paradoxical coincidence, despite using different editorial goals, lie in the appreciation that Q1, although a 'pirate' edition, is a relatively good text[29] and that Edwards practised a rather conservative editing. For instance, in his footnote to III.iv.81, he suggests that 'see' in Lorenzo's 'The only thing is uneffected yet / And that's to see the executioner' could be emended to 'fee' as 'the remark would be more in character and more powerful', yet Edwards retains Q1's 'see' because 'one cannot tamper with a reading which makes good sense'.

Quantitatively, I have been slightly more conservative than Edwards since a number of those ten differences are in fact preservations of Q1 readings. One example appears in the first speech of the play, when Andrea describes his descent into hell. After he sees the three judges, whom he approaches, Andrea says (in the Q1 text):

> But *Minos* ingrauen leaues of Lotterie,
> Drew forth the manner of my life and death.
> (A2ᵛ 10; I.i.36–7)

In fact, it is not clear in Q1 whether there is a space between 'in' and 'grauen'.[30] Editorial tradition since Q2 reads the first line as 'Minos, in graven leaves of lottery', so that the judge of the underworld, Minos, is the subject of the verb 'Drew forth' in the second line. 'Lottery' means 'what one is allotted to, i.e. his lot, his destiny', and 'leaves of lottery' is understood as 'slips' or 'records of allotted life', as glossed by Gibson. Since Minos shakes an urn and discerns 'lives and crimes' in Virgil's *Aeneid* (6.568–72), Edwards interprets 'Drew forth' literally and assumes that 'Minos draws from his urn the lottery slip on which was engraved the manner of life which Andreas has now fulfilled, i.e.

what has been his lot'. But in Virgil there is no reference to a drawing out of 'leaves'.³¹ From a fresh examination of the text, and forgetting the received text of *The Spanish Tragedy*, one can interpret the first line as a single noun phrase 'Minos' engraven leaves of lottery', with the 'inscribed leaves' as its head, and therefore as the subject of the verb 'Drew forth', meaning 'displayed' or 'delineated' (as John Jowett has privately suggested) the manner of life and death of Andrea.

However, I have not been as conservative – in qualitative terms – as to reject the possibility of emending a Q1 reading that makes sense but is suspected of resulting from error. In one example, I have entertained an emendation of a Q1 reading that Edwards and all editors consulted retain. In the last line of the following lament by Isabella, Q1 reads 'dyde, I', but Q2 has 'liu'd, I', followed by Q3 ('liu'd: I,') and Q4:

> To heauen, I there sits my *Horatio*,
> Backt with a troup of fiery Cherubins,
> Dauncing about his newly healed wounds
> Singing sweet hymnes and chaunting heauenly notes,
> Rare hermony to greet his innocence,
> That dyde, I dyde a mirrour in our daies.
>
> (G1ʳ 6–11; III.viii.17–22)

Q2's innovation 'liu'd I' has been neglected by editors because Q1 is defensible in its own terms. Q2 commits more unauthorised changes (seventy, such as 'vnbowed' I.ii.61) than it corrects. However, we cannot take for granted that the only surviving copy of Q2 was printed from the only surviving copy of Q1. It may well be that the Q1 compositor wrongly duplicated the first 'dyde' because of the closeness of the second 'dyde' and the similarity in the letters. With 'lived, ay, died a mirror in our days', Isabella first refers to Horatio when he lived, then immediately corrects herself as she recognises the fact that her son has died. Rather than explaining Q2's 'liu'd' as a compositor's erroneous substitution, it is more probable that our only surviving copy of Q1 contains an erroneous repetition, corrected in other exemplars, and that our only surviving Q2 copy was set from one of these exemplars, now lost.

The conclusion to my assessment of the contribution of a new edition of *The Spanish Tragedy* in the early twenty-first century, is threefold. Firstly, although some scholars would expect the choice of Q4 as copytext, especially for its 'Additions' that develop Hieronimo's madness, a Q4-based edition would incorporate about 150 corrections from Q1 and would be almost identical, with exceptions, to a Q1-based edition. Secondly, if readers are interested in *The Spanish Tragedy* as a seminal play in the development of English tragedy, best represented in Q1, and are also interested in the added material (perhaps post-dating *Hamlet*), a new edition can serve both interests by using Q1 as copy-text and inserting the Q4 'additional' text in the main text. These elements are to be typographically distinguished from Q1, and, at the same time, the mutually exclusive Q1 lines and speech prefixes are also to be marked off, so that readers can easily discern both versions. Thirdly, a Q1-based edition reconstructing its publisher's text, thus endorsing a more social and collaborative view of the work instead of the traditional author-oriented approach, does not result in a markedly different edited text. The only claims to an original contribution would lie in the typographical distinction of Q1-only elements and in local decisions to retain or emend readings.

If finally adopted, 'Minos' engraven leaves of lottery' (I.i.36) and 'lived, ay, died a mirror in our days' (III.viii.22) have not been put forward by any previous editor. More than relieving – to some extent – one's anxiety to justify a new edition of the play, these readings vindicate that there is always room for fresh re-examination of the texts, and that one can never call an edition 'definitive'. As Tanselle keeps evangelising, 'it is in the nature of all works in intangible media [such as verbal language] that their intended form (or forms) can never be precisely known and must be continually reconstructed'.[32] The texts of verbal works are always indeterminate and therefore in need of 'endless reconsideration',[33] much as the victims in *The Spanish Tragedy* are doomed to suffer an *endless tragedy*.

NOTES

1 This chapter was part of Research Projects FFI 2009-12730 and CSD 2009-00033 and BBF 2003 – 06096, funded by the Spanish government. I would like to thank Nicoleta Cinpoeş for inviting me to participate in the conference *Doing Kyd* (2006) and the University of Warwick for its hospitality.
2 West, *Textual Criticism and Editorial Technique*, p. 61.
3 Ibid.
4 Tanselle, 'Varieties of scholarly editing', pp. 10–11.
5 For Shakespearian multi-reading texts, see Kliman's 'The enfolded *Hamlet*' and *The Enfolded Hamlets: Parallel Texts*, and Tronch-Pérez's *A Synoptic Hamlet* and 'Dual-reading'.
6 West, *Textual Criticism and Editorial Technique*, p. 61.
7 The Editorial Guidelines (a private document made by the general editors Suzanne Gossett, John Jowett and Gordon McMullan) do not specifically mention author's intentions; they refer to 'restor[ing]' the early text(s) by 'correcting the text [...] where it is certainly or probably corrupt' (1a2).

8 Although in technical terms an 'octavo-in-fours', I designate the earliest edition (and also the 1594 printing) as a 'quarto'. For arguments, see Arthur Freeman, 'The printing of *The Spanish Tragedy*' 198; and G. T. Tanselle, 'The concept of format', 90. The date 1592 and 'piratical' nature of the edition are inferred from evidence in the Register of the Stationers' Company. On 18 December 1592, Edward White was fined by the Stationers' Company for 'transgressing the ordonance' by 'hauinge printed the spanish tragedie belonging to [Edw. *deleted*] Abell Ieffes', according to Greg's argument in *A Bibliography of English Printed Drama to the Restoration*, vol. 2 (1970), p. 9. Jeffes had secured his rights over *The Spanish Tragedy* by entering it in the Register of the Company on 6 October (Greg, p. 8). Incidentally, White had acquired rights over *Arden of Faversham* on 3 April (Greg, p. 7), and Jeffes was similarly fined for 'having printed the tragedie of arden of kent belonging to Edw White' (Greg, p. 9). Both White and Jeffes had their illegal editions confiscated. Unfortunately, Jeffes's edition of *The Spanish Tragedy* is now lost; only one copy of White's 'pirate' quarto, now in the British Library (C.34.d.7), has come down to us.

9 Although the second 'Addition', located after III.ii.67, contains a two-line substitution, and the fifth one, placed after IV.iv.167, comprises addition, transposition and substitution, I will continue to call them 'Additions' for the sake of brevity.

10 Greg, *A Bibliography of English Printed Drama*, p. 16.

11 I exclude from this counting variant spellings (e.g., Q1 'Cipresse' / Q4 'Cypers' I.i.44), uncertain metrical variants (e.g., 'knowst / knowest' II.i.45) and obvious typographical errors in Q1 and in Q4 (e.g. Q1 'fortuues' I.iii.10, Q4 'aud' I.i.33). For comparison of variants, I will juxtapose them (as in Kliman's 'The enfolded Hamlet') and mark them off with corresponding superscript abbreviated references (as in Foakes's Arden 3rd series *Lear* edition).

12 In some places Q4 corrects a Q3 reading by reverting to Q1: for instance, at signature I1v 31 (III.xiii.83), Q3 wrongly reads 'Balthazar' and Q4 rightly restores 'Bazulto'. In other places Q4 corrects Q3 without recourse to Q1: for instance, at signature L1^v 11 (IV.ii.32), Q4 emends 'Ah na' in Q3 (and in Q2) to 'Ah ha', while Q1 reads 'Ah nay'.

13 In '*Hiero.* But wherefore Q1stands yonQ1 Q4stand youQ4 silly man so mute' (H2r 23; III.xiii.67), the Q3 exemplar used as printer's copy probably read Q2's 'stands you', so that either the compositor or an 'editor' corrected the verb.

14 Not counting five regularisations, such as IV.i.147 SD '*Giues*' for Q1 'He giueth', IV.iv.0 '*Duke*' for Q1 'the Duke', IV.iv.10 '*giues*' for Q1 'giveth', IV.iv.88 '*He shews*' for Q1 'Shewes'.

15 'Almost identical' means considering that together, within those 120 emendations resorting to Q1, we count those twenty or thirty readings first appearing in Q4 that are also emended to Q1, six emendations of Q1 readings resorting to Q4, and those correct readings provided by Q2, Q3 and modern editions that an edited Q4 and edited Q1 would have in common.

16 Namely, the stage directions '*Draw his sword*' II.i.67, '*Offer to kill him*' II.i.77, and the absence of speech prefixes for Bel-imperia's letter in III.ii. The added stage directions in IV.i are not counted since they would as well appear in a critically edited Q1.
17 Gibson (1997) excludes the 'Additions' except the fourth one, the so-called Painter scene, which he prints in Appendix I not at the end of the play but at the end of all the six Renaissance tragedies of his edition.
18 Hazlitt wrongly closes the square brackets after '*nunc caede, manus*,' and omits Q4's 'Now to express the rupture of my part'.
19 Prouty simply adds a concise '[*Fifth of the 1602 Additions, designed to replace ll. 197–221*]' and closes the Addition with equally brief '[*End of Fifth Addition*]'. Cairncross simply prints '[Fifth passage of additions.]' to the added Q4 fragment between square brackets, and in a footnote repeats Boas's specification: '*replacing ll. 168–190, but incorporating, in transposed order, ll. 168–178 (…stab him) and l. 190 of the original text.*'
20 Similarly, for their edition of *Hamlet* based on the Second Quarto text, Mowat and Werstine print Folio-only words between pointed parentheses, Second Quarto-only lines between square brackets and editorial emendations between superior half-brackets (*Hamlet* l).
21 Foakes, *Lear*, p. 149.
22 Fotheringham (ed.), '*The House that Jack Built*', p. 235.
23 Freeman, 'Printing', pp. 195 and 197.
24 There is no doctoral thesis on this topic, though there were many such studies, conducted from the 1960s to the 1980s, on Shakespeare's compositors.
25 Proudfoot, 'New conservatism and the theatrical text', p. 134.
26 Ibid., p. 133.
27 Kastan states: 'I have, however, departed from Qo and Q1 only when they are evidently in error. In this I have been more conservative than many editors' in his introduction to *King Henry IV, Part 1*, The Arden Shakespeare (p. 119). Thompson and Taylor state: 'our editorial approach is to produce a conservative edition of each of the three texts, while providing the reader with enough information to entertain a less conservative edition. [...] we print the copy-text reading wherever we can reasonably defend it and emend only when, to us, it is implausible' in their introduction to *Hamlet*, The Arden Shakespeare (p. 510).
28 See also Bate 'The case for the Folio', p. 49.
29 Having said that, it is not as clean as the Folio text of *The Winter's Tale* or *Julius Caesar* or the first quarto of *Much Ado About Nothing* but quantitatively comparable to *Antony and Cleopatra* or *A Midsummer Night's Dream*.
30 Similar problems of spacing appear in 'ouer spread' (A4^r 19; I.ii.62) and 'in expected' (E4^v 11; III.iv.5).
31 The *OED* specifies that in Ancient Greece the decision was given by the first 'lot' to fall out of a receptacle that was shaken (lot *n.* 1). Contrastingly, the *OED* quotes Statius describing Minos as shaking the souls of the dead

in his inexorable urn in order to force them to confession (*Thebaid* 4.520).
32 Tanselle, 'The text of Melville', p. 342.
33 Ibid., p. 343.

REFERENCES

Anonymous, 'The House that Jack Built', in R. Fotherigham (ed.), *Australian Plays for the Colonial Stage 1834–1899* (St Lucia: University of Queensland Press, 2006), pp. 217–314.
Bate, J., 'The case for the Folio', 2007. www.rscshakespeare.co.uk/pdfs/Case_for_Folio.pdf [last accessed 30 January 2014].
Bate, J. (ed.), *Titus Andronicus*, The Arden Shakespeare (London and New York: Routledge, 1995).
Bate, J. and E. Rasmussen (eds), *The RSC Shakespeare Complete Works* (Basingstoke and New York: Palgrave Macmillan, 2007).
Foakes, R. (ed.), *King Lear*, The Arden Shakespeare (London: Thomson, 1997).
Freeman, A., 'The printing of *The Spanish Tragedy*', *The Library*, Fifth series 24:3 (1969): 187–99.
Greg, W. W. (ed.), *A Bibliography of English Printed Drama to the Restoration*, vol. 2 (London: The Bibliographical Society, 1970).
Kastan, D. S. (ed.), *King Henry IV, Part 1*, The Arden Shakespeare (London: Thomson Learning, 2002).
Kliman, B. (ed.), 'The enfolded *Hamlet*', *The Shakespeare Newsletter*, Extra Issue (1996): 1–44. http://triggs.djvu.org/global-language.com/ENFOLDED/ [last accessed 30 January 2014].
Kliman, B., *The Enfolded* Hamlets: *Parallel Texts of <F1> and {Q2}* (New York: AMS Press, 2004).
Marcus, L., *Unediting the Renaissance: Shakespeare, Marlowe, Milton* (London and New York: Routledge, 1996).
McLeod, R., 'UN *Editing* Shak-speare', *Sub-Stance* 33–4 (1982): 26–55.
McLeod, R., 'Introduction', in R. McLeod (ed.), *Crisis in Editing: Texts of the English Renaissance: Papers Given at the Twenty-fourth Annual Conference on Editorial Problems, University of Toronto, 4–5 November 1988* (New York: AMS Press, 1994), pp. ix–xiii.
Mowat, B. and P. Werstine (eds), *Hamlet*. The New Folger Shakespeare (New York. Washington Square Press, 1992).
Orgel, S. and A. R. Braunmuller (gen. eds), *The Pelican Shakespeare* [series of individual editions] (New York and London: Penguin Books, 1999–2002).
Proudfoot, R., 'New conservatism and the theatrical text', *Shakespeare International Yearbook* 2 (2002): 127–42.
Statius, *Silvae. Thebaid I–IV*, ed. and trans. J. H. Mozley (London: William Heinemann, 1967).
Tanselle, G. T., 'Varieties of scholarly editing', in D. C. Greetham (ed.), *Scholarly Editing: A Guide to Research* (New York: The Modern Language Association of America, 1995), pp. 9–32.

Tanselle, G. T., 'The text of Melville in the 21st century', in J. Bryant and R. Milder (eds), *Melville's Evermoving Dawn* (Kent, OH: Kent State University Press, 1997), 332–45.
Tanselle, G. T., 'The concept of format', *Studies in Bibliography* 53 (2000): 67–116.
Thompson, A. and N. Taylor (eds), *Hamlet*. The Arden Shakespeare, 3rd series (London: Thomson Learning, 2006).
Tronch-Pérez, J., *A Synoptic* Hamlet: *A Critical-Synoptic Edition of the Second Quarto and First Folio Texts of* Hamlet. SEDERI Monografías 3 (València: Publicacions de la Universitat de València; Zaragoza: Sederi, 2002).
Tronch-Pérez, J., 'Dual-reading editions for Shakespeare's two-text plays in the example of *Troilus and Cressida*', *Text* 17 (2005): 117–44.
Virgil, *Eclogues; Georgics; Aeneid I–VI*, trans. H. Rushton Fairclough. The Loeb Classical Library, vol. 63 (Cambridge, MA: Harvard University Press; London: Heinemann, 1986).
Werstine, P., 'The editorial usefulness of printing house and compositor studies', in G. B. Shand and R. C. Shady (eds), *Play-texts in Old Spelling: Papers from the Glendon Conference* (New York: AMS Press, 1984), pp. 35–64.
Werstine, P., 'Housmania: Episodes in twentieth-century "critical" editing of Shakespeare', in L. Erne and M. J. Kidnie (eds), *Textual Performances: The Modern Reproduction of Shakespeare's Drama* (Cambridge: Cambridge University Press, 2004), pp. 49–62.
West, M. L., *Textual Criticism and Editorial Technique Applicable to Greek and Latin Texts* (Stuttgart: B. G. Teubner, 1973).

Select bibliography of modern editions of *The Spanish Tragedy* consulted
Barker, S. and H. Hinds (eds), *The Routledge Anthology of Renaissance Drama* (London: Routledge, 2003).
Bevington, D. and E. Rasmussen (eds), '*The Spanish Tragedy*', in D. Bevington, L. Engle, K. Eisaman Maus and E. Rasmussen (eds), *English Renaissance Drama: A Norton Anthology* (New York: W. W. Norton 2002), pp. 3–73.
Bevington, D. (ed.), *The Spanish Tragedy*, Revels Student Editions (Manchester: Manchester University Press, 1996).
Boas, F. (ed.), *The Works of Thomas Kyd* (Oxford: Clarendon Press, 1955 [1901]).
Brooke, C. F. T. and N. B. Paradise (eds), *English Drama 1580–1642* (Boston: Heath, 1933).
Cairncross, A. S. (ed.), *The First Part of Hieronimo and The Spanish Tragedy*, Regents Renaissance Drama (Lincoln, NE: University of Nebraska Press, 1967).
Craik, T. W. (ed.), *Minor Elizabethan Tragedies* (London: Dent, 1974).
Dodsley, R., *A Select Collections of Old Plays*, vol. 2 (London, 1744).
Edwards, P. (ed.), *The Spanish Tragedy*, The Revels Plays (London: Methuen, 1959; rpt Manchester: Manchester University Press, 1977).
Gibson, C. (ed.), *Six Renaissance Tragedies* (Basingstoke: Macmillan, 1997).
Hawkins, T. (ed.), *Origin of the English Drama*, vol. 2 (London, 1773).

Hazlitt, W. C. (ed.), *Dodsley's Select Collection of Old Plays*, vol. 4 (London, 1874).
Kinney, A. (ed.), *Renaissance Drama: An Anthology of Plays and Entertainment* (Oxford: Blackwell, 1999).
Manly, J. M. (ed.), *Specimens of the Pre-Shakespearean Drama*, vol. 2 (London, 1897).
Matthews, B. and P. R. Lieder (eds), *The Chief British Dramatists, Excluding Shakespeare* (Boston: Houghton Mifflin, 1924).
Maus, K. Eisaman (ed.), *Four Revenge Tragedies*, The World's Classics (Oxford: Oxford University Press, 1995).
McIlwraith, A. K. (ed.), *Five Elizabethan Tragedies*, The World's Classics (Oxford: Oxford University Press, 1938).
Mulryne, J. R. (ed.), *The Spanish Tragedy*, New Mermaids (London: Benn, 1970; 2nd edn London, New York: A & C Black; W. W. Norton, 1989).
Neilson, W. A. (ed.), *The Chief British Dramatists, Excluding Shakespeare* (Boston: Houghton Mifflin, 1911).
Prouty, C. T. (ed.), *The Spanish Tragedy*, The Crofts Classics (Arlington Heights, IL: AHM Publishing Corporation, 1951).
Ross, T. W. (ed.), *The Spanish Tragedy*, Fountainwell Drama Texts (Berkeley and Los Angeles: University of California Press, 1968).
Schick, J. (ed.), *The Spanish Tragedy: A Play Written by Thomas Kyd*, The Temple Dramatists (London: Dent, 1898).
Smith, E. (ed.), *'The Spanish Tragedie' with 'The First Part of Jeronimo'*, Renaissance Dramatists (Harmondsworth: Penguin Books, 1998).
Thorndike, A. (ed.), *Minor Elizabethan Drama*, vol. 1, *Pre-Shakespeare Tragedies* (London: Dent, 1964).
Tydeman, W. (ed.), *Two Tudor Tragedies*. Penguin Classics (Harmondsworth: Penguin Books, 1992).

PART III

'Chronicles of Spain' or tales of Albion?

CHAPTER 7

How Spanish is *The Spanish Tragedy?* Dynastic policy and colonial expansion in revenge tragedy

Clara Calvo

The Spanish Tragedy seems at times a play more about Italian city-states and their scheming, vengeful dukes than about Habsburg Spain. Frank Ardolino, who in *Apocalypse and Armada* has read it as an Armada play depicting Spain as both Babel and Babylon, has voiced the common feeling that Italy lurks behind the Spanish court of Kyd's tragedy: 'In *The Spanish Tragedy* Hieronimo has taken a brutal revenge against his son's killers with his creation and enactment of the Italian tragedy'.[1] His suggestion that Hieronimo's revenge is modelled on Lorenzo de' Medici's cruel and bloody reaction to the Pazzi plot against his life supports a view of Italy as the effectual setting of the play.[2] Italian words, together with the discourse of revenge and the rhetoric of cruelty, mediate the representation of Spain throughout the text of Kyd's tragedy, and Italy, through its language and its Machiavellian villains, hovers distinctly over the play.[3]

Is *The Spanish Tragedy* a play about Spain at all? Is there anything Spanish about the characters, the plot, the manners, the language or the play as a whole? Philip Edwards thinks that Kyd 'chose Spain and Portugal without much thought of the real Spain and the real Portugal' and 'is innocent of contemporary allusions'.[4] Challenging this critical tradition, Steven Justice (1985) and José Manuel González (1989) have independently stressed the play's concern with Spain. Steven Justice argues that 'Kyd uses revenge tragedy to give form to popular images of Catholic Spain' and suggests that 'Kyd shows his Spain' in terms that resemble Robert Greene's anti-Spanish rhetoric in his pamphlet *The Spanish Masquerado* (1589).[5] With the Spanish Armada and the projected invasion of Britain in mind, he also concludes: 'It would be well to remember that the tragedy of *The Spanish Tragedy* is Spanish. Spain was much on English minds during the 1580s when the play was written.'[6] González also reads the play as anti-Spanish, the logical outcome of two countries, Spain and England, at war with each other. The negative view of Spain, fostered also by the Black Legend,[7] offered Kyd a suitable space for the creation of a dramatic universe presided over by injustice and chaos, from which horror, murder and revenge easily ensue.[8] Andrew Hadfield, instead, has gone beyond the reading of *The Spanish Tragedy* as an anti-Spanish play *about* Spain and suggests that '*The Spanish Tragedy* does not simply present us with a bigoted representation of the major Catholic power in contemporary Europe, but also reflects on the state of the English realm'.[9] Before Hadfield, Ardolino had already read *The Spanish Tragedy* as an Apocalypse play in which Hieronimo represents England, the true Protestant spirit that destroys Spain, the new Babylon.[10] But to see Hieronimo as a Protestant martyr requires stretching the text considerably. In spite of Hieronimo's sympathy for England in his 'pompous jest' (I.iv.137), the play's concern with religious controversy seems slight. Readings of *The Spanish Tragedy* as an Armada play that feeds on Anti-Catholic sentiment ignore the fact that in *The Spanish Tragedy* there is no mention of either the Pope or the Catholic Church. Unlike Greene's *The Spanish Masquerado*, Kyd's play betrays no hatred of fat priests or fear of the antichrist. As Philip Edwards points out, 'Marlowe' – the allegedly "atheist" playwright of *Tamburlaine* and *Dr Faustus* – 'never wrote a less Christian play than [Kyd's] *The Spanish Tragedy*'.[11] Kyd was arrested and tortured by the Privy Council for having in his possession atheistic writings, so he may well have drawn inspiration from them for the pagan, nihilistic ending of *The Spanish Tragedy*, even if the papers did ultimately belong, as he claimed, to Marlowe.

The Spanish characters in *The Spanish Tragedy* do not seem particularly Spanish. The courts of Portugal and Castile are unashamedly similar and do not represent distinct nations and peoples. This lack of difference between Spanish and Portuguese characters in *The Spanish Tragedy* and the similarity of both their courts to Quattrocento and Cinquecento Italian courts suggest that early modern English authors and audiences did not always deem it necessary to distinguish between southern Europeans as individuals belonging to differentiated nations with an individualised national identity.[12] In spite of religious and racial differences, the Mediterranean in early modern Europe was, through trade and war, a theatre of contact and exchange.[13] Mediterranean countries shared a common cultural space that fostered familiarity and downplayed cultural alterity, at least amongst Christian states, but also, occasionally if the arts or commerce were involved, with the Ottoman Empire. For many, it might have been hard to distinguish between the Italians, the Portuguese and the Spanish, as Philip II was

HOW SPANISH IS THE SPANISH TRAGEDY? 113

Duke of Milan since 1540, King of the Two Sicilies (i.e., Sicily and Naples) since his father's abdication in 1555, and King of Portugal since 1580. Critical discussion on *The Spanish Tragedy* should perhaps move beyond debating whether the play reflects Habsburg Spain or Renaissance Italy to considering how it portrays Mediterranean culture (Spanish, Portuguese, Italian, French and Ottoman) in relation to early modern England and its desire to play a role in the European colonial expansion.

This chapter will aim to show how *The Spanish Tragedy* simultaneously favours a view of corrupt Mediterranean monarchies and contemplates future imperial dreams for England. While questioning Spanish imperial power in the light of Portugal's diminished might, Kyd's tragedy suggests that the Habsburgs' policy of marital alliances and colonial expansion can be thwarted by the threat of dynastic crisis. Before doing so, it seems useful to explore how *The Spanish Tragedy* deals with cultural alterity and racial otherness, and how it distances itself from the ways in which alterity and otherness are signalled in contemporary plays that dramatise race and foreignness.

REPRESENTING CULTURAL ALTERITY

Early modern English playwrights construed national identity through a diverse array of dramatic devices. In *Titus Andronicus*, a play very much modelled on *The Spanish Tragedy*,[14] otherness is signalled through significant, outstanding racial features or through differences in attitudes to the world. The Goths are made to look different from the Romans through a well-known resource of epic poetry, the epithet; premodification is what distinguishes the Goths as a nation, since they are described as barbarous ('the barbarous Goths', 1.1.28) and traitorous ('these traitorous Goths', 4.1.92). The Goths are represented as a warmongering nation; consequently, 'warlike' is the adjective most often placed before the noun Goths:

1. Aaron: 'Now by the gods that **warlike Goths** adore' (2.1.61)
2. Marcus Andronicus to Titus: 'Thy **warlike hand**, thy mangled daughter here' (3.1.254)
3. Saturninus: 'Is **warlike Lucius** general of the Goths? (4.4.68)
4. Tamora: 'Say that the emperor requests a parley / Of **warlike Lucius**, and appoint the meeting' (4.4.100–1)
5. Tamora: 'To pluck proud Lucius from the **warlike Goths**' (4.4.109)
6. Tamora to Titus: 'To send for Lucius, thy thrice-valiant son, / Who leads towards Rome a band of **warlike Goths**' (5.2.112–13)
7. Titus: 'Welcome, ye **warlike Goths**; welcome, Lucius' (5.3.27)

The word 'warlike' occurs seven times, four to modify Goths, once to modify Titus's hand and two to modify Lucius, Titus's son, after he has joined the Goths. Tamora, once she is the wife of the Roman Emperor, applies the adjective 'warlike' to Lucius once and uses it twice to describe her own people.

If the Goths are given a national identity through moral and psychological features (barbarous, treacherous, warlike) and not through racial difference, Aaron the Moor, instead, is shaped out of blackness. When he is on stage, the adjective 'black' recurs in the dialogue. There are fourteen occurrences of the word 'black' in the play; in twelve of these, 'black' is used to describe either the Moor or his child by Tamora. Aaron himself signals his alterity by referring to his racial identity: 'Aaron will have his soul **black** like his face' (3.1.204). Marcus Andronicus compares 'a **black** ill-favoured fly' with 'the Empress' Moor' (3.2.66–7). Titus makes use of the simile to establish the superiority of the Romans as a race to a 'coal-**black** Moor' as he displays his feelings and intentions regarding Aaron:

> Yet I think we are not brought so low
> But that between us we can kill a fly
> That comes in likeness of a coal-**black** Moor.
>
> (*Titus Andronicus*, 3.2.75–7)

In *Titus*, blackness is also what is unlike 'us Romans'. The Nurse who has been entrusted with Tamora's child clearly establishes, in 4.2, a distinction between Moors and Romans through difference in skin colour:

> A joyless, dismal, **black**, and sorrowful issue.
> Here is the babe, as loathsome as a toad
> Amongst the fair-faced breeders of our clime.
> The Empress sends it thee, thy stamp, thy seal,
> And bids thee christen it with thy dagger's point.
>
> (*Titus Andronicus*, 4.2.66–70)

For the nurse 'black' is not only different from 'fair' – it is also ugly ('loathsome as a toad'). Aaron questions this equation 'is **black** so base a hue?' (71) and calls his child 'a beauteous blossom' (72). White, for Aaron, can be hideous: it becomes an insult when he addresses Tamora's sons as 'ye sanguine, shallow-hearted boys, / Ye whitelimed walls, ye alehouse painted signs' (96–7), and shows racial pride when he claims: 'Coal-**black** is better than another hue / In that it scorns to bear another hue' (98–9). White skin, in fact, Aaron says, is a 'treacherous hue, that will betray with blushing / The close enacts and counsels of thy heart' (116–17). This advantage of black skin over fair one is shown in action later in the play:

A GOTH: What, canst thou say all this and never blush?
AARON: Ay, like a black dog, as the saying is.
(*Titus Andronicus*, 5.1.121–2)

Alterity is construed differently in the comedies, often relying on speech differences. Foreigners are those who do not speak like us. In *The Merry Wives of Windsor*, national character emerges in discourse, as a foreigner is someone who, like the Welsh Priest and the French doctor, speaks bad English. Linguistic nationalism enters the play through remarks on how foreigners abuse the English language. The presence of a Welsh priest (Sir Hugh Evans) – addressed by Pistol as 'thou mountain-foreigner!' (1.1.133) – and a French Doctor (Doctor Caius) provides ample occasion for linguistic merrymaking and nationalistic assertion at their expense. The Welsh priest cannot deal properly with voiced initial consonants /v/ and /b/, so he replaces them with voiceless /f/ and /p/ respectively; he also seems to have trouble with final voiced /d/, which becomes voiceless /t/: 'It is petter that friends is the sword and end it. And there is also another device in my prain, which peradventure prings goot discretions with it' (1.1.36–8); 'It is that fery person of all the 'orld, as just as you will desire' (1.1.42–3). In *Henry V*, Captain Fluellen, who is also Welsh, has the same problem with initial voiced consonants, giving 'falorous' for 'valorous' and 'porn' for 'born'. Besides having trouble with sounds, the Welsh priest sometimes ignores the fact that in English certain grammatical functions require a given part of speech and replaces verbs and adjectives with a noun: '*Evans*: Master Slender, I will description [i.e. describe] the matter to you, if you be capacity [i.e. capable] of it' (1.1.180–1).

The French Doctor has phonetical troubles too, since he cannot pronounce certain English phonemes; in his speech, initial /w/ is replaced by /v/, /th/ by /d/ and /f/ by /v/: 'Vat is you sing? I do not like dese toys. Pray you go and vetch me in my closet *un boîtier vert* – a box, a green-a box. Do intend vat I speak?' (*The Merry Wives of Windsor*, 1.4.38–40). His phonetic disabilities are accompanied by a sort of Franglais which include false friends ('intend' for *entendre*), grammatical errors such as the absence of personal pronouns (Do you hear what I say?), lexical errors ('speak' for 'say') and French borrowings ('*un boîtier vert*'). Besides, he cannot always decipher the meaning of English lexemes, particularly when they contain a pun, and the Host rushes to explain them, as in 'Mockwater, in our English tongue, is valour, bully' (2.3.52).

This non-standard use of the English language by a Welshman and a Frenchman is noticed by Mistress Quickly, Sir John Falstaff and the Host of the Garter. Quickly finds Doctor Caius's lack of linguistic competence in English unbearable:

> What, John Rugby! [*Enter* JOHN RUGBY] I pray thee, go to the casement and see if you can see my master, Master Doctor Caius, coming. If he do, i'faith, and find anybody in the house, here will be an old abusing of God's patience and the King's English.
>
> (*The Merry Wives of Windsor*, 1.4.1–5)

Sir John Falstaff's bad humour once the wives' pranks are revealed finds an outlet in pointing out the Welshman's phonetical disabilities:

> EVANS: Seese is not good to give putter; your belly is all putter.
> FALSTAFF: 'Seese' and 'putter'? Have I lived to stand at the taunt of one that makes fritters of English? This is enough to be the decay of lust and late walking through the realm.
>
> (*The Merry Wives of Windsor*, 5.5.134–7)

The Host brings the dispute between Caius and Evans to an end, knowing that they can be stopped from delivering blows to each other, but not deterred from mangling English linguistic structures:

> Disarm them and let them question. Let them keep their limbs whole, and hack our English.
>
> (*The Merry Wives of Windsor*, 3.1.66–7).

English – 'our English' according to the Host – stands in need of being defended from the attack of foreign speech, just as much as England needs to protect its land from invasion. This shared feeling of the need to look after the national language – which the possessive pronoun 'our' turns into a sort of commodity owned by Englishmen, part of the private property or patrimony of those who constitute the English nation – betrays a certain amount of anxiety at a time when English is struggling to find a place as a strong European vernacular language and England is eagerly looking for means to establish itself as a European colonial power.

None of these means available to early modern playwrights for the stage construction of foreign identities is deployed in *The Spanish Tragedy*. The play shows no interest in presenting the Spanish and the Portuguese through individualised national features, nor does it construe them as aliens to an English audience. Kyd's Spaniards are not represented as racial 'others' (like Aaron in *Titus* or Othello) or as foreigners (like Evans, the Welsh Priest and Doctor Caius in *Merry Wives*). Hieronimo, Lorenzo, the Duke of Castile and Bel-imperia

HOW SPANISH IS *THE SPANISH TRAGEDY*? 117

have no single character trait that identifies them as 'Spanish'. There is nothing that can be pointed at as specifically 'Portuguese' about Balthazar and no attempt is made to make him stand apart from the Spanish characters in the court of Spain where he is more a guest than a prisoner. Names of characters do not signal nationality either. The *dramatis personae* contain no particularly Spanish names, apart from Pedro and possibly Pedringano, a combination of Pedro and the Spanish morpheme found in *fulano, zutano, mengano, perengano* (meaning 'this, that and the other'). Lorenzo could be Spanish – Philip II's *magnum opus* at El Escorial may have provided inspiration. But Lorenzo is also an Italian name, as in Lorenzo de' Medici, and Frank Ardolino has seen a connection between the name of the character and the Pazzi plot to kill the Duke of Florence in Hieronimo's allusion to the Italian tragedians, since the Medicis celebrated marriages with intermezzi, i.e. theatrical entertainments.[15] Other Italian-sounding names in the play are Andrea, Alexandro and Isabella (although the Spanish 'Isabel' also occurs) – and Lorenzo asks Pedringano to meet Serberine at St Luigis's Park. Several characters have Latin names: Bel-imperia, Villuppo, Christophil, Horatio and Hieronimo. Hieronimo has equivalents in both Spanish (Jeronimo) and Italian (Girolamo). Don Cyprian, the Duke of Castile, sounds more Portuguese than Spanish and Don Pedro, the Viceroy's brother, more Spanish than Portuguese.

DYNASTIC CRISIS AND THE ANXIETY OF SUCCESSION

National identity and the peculiarities of national character are not, therefore, a concern of the play. Instead, the play pays attention to the fate of monarchs and their dynastic lines, and shows how the actions of kings and rulers impinge on the history of countries as geo-political entities. Spain is construed throughout the play as a colonial power that extends and manages its empire through war and taxes demanded of conquered lands. In Hieronimo's masque (I.iv), Spain is also given a national identity as England's opponent. *The Spanish Tragedy* has often been discussed in relation to the Armada, the Pope's command to invade England and kill Elizabeth I, and religious conflict in early modern Europe. There is room, however, in Kyd's revenge tragedy to undertake an exploration of Spain's role as England's greatest rival and antagonist beyond the fear of invasion awaken by the Armada and also beyond its fervent Catholic zeal against Protestant England. *The Spanish Tragedy* extends its interests beyond home affairs and religion, and casts its nets into the deep of colonial desires and imperial politics. In this sense, Kyd articulates Spain as a touchstone

England has to measure itself against. It is Spain's colonial might that England wants to equal and surpass; it is Spain's capacity to go over its geographical boundaries and collect taxes, therefore increasing its power, that is feared and needs to be contained. At the end of the play, Spain's pride and power has been dealt a blow with the suspension of dynastic continuity and the political instability that the lack of an heir apparent generates. Kyd's early audience may have been familiar with *Gorboduc*, a play in which the lack of a hereditary line and heir apparent leads to civil war, economic depression and ruin, and the ending of *The Spanish Tragedy* may have triggered expectations of a similar fate for Spain. The topicality of Kyd's play, therefore, extends beyond the Armada anxiety to a greater and more tangible fear – Elizabeth's inability to produce an heir. The fate of Spain at the end of the play could easily be decoded on the Elizabethan stage as the possible fate of England.

If *The Spanish Tragedy* is about Spain as a mirror for England, how is Spain imagined in the play? After the masque that Hieronimo puts up to entertain the court, the Portuguese Ambassador displays his approval of a dumb show that celebrates a scenario dear to his heart:

That Spain may not insult for her success,
Since English warriors likewise conquer'd Spain
And made them bow their knees to Albion.

(I.iv.169–71)

In the Ambassador's speech, Spain is first imagined as a monarchy or political entity, personified as proud and able to insult with its arrogance, in terms not unlike those Greene uses in *The Spanish Masquerado* (1589). In the second of these lines, Spain is imagined in terms of space, as a kingdom, a geographical entity with known boundaries, a plot of land that can be conquered. The use of the pronoun 'them' in the last line is unsettling but telling. It is certainly ungrammatical, since it introduces a lack of grammatical concord, given that the antecedent of 'them' is 'Spain'. Spain is here finally presented momentarily as a group of individuals. In most of Kyd's revenge tragedy, though, the geographical reality of space takes over the Spanish as individuals and Spain becomes a territorial entity, a space defined in opposition to others (Portugal, England) that can be expanded through colonisation or diminished through invasion. In this light, the Ambassador's remark after Hieronimo's masque seems a retort to the King of Spain's lines before the masque, when he orders, rather than invites his guests to sit for the banquet:

HOW SPANISH IS *THE SPANISH TRAGEDY*? 119

> Sit down young prince, you are our second guest:
> Brother sit down, and nephew take your place:
> Signior Horatio, wait thou upon our cup,
> For well thou hast deserved to be honour'd.
> Now lordings fall to, Spain is Portugal,
> And Portugal is Spain, we both are friends,
> Tribute is paid, and we enjoy our right.
>
> (I.iv.128–34)

The long list of imperatives in these conciliatory but otherwise arrogant lines places the King of Spain in a clear position of authority over his guests. After the last line, 'Tribute is paid, and we enjoy our right', the declaration that Spain is Portugal and Portugal Spain acquires its true meaning, i.e. that the King of Spain is also King of Portugal. The two countries remain distinct geographical units, bound by a single monarch, and their union articulated though the payment of tribute. Later, this union based on economic exchange is rearticulated through the proposed marriage of Balthazar and Bel-imperia, which is graced with an 'uncle's gift' (the tribute is waived) and which could seal the union with the production of a suitable heir, as the King of Spain explains to the Portuguese Ambassador:

> I'll grace her marriage with an uncle's gift,
> And this it is: in case the match go forward,
> The tribute which you pay shall be releas'd,
> And if by Balthazar she have a son,
> He shall enjoy the kingdom after us.
>
> (II.iii.17–21)

At the end of the play, the dream of union is shattered. By fulfilling his revenge on the Duke of Castile, his son and his daughter, Revenge, with Hieronimo's aid, brings about the end of a dynastic line and unleashes a political crisis, as the play-within-the-play gives way to a void in the succession to the Spanish throne. The fall of the house of Spain is announced, in a state of semi-shock, by the King himself:

> What age hath ever heard such monstrous deeds?
> My brother, and the whole succeeding hope
> That Spain expected after my decease!
>
> (IV.iv.202–4)

Oblivious to the corpses of his niece and nephew, the King gives orders only for the removal of Castile's body. Striking as it may seem, singling out Castile at this point has an important structural function. Castile's death launches the ultimate political crisis:

> Go bear his body hence, that we may mourn
> The loss of our beloved brother's death,
> That he may be entomb'd whate'er befall:
> I am the next, the nearest, last of all.
>
> (IV.iv.205–8)

If the death of Castile leaves Spain without its heir apparent, the death of Balthazar also brings the end of the Portuguese dynastic line – the Viceroy asks to be set adrift on a ship with the body of Balthazar, since 'Spain hath no refuge for a Portingale' (IV.iv.217). With Balthazar and Bel-imperia dead, the dream of political union through the birth of an heir collapses and the Viceroy's words challenge the King's earlier confident statement (I.iv.122–3). Spain and Portugal may be ruled by the same king, but they remain, at the end of the play, distinct, separate countries, divided by murder. Except for the final scene in which Andrea and Revenge give the list of punishments and rewards, the play's action technically ends at this point, with the bearing away of the bodies of those who were next in line to the throne, as in *Hamlet*, but also with an unequivocal message: no good comes out of Spain, particularly for a Portuguese.

Reading *The Spanish Tragedy* as a play about dynastic policy and the anxiety of succession helps to account for Castile's death. Castile's murder is often read as a gratuitous act of unnecessary violence on Hieronimo's part, and it is usually singled out as an example of the serious structural shortcomings the play presents, and, in particular, of its loose ends. Hieronimo's revenge may be initially directed towards his son's murderers – but Revenge's revenge for Don Andrea's sake is more complex and far-reaching. Its aim is the destruction of the entire dynastic line to the thrones of Spain and Portugal. To be complete, this aim requires the deaths of both Castile, the heir apparent to date, and Bel-imperia, who could have provided an heir to secure the continuity of the House of Spain, besides bringing into effect the union between the two countries.

CHRONICLE PLAY AND MORALITY PLAY

When *The Spanish Tragedy* is read as a chronicle play about past events rather than as a tragedy reflecting on contemporary Spanish affairs, a series of connections between Spanish history and Kyd's play emerge.[16] The planned marriage between Bel-imperia and Balthazar, proposed as a political union between the two countries, hopefully leading to their effective union through the couple's offspring, echoes the Habsburgs' policy of marital alliances. Charles V married Isabel of

HOW SPANISH IS *THE SPANISH TRAGEDY*? 121

Portugal (d. 1539) in 1526 and in 1543 Philip II married his first wife, Maria, also a Portuguese princess. The dynastic policy and succession line of Kyd's Spain also resemble closely the actual hereditary practices of the Habsburgs. After the death of King Sebastian, Philip II could claim the Portuguese crown on the strength of his mother's rights. His father's abdication and retirement to the monastery at Yuste, in 1556, is echoed in the Viceroy's abdication in favour of his son Balthazar: 'Here take my crown, I give it her and thee, / And let me live a solitary life, / In ceaseless prayers' (III.xiv.31–3). When Charles V retired from government, his son Philip II succeeded him as King of Spain and its colonial empire in the New World but it was his brother Ferdinand I, who had been effectually ruling the Austrian side of the Habsburg empire for some years, who eventually succeeded him as Holy Roman Emperor, just as in Kyd's play Castile is presented as heir to his brother, the King of Spain. Bel-imperia's imprisonment by her brother on the grounds that it was primarily for her sake, due to her state and their father's anger – 'Your melancholy, sister, since the news / Of your first favourite Don Andrea's death / My father's old wrath hath exasperate' (III.x.71–3) – echoes Joanna of Castile's forced confinement in Tordesillas. Joanna was Queen of Castile between 1504 and 1555, but she lived deprived of freedom and royal power, first by her husband, the Archduke Philip of Flanders (also known as Philip the Handsome), then by her father, Ferdinand of Aragon, and later by her son, Charles V. On the grounds of mental illness, variously diagnosed as melancholia, depression and schizophrenia, she was kept from government, effectively a prisoner in the castle in Tordesillas. She retained the titles of Queen of Castile, Leon, Aragon, Naples and Sicily while her husband, father and son effectively reigned as regents. Lorenzo's linking Bel-imperia's melancholy to the news of Don Andrea's death echoes Joanna's grief and destructive reaction to the untimely death of her husband, documented by contemporary sources and later depicted by nineteenth-century romantic artists (Pradilla Ortiz) and playwrights (Tamayo y Baus), and mythologised by twentieth-century historians.[17]

The dynastic anxiety *The Spanish Tragedy* encodes in its final scene is a recurrent topic in the play. At the opening of Act III, when news of Balthazar being safe and sound at the Spanish court has not yet reached his father's ears, Portugal's Viceroy laments the 'Infortunate condition of kings' (III.i.1) and invites his courtiers to 'look upon your king, / By hate deprived of his dearest son / The only hope of our successive line' (III.i.12–14). This anxiety about the 'successive line' of Portugal could be read as a warning for England, as there was no longer any hope of Elizabeth producing an heir. The play ends with two kingdoms, Spain and Portugal, left devoid of an heir apparent. In *Hamlet*, the dynastic void is filled – and the problem sorted out – with the arrival of Fortinbras, for whom Hamlet casts his vote just before he expires. In *The Spanish Tragedy*, by contrast, the play ends with an unresolved succession to the crown of the two leading colonial empires in sixteenth-century Europe. Freeman has pointed out the ahistoricity of this situation, which bears no parallel with contemporary events in Spain, even though reports of the death of Philip II's son Don Diego, Prince of Asturias, may have reached England.[18] Even if the events in *The Spanish Tragedy* are not historically true, they encode an anxiety that was entirely justified. Don Diego was the third heir apparent to die since Philip II's coronation: Don Carlos died in 1568, Don Fernando in 1578 and Don Diego in 1582. After Don Diego's death, Don Felipe, the future Philip III, then a mere infant, assured nevertheless the continuity of the dynastic line, but, given the fate of his brothers, one could wonder for how long.

The dynastic void *The Spanish Tragedy* ends with was not an accurate reflection of the contemporary state of affairs in Spain, but, in the case of the English monarchy, the dynastic crisis the play envisages after Hieronimo has accomplished his revenge was a far more likely scenario. If Andrew Hadfield is right and Kyd, while writing his play, had in mind the Alençon match, that is the failed marriage proposal that Francis, Duke of Alençon made to Elizabeth in 1579 and 1580, then *The Spanish Tragedy* is also, in this respect, a play about England.[19] The dynastic crisis the play portrays could be read as an indirect warning for the Crown – and an incentive to name an heir. *The Spanish Tragedy* may have worked on the stage of Elizabethan London as a morality play, showing England the ills derived from the lack of an heir apparent.

The Spanish Tragedy is, in any case, a play that involves four nations: Spain, Portugal, Italy and, to some extent, England.[20] Through Hieronimo's masque and through the play's final, unresolved, dynastic crisis, England is decidedly present in the play. The hangman and Pedringano's execution (III.vi) also invite the audience to connect what was displayed on stage with everyday English life off stage. Italy, present through its association with Machiavellian dukes and revenge, is also part of the play in a geographical or territorial sense, given contemporary Spanish control of Milan, Sicily and Naples. Little attempt has been made so far to regard *The Spanish Tragedy* as a play about Spain, Portugal, Italy and England, that is, a play about the relations between England and the north-west Mediterranean quadrant, particularly with regard to the colonial aspirations of their respective rulers

HOW SPANISH IS *THE SPANISH TRAGEDY*? 123

in both North Africa and the West Indies, and their always tense relations with the Turks. Freeman, in *Thomas Kyd: Facts and Problems*, considers *The Spanish Tragedy* a play about Hispano-Portuguese relations but on closer inspection the play seems to deal with them in connection with the much wider context of Mediterranean politics at the time and the colonial policies of European monarchs.

IMPERIAL MONARCHIES

Relations between Spain and England have always been articulated from the perspective of the English fear of an invasion unleashed by the Armada, but Spain and England can be cast in a different light, as countries fighting for imperial influence on other Mediterranean kingdoms and their colonies. After the Battle of Alcantara (1580) that obtained for Philip II the Portuguese crown, the Pretender to the throne of Portugal, Don Antonio, Prior of Crato, found refuge at the English court. The rebellion at Terceira, the second largest of the Azores, and the naval battle that ensued, probably had the support of, and possibly some aid from, the English Crown.[21] The battle of Terceira (1582) was followed by the slaughter of prisoners ordered by the Marquis of Santa Cruz. If Kyd did not hear of this historical event or read a printed report of it, he could have learnt about it from Thomas Lodge, who visited the island in 1585.[22]

In the light of these historical events, Hieronimo's masque can be read as establishing the grounds for dispute between two competing colonial powers, a dominant Spain and an emergent England in front of a third country, Portugal, and most crucially, its colonies. Portuguese colonial expansion began in the fourteenth century and was directed to the North of Africa; the year 1415 – in which the English under Henry V fought, in Harfleur and Agincourt, for their colonial expansion into France – is also the year Portugal conquered the North African town of Ceuta.[23] Later, the discovery of America added Brazil to Portuguese possessions. Kyd presents Portugal's colonial power as residual when he makes the King of Spain say:

> And now to meet these Portuguese,
> For as we now are, so sometimes were these,
> Kings and commanders of the western Indies.
>
> (III.xiv.5–7)

With these lines, the King of Spain clearly states that Portugal's colonies, together with its crown, are now under Spanish rule, enlarging its empire in America.

It is perhaps no coincidence that *The Spanish Tragedy* and George Peele's *The Battle of Alcazar* (1594) are related because, unlike other early modern English revenge plays, they are not primarily concerned with either Greek or Roman history and classical settings or with the matter of Britain and the remote, legendary past of the British Isles. Greeks and Romans are no foreigners but predecessors, given Brutus's role in the formation of England, so *The Spanish Tragedy* is one of the very first plays to deal with contemporary European concerns in a revenge play. The colonial interest of the play is resurrected in *The Battle of Alcazar*, a play that serves as historical introduction to why Portugal is in the hands of Spain at the opening of *The Spanish Tragedy*. *The Battle of Alcazar* also connects again dynastic trouble and colonial ambition, and it is not difficult to imagine that it may have been written to cash in on *The Spanish Tragedy*'s success. The dynastic void arising from the disappearance of the Portuguese king in the North of Africa did not remain a matter of internal national conflict and soon involved European kingdoms. By taking under his care the crown of Portugal as a result of the dynastic void ensuing from the loss of King Sebastian, the Spanish king also obtained the control of Portuguese colonies in both the North of Africa and the West Indies. Thus, *The Spanish Tragedy* and *The Battle of Alcazar* result from an English interest in Iberian affairs that stretches beyond the Armada and religious conflict, and points in the direction of colonialism, territorial expansion and imperial dreams.

An interest in Portuguese affairs existed in Elizabethan England, as suggested by the publication, in 1600, of a book, translated from Italian and dedicated by the publisher Edward Blount to Henry Wriothesley, third Earl of Southampton, *The historie of the uniting of the kingdom of Portvgall to the Crowne of Castill. Containing the last warres of the Portugals against the Moores in Africke, the end of the house of Portugall, and change of that Gouernment*. The Italian original, by Girolamo Franchi di Conestaggio of Genoa, *Dell' unione del regno di Portogallo alla corona di Castiglia, istoria del Sig. Jeronimo di Franchi Conestaggio*, had been published in Genoa in 1585. The author of the original Portuguese text on which the Italian translation is based is assumed to have been Juan de Silva, fourth Count of Portalegre. Conestaggio's history of Portugal, like *The Spanish Tragedy*, links colonial ambition and dynastic crisis, the result of this lethal combination being annexation by a foreign Crown.

In Hieronimo's masque, Kyd is dealing with historical facts, even if, as Philip Edwards says, he has got them upside-down. The degree of accuracy in Kyd's historical facts is not the crucial issue here, since what matters is how an early modern English audience watching the play were invited to envisage or imagine a colonial future for their own country. If Portugal, formerly a country of 'Kings and commanders of the Western Indies' has fallen under Spanish rule, perhaps one day England could take over Spain in the control of Portugal and its colonies. This is the future for England that the play articulates. Through Hieronimo's masque *The Spanish Tragedy* shows how a colonial power – Portugal – can be conquered and has to pay homage and tribute to another – Spain – and how this country in turn can be, since it has been in the past, subdued by an emergent colonial power – England. Hieronimo's masque presents Portugal as a country that has been twice invaded by English knights, and the masque seems to suggest that what has been accomplished in the past could be achieved once again. In Kyd's rewritten history of Anglo-Portuguese relations, the first Portuguese ruler deposed by an English knight was a Saracen king, possibly a Muslim corsair, suggesting perhaps that England could take an active part in Christian Europe's fight against the Turks. The ending of the play, with no heir apparent to the Spanish and Portuguese thrones, invites the audience to imagine a country moving in the direction of anarchy and chaos and civil war – like England at the end of *Gorboduc*. England would clearly benefit from a power void in Spain – anarchy and civil war always leave a country emasculated. Given historical reality, this vision of European affairs Kyd presented in his *Spanish Tragedy* may be deemed nothing but wishful thinking – but this is exactly the power allowed to the stage through performance and dramatic illusion.

Unlike other early modern English plays, *The Spanish Tragedy* is not concerned with nations and national identity or with the peculiarities of foreigners and cultural alterity. Rather, it is a play that explores dynastic crisis in the context of western Mediterranean imperial politics. As such, it is as much concerned with Spain and Portugal as with Italy and England – and, to a certain extent, with the Ottoman empire. The play questions the expansive policies of the houses of Aragon and Habsburg through marital alliances. It repeatedly encodes the anxiety of a reigning monarch who is left without an heir apparent and the fear that dynastic crisis may lead to anarchy. In a more minor key, the play also toys with nationalistic aspirations and dreams, seeing England as a European colonial monarchy, rising to imperial pre-eminence after the decline of Portugal and Spain as colonial leaders. Through the enactment on stage of the dynastic crisis of Spain and Portugal, *The Spanish Tragedy* envisages a role for England as the future imperial monarchy of the western Mediterranean.

NOTES

1 Ardolino, *Apocalypse and Armada*, p. 99.
2 Kyd had other models for Hieronimo's revenge, as Ardolino himself suggests, when he reads Hieronimo's reference to the French tragedians as an allusion to the St Bartholomew's Day massacre of Protestants, arranged by Catherine de' Medici and the Duke of Guise. See *Apocalypse and Armada*, pp. 100–20.
3 Hoenselaars, however, has shown that Italy in Renaissance drama is not merely the land of vice but a real nation. See 'Under the dent of the English pen', pp. 272–91.
4 Edwards, 'Introduction', in *The Spanish Tragedy*, p. xxv.
5 Justice, 'Spain, tragedy, and *The Spanish Tragedy*', pp. 272, 274.
6 Ibid., p. 274.
7 The phrase 'Black Legend' is often used to refer to anti-Spanish sentiment and propaganda fostered mainly by Protestant and Calvinist writers since the sixteenth century. Accounts of the cruelty and inhuman behaviour of Spanish rulers and settlers against native Indians in Spanish colonies in the New World were used to disqualify Spain and its people at a time when the country was a world superpower. The work of a Spanish priest, Bartolomé de las Casas, *A Short Account of the Destruction of the Indies* (1552), soon translated into several European languages, helped to create a widespread state of opinion that regarded Spanish colonial practices as criminal. The activities of the Spanish Inquisition on both sides of the Atlantic also contributed to the negative portrayal of the country as morally and politically corrupt. In Protestant countries, such as England and the Netherlands, anti-Spanish feeling was used to suggest that Spanish imperial expansion had to be counteracted by increasing the presence of other nations in the New World. See Maltby, *The Black Legend in England*, and Cárcel, *La leyenda negra: historia y opinión*.
8 González, 'Lo Español en *The Spanish Tragedy*', pp. 95–6.
9 Hadfield, '*The Spanish Tragedy*, the Alençon marriage plans', p. 43.
10 Ardolino, *Apocalypse and Armada*, passim.
11 Edwards, *The Spanish Tragedy*, p. lii.
12 It is nevertheless true that national stereotypes were often exploited in early modern plays. For a study of national character and Renaissance drama see Hoenselaars, *Images of Englishmen and Foreigners*.
13 See Braudel, *The Mediterranean and the Mediterranean World in the Age of Philip II*.
14 Bate, in 'The performance of revenge: *Titus Andronicus* and *The Spanish Tragedy*', has pointed out the close relationship existing between these two plays, both of which seem to lack a single source.
15 Ardolino suggests: 'Hieronimo also alludes to the famous Pazzi plot in 1478 to kill Lorenzo de' Medici during High Mass at the cathedral when the sanctus bell was rung. However, the conspirators only wounded Lorenzo, who hunted down, tortured, and brutally executed those connected with

the assassination attempt.' In *The Spanish Tragedy* Hieronimo reverses this outcome by killing Lorenzo, whose name, Catholicity and Machiavellian activities link him with Lorenzo de' Medici, Duke of Florence. See Ardolino, *Apocalypse and Armada*, p. 96.
16 Ardolino sees *The Spanish Tragedy* as a history play about Italy, not Spain, in *Apocalypse and Armada*, pp. 83–99.
17 See Gómez, Juan-Navarro and Zatlin, *Juana of Castile*.
18 Freeman, *Facts and Problems*, p. 54.
19 Hadfield, 'The Spanish Tragedy, the Alençon marriage plans', *passim*.
20 Although events in the play never take place beyond the boundaries of the Iberian Peninsula (with, perhaps, the only exception of the island of Terceira), a fifth colonial monarchy has to be added to this list, if the play-within-the-play is taken into account – the Ottoman empire.
21 Freeman, *Facts and Problems*, p. 52.
22 Ibid., p. 52.
23 For an illuminating study of Anglo-Portuguese relations and early modern drama, see Homem, 'Cross-histories, straying narratives', pp. 45–55.

REFERENCES

Ardolino, F., *Apocalypse and Armada in Kyd's Spanish Tragedy* (Kirksville: Sixteenth Century Journal Publishers, Northeast Missouri State University, 1995).
Bate, J., 'The performance of revenge: *Titus Andronicus* and *The Spanish Tragedy*', in François Laroque (ed.), *The Show Within: Dramatic and Other Insets: English Renaissance Drama (1550–1642)*, 2 vols (Montpellier: Université Paul-Valéry, 1992), vol. 2, pp. 267–84.
Bate, J., 'Shakespeare's islands', in T. Clayton, S. Brock and V. Forés (eds), *Shakespeare and the Mediterranean* (Newark, DE: University of Delaware Press, 2004), pp. 289–307.
Braudel, F., *The Mediterranean and the Mediterranean World in the Age of Philip II*, 2 vols, trans. Siân Reynolds (Berkeley, CA: University of California Press, 1966; 1995).
Cárcel, R. G., *La Leyenda Negra: historia y opinión* (Madrid: Alianza, 1992).
Edwards, P. (ed.), *The Spanish Tragedy*, The Revels Plays (London: Methuen, 1959).
Freeman, A., *Thomas Kyd: Facts and Problems* (Oxford: Clarendon Press, 1967).
Gómez, M. A., S. Juan-Navarro and P. Zatlin (eds), *Juana of Castile: History and Myth of the Mad Queen* (Cranbury, NJ: Associated Presses, 2008).
González, J. M., 'Lo español en *The Spanish Tragedy*', *Revista Alicantina de Estudios Ingleses* 2 (1989): 91–100.
Hadfield, A., 'The Spanish Tragedy, the Alençon marriage plans, and John Stubbs's *Discoverie of A Gaping Gulf*', *Notes and Queries* 47 (2000): 42–3.
Hoenselaars, A. J., *Images of Englishmen and Foreigners in the Drama of Shakespeare and His Contemporaries: A Study of Stage Characters and*

National Identity in English Renaissance Drama, 1558–1642 (Rutherford, NJ: Farleigh Dickinson University Press, 1992).
Hoenselaars, A. J., 'Mapping Shakespeare's Europe', in A. J. Hoenselaars (ed.), *Reclamations of Shakespeare* (Amsterdam: Rodopi, 1994), pp. 223–48.
Hoenselaars, A. J., '"Under the dent of the English pen": The language of Italy in English Renaissance drama', in M. Marrapodi, A. J. Hoenselaars, M. Capuzzo and L. F. Santucci (eds), *Shakespeare's Italy: Functions of Italian Locations in Renaissance Drama* (Manchester: Manchester University Press, 1993; rev. edn, 1997), pp. 30–48.
Homem, R. C., 'Cross-histories, straying narratives: Anglo-Portuguese imbrications and Shakespeare's history plays', in M. Gibinska and A. Romanowska (eds), *Shakespeare in Europe: History and Memory* (Cracow: Jagiellonian University Press, 2008), pp. 45–55.
Hunter, G. K., *Dramatic Identities and Cultural Tradition* (Liverpool: Liverpool University Press, 1978).
Justice, S., 'Spain, tragedy, and *The Spanish Tragedy*', *Studies in English Literature* 25 (1985): 271–88.
Maltby, M. S., *The Black Legend in England: The Development of Anti-Spanish Sentiment 1558–1660* (Durham, NC: Duke University Press, 1971).

CHAPTER 8

Kyd's use of Antonio Pérez's *Las Relaciones* in *The Spanish Tragedy*

Frank Ardolino

Building on the insights of S. F. Johnson and Ronald Broude, scholars have delineated the anti-Spanish themes of *The Spanish Tragedy*. Johnson noted the identification of Spain with Babylon, which is established in Hieronimo's declaration, directly before the performance of the revenge playlet, 'Now shall I see the fall of Babylon / Wrought by the heavens in this confusion' (IV.i.195–6). Relating Hieronimo's prediction with the confusion of the sundry tongues of the playlet, Johnson concluded that Kyd uses the analogy of Babylon/Babel to depict the fall of Babylon/Spain engineered by Hieronimo, the Spanish justice-figure who paradoxically represents for Elizabethan audiences the Protestant revenger.[1] Similarly, in three significant articles, Ronald Broude (1971, 1973, 1975) maintained that Kyd's depiction of a merciless revenge exacted upon Babylon/Spain fits the age in which Sir Francis Drake and his ship the *Revenge* helped to defeat the Spanish Armada in 1588.[2]

Like Broude, Eugene Hill argued that *The Spanish Tragedy* involves the transfer of empire from Spain to England, which is enacted symbolically in Hieronimo's playlet where the sundry languages emblematic of Babylonian confusion are replaced by the English vernacular.[3] Stephen Justice explained that Kyd uses the Black Legend to attack Catholic Spain as a tyranny in which no justice is possible 'because it had rejected Christ's new dispensation'.[4] Further, in '"In Paris? Mass, and well remembered"', I maintained that Hieronimo's *Soliman and Perseda* playlet, which ostensibly is performed to celebrate the marriage between Balthazar and Bel-imperia, alludes to the fateful marriage between Henry of Navarre and Margaret of Valois in Paris on St Bartholomew's Day in 1572, when Huguenots were massacred by Catholic conspirators. In effect, Hieronimo's revenge playlet reverses the earlier historical event. Finally, in *Apocalypse and*

Armada in Kyd's Spanish Tragedy, I argued that the play contains a subtext that concerns the defeat of the Spanish Armada in 1588.

The purpose of this chapter is to demonstrate that in the episodes dealing with the murder of Serberine and the execution of Pedringano for this crime (III.ii–vii), Kyd creates a political subtext that is related to the play's anti-Spanish themes.[5] Critics have maintained that the betrayal of Pedringano by Lorenzo is adapted from *Leicester's Commonwealth*, also known as *The Copie of a Leter*, and *The Leter of Estate*, two anti-Leicester libels written between 1584 and 1586 that attacked Robert Dudley as a Machiavellian villain who betrayed his accomplices after they carried out his criminal orders. However, Kyd combines aspects of the anti-Leicester tradition with elements of the Spanish Black Legend as expressed in Antonio Pérez's *Las Relaciones* in order to depict Spain under Philip II as the evil enemy of Protestant England. First published in France in 1591, *Las Relaciones* perhaps did more to undermine Philip II's image as a responsible and prudent monarch than any work in the anti-Hispanist tradition.[6]

Kyd combines two traditions that are similar and yet opposed to each other. *Leicester's Commonwealth* was written by Catholic dissidents determined to defame the leader of the militant Protestant faction in Elizabeth I's government, while Pérez's revelations about Philip's treachery were welcomed in England by Leicester's faction. Kyd's joining of rival legends to depict Lorenzo as a Spanish Machiavel analogous to Philip II demonstrates the propagandistic similarities in the ideological war between Spain and England. The charges against Leicester and Philip II are very close: both men are vain, arrogant and cruel Machiavellian villains who reward loyal service with treachery and are determined to maintain secrecy about their many crimes. Kyd appropriates the attacks on Leicester to create an assault on Philip's character and, by extension, on Spain itself.

Robert Dudley (1532?–88), the Earl of Leicester and Queen Elizabeth's favourite, was a focal point for political attack. In his career rise he was the Master of the Queen's horse, a member of the Privy Council, Chancellor of Oxford University, reputed secret lover of Elizabeth and aspirant for the English Crown, leader of the expeditionary force to the Netherlands and commander of the land forces against the Armada. Because of his enormous power, political machinations and opposition to Elizabeth's marriage to Duc d'Alençon, Leicester earned the hatred of English and foreign Catholics, whose attacks denounced him as a power-mad politician and inveterate seducer who murdered his wife, Amy Robsart, to marry Lettice Knollys, the wife of the first Earl of Essex, whom he reputedly also had murdered.

In 1584, the anonymous *The Copie of a Leter, Wryten By A Master Of Arte Of Cambridge* was published. Also known as *Leicester's Commonwealth*, the book was written by a group of English exiles in France, including Charles Arundell, Lord Paget, Thomas Fitzherbert, William Tresham and Thomas Throgmorton, all of whom had supported Alençon's attempt to marry Elizabeth and, subsequently, had been hounded from England by Leicester. The work consists of a dialogue among a gentleman, a lawyer and a scholar who, by recounting the many crimes of Leicester, make Mary Queen of Scots and the English Catholics appear as the innocent victims of his infamy. *Leicester's Commonwealth* was translated into French and Italian in 1585, and it quickly became the definitive source for writers eager to defame Leicester and undermine his supporters.[7] Some time after Leicester died on 4 September 1588, another libellous satire entitled *News from Heaven and Hell* was published, which purported to be an account of Leicester's judgement at the gates of heaven. The infamous Earl is condemned for his numerous villainies and sent to Hades for a gruesome but appropriate punishment.

The publication and dissemination of these attacks sparked a concomitant defence of Leicester. The libels were attacked vigorously by Elizabeth, who ordered that all copies be brought to the Privy Council, which declared that the books against Leicester were so malicious, false and slanderous that 'only the devil could believe them true'.[8] Sir Philip Sidney read *Leicester's Commonwealth* during the winter of 1584-85 and composed a *Defense of Leicester*, which, however, was never published. Primarily, Sidney defends the lineage and meritorious service of Leicester, whom he identifies with the Queen and the efficacious government of England:

> Of late there hath been printed a book in form of Dialog to the defaming of the Earl of Lester full of the most vyle reproches. [...] no man hath born a hatefull hart to this Estate but that at the same time he hath shewed his enmity to this Earl testefying [...] herebi, that his faith is so lynked to her Majesties service, that [...] who hates England, and the Queen, must also [...] hate the Earl of Lester.[9]

Similar praise for Leicester was provided by Alberico Gentili, a Protestant Italian exile who, in 1581, received a doctorate of civil laws at Oxford as a result of Leicester's support. In 1585, Gentili wrote *De Legationibus Libri Tres*, a treatise on the qualities of good ambassadors, and in his dedication to Sidney he pays tribute to Leicester and condemns his slanderers who 'in their madness [...] bear testimony to the virtues of Leicester quite as effectively as the good citizens'.[10]

Finally, in 1593, *The Dead Man's Right*, a prose eulogy of Leicester, was published as the introductory piece in the poetic anthology *The Phoenix Nest*. The anonymous tribute gives the dead Leicester his due as England's great politician '[a]gainst whom [...] they forged millions of impieties, abusing the people by their divelish fictions, and wicked wresting of his actions; all to bring his vertues & person in popular hatred'.[11] The eulogy maintains that, instead of being reviled, Leicester's memory should be revered for his staunch defence of Protestantism.

Fredson Bowers compared the scenes involving Pedringano to the story of the death of Leicester's criminal accomplice Gates, as recounted in *The Copie of a Leter*. Leicester promotes Gates's criminal activities for his own gain, but, when Gates is apprehended, Leicester, despite his promise of a pardon, ensures that he is hanged to prevent disclosure of his villainy. Similarly, Lorenzo arranges to have Pedringano murder another accomplice, Serberine, and at the same time to be apprehended in the act. Lorenzo subsequently promises the condemned man a pardon to be delivered in a box, but Pedringano goes to his death imagining that it will be produced by the Page, who taunts him by pointing to the empty box.

Bowers concluded 'that the account of Gates and Leicester in 1584 [...] gave Kyd the idea for the Pedringano incident in *The Spanish Tragedy*, which followed shortly after *The Copie of a Leter* in 1585–88 when the scandalous book was still fresh in the mind of the audience'.[12] As further proof of his contention that Lorenzo was identified with Leicester as a Machiavellian villain, Bowers adduced Thomas Rogers's *Leicester's Ghost* (1605), a metrical account of the events detailed in *Leicester's Commonwealth*, in which Dudley's ghost returns from the otherworld to recount his evil deeds. To enhance Leicester's villainy, Rogers borrows the box motif from *The Spanish Tragedy*: 'For his reprivall, like a crafty fox, / I sent noe pardon, but an emptie box'.[13] By using the Kydian box ruse in his anti-Leicester poem, Rogers demonstrates, according to Bowers, that *The Spanish Tragedy* was perceived by Elizabethan audiences as belonging to that tradition. However, Rogers's use of the box motif does not prove he interpreted *The Spanish Tragedy* as anti-Leicester, but, even if he did, one contemporary placement of the play within that tradition does not demonstrate that Kyd intended it to be anti-Leicester or that Elizabethan audiences perceived it as such.

In an effort to prove the early composition date of 1583–84 for *The Spanish Tragedy*, T. W. Baldwin argued that Kyd's depiction of the Pedringano episode is the source of the versions of Leicester's Machiavellian treatment of his accomplices in both *The Copie of a Leter* and the anonymous manuscript libel of Leicester, *The Leter of Estate*.[14] Baldwin contended that there is a direct line from play to manuscript to printed book. *The Leter of Estate* contains an account of Leicester's betrayal of another accomplice, a Yorkshire gentleman. In debt because of the extravagance forced upon him by Leicester, the gentleman commits a murder for his master, who promises to relieve the debt as his reward. When he is apprehended for the crime, Leicester promises him a pardon, but he never delivers it. On the scaffold, the gentleman repents his sins, declares Leicester's villainy and is executed. Leicester had promised him 'mountaines', but 'to this great prefermente hee [Leicester] prefered him after he had consumed all his patrimony in his servis and lastly his life'.[15]

Baldwin concluded his argument by stating that *The Copie of a Leter* contains another reference to *The Spanish Tragedy* in Gates's threat to reveal Leicester's villainy.[16] After he was apprehended, Gates was reluctant to issue a public denunciation of Leicester, but he 'disclosed the same onely to a gentleman [...] whose name [...] beginneth with H'.[17] Baldwin maintained that this reference is to Hieronimo, and it proves that the libels are actually fictions that borrow their accounts from Kyd's dramatic version. However, D. C. Peck countered Baldwin by demonstrating that the *Leter of Estate* is not an earlier version of *The Copie of a Leter* but is, in fact, a later tract with its own versions of Leicester's crimes.[18] Moreover, Arthur Freeman argued that the libellers, who wanted their works to be perceived as the truth, would not have used a popular play as the source of their libels.[19] Thus, it is more probable that Kyd used the printed and manuscript libels as the source for some of the major elements in the Pedringano episode.

The Copie of a Leter, the *Leter of Estate* and *The Spanish Tragedy* share a basic pattern in the depiction of Leicester/Lorenzo's treatment of their accomplices: a subordinate is ordered to commit a murder, is apprehended and, expecting a pardon, is executed to prevent secrets from being revealed. Further, the works establish a paradoxical relationship between secrecy and revelation. Although Gates and the Yorkshire gentleman are silenced, the crimes enumerated in the tracts are sufficient proof of Dudley's villainy. In addition, *The Copie of a Leter* ends with the threat that further infamies have been disclosed to H, who will publish them in the future. However, despite all of this evidence, Leicester remains unpunished for his crimes. But in

The Spanish Tragedy, Pedringano's posthumous letter is the means of disclosing to Hieronimo Lorenzo's role in the murder of Horatio. It is as if Kyd completes the promise of punishment made in the libels as the man whose name begins with 'H' – Hieronimo, the Lord Marshal – punishes Lorenzo in the revenge playlet. In sum, although it is obvious, as Bowers and Baldwin have argued, that Kyd uses elements found in *The Copie of a Leter* and *The Letter of Estate*, neither of these libels contains the major element of the villain arranging to have one accomplice murdered by another accomplice who, after his execution, leaves behind an incriminatory posthumous letter that leads to the punishment of the mastermind. For this development, I suggest, Kyd drew upon the scandalous revelations of Antonio Pérez (1540?-1611), which provided a sustained and effective denunciation of Philip II on political and moral grounds.

Pérez's *Las Relaciones* contains the account of his persecution by Philip II for the murder of Juan de Escobedo. Pérez had been Philip's secretary and favourite, but after the murder of Don John's secretary and favourite, Juan de Escobedo, in 1578, Pérez was pursued by Philip for twelve years for the assassination, which he claimed had been ordered by Philip himself. Pérez recounted the events leading to his arrest, on 28 July 1579, and subsequent imprisonment. After his escape to Aragon in 1590, he learned that he had been tried *in absentia* on charges of heresy and witchcraft, and sentenced to be hanged, drawn and quartered.[20] When the King ordered the Castilian army to invade Aragon, Pérez fled to France in 1591, where he published the first edition of *Las Relaciones*, which was known as the *Librillo*. After Henry IV led a failed invasion of Aragon in 1592, Pérez travelled to England and became a member of the Essex circle, which was devoted to the continuation of Leicester's anti-Spanish policies. In 1594, Pérez published the expanded second edition of *Relaciones*, *Pedaços de Historia, o Relaciones, assy llamadas por sus Auctores los Peregrinos*, which was dedicated to the Earl of Essex and distributed in the Netherlands and Spain to continue to arouse resentment against Philip II.[21]

One year after the publication of the second edition, an English translation was completed, but never published, by Arthur Atey, former secretary of Leicester and, subsequently, a member of the Essex anti-Spanish faction. Entitled *Pieces of the storye or Relaciones so called (by the) Peregrini their Authors*, Pérez's work is presented by Atey in 'The Translatour to the Reader' as a providential history with a cast of royal and high-ranking actors in 'A very tragedye [...] full of imprisonmente, [...] confiscations, [...] executions: [...] suttle practises, conning dissimulations, fowle treachouryes'.[22] For Atey, the major theme of Pérez's account of Philip's behaviour is that English Catholics cannot expect support from this ruler who sent the ill-fated Armada to England in 1588 and, on a more personal level, betrayed his favourite for a crime Philip had ordered:

> [Perez is] a paterne to frame [...] a doctrine by. Have you done the kinge service for which you should looke for recompense? [...] More than Senor Antonio Perez? his principall Secretorye of Estate and specially trusted man [...] in this deathe of Escovedo? for which his requitall is suche extreame persecution as you shall here see? Hath he promised to do any thinge for you [...] more then to [...] Perez [...] by wordes [...] before most honourable witnesses? by wrytinge of his owne hande? by [...] pledges [...] so [...] secret [...] after the deathe of Escovedo, and for his speciall service therein [...] that man from man can not imagine more, and yet hath fayled in all?[23]

Philip II had ordered Pérez to murder Escobedo for political reasons and then, having promised him immunity, Philip pursued him remorselessly in the courts in order to prevent the revelation of his role in the death of Escobedo and other political crimes. This is the essence of the parallels between Pérez's history and Kyd's play: the attempts by Machiavellian villains to silence dangerous subordinates are foiled by incriminatory written revelations.

Atey completed the translation of Pérez's *Las Relaciones* three years after the first recorded performance of *The Spanish Tragedy*, and his observations in 'The Translatour to the Reader' epitomised the political lessons that Kyd's generation wished to take from Pérez's story. His evaluation of *Las Relaciones* as a providential tragedy with a high-ranking cast is paralleled by Kyd's adaptation in his anti-Spanish '*Tragedia cothurnata*' (IV.i.160) of the relevant episodes in Pérez's account of his troubles. Kyd does not provide a transparent analogy with Pérez's narrative elements, but rather he fashions a dramatic mosaic of similar characters, themes, and motifs, which include: Pérez's pseudonymous persona 'Peregrino'; the network of dynastic ambitions and romantic jealousies that results in betrayal, murder and legal prosecution; and the opposition between secrecy and revelation as delineated in the publication of secrets. The question of how much of the Pérez story Kyd could have known before writing *The Spanish Tragedy* must be considered. Critics have dated *The Spanish Tragedy* from 1587 to 1591, and its first recorded performance occurred on 14 March 1592, as Philip Henslowe noted in his diary.[24] During this period, the scandalous events of the Pérez affair had become common knowledge in England and on the continent. At the outset of the scandal in 1579, Edward Wotton wrote to Sir Francis Walsingham from Madrid that 'the princesse of Evoly [...] and Antonio Pérez, the kinges chiefest secretary, were by the kinges commaundement committed to prison [...] aboute the death of Escovedo'.[25] In Saragossa when Pérez fought against prosecution by the Inquisition, he had copies of the account of his legal troubles with Philip II distributed to important persons in Aragon, England and the continent.[26]

After his escape to France, Pérez wrote a letter to Catherine of Bourbon, in which he declared 'there cannot be on earthe any corner [...] whither the sounde of my persecutions [...], according to the great noyse of them, hath not come'.[27] Finally, in a letter to the English court in April, 1592, which accompanied the presentation of his book, Pérez summarised his significance for the anti-Spanish forces:

> [W]ee hope you will favor the afflicted, uniustly pursued, inasmuche as the offences wherewith he is charged are [...] sleights for his great fidelytie towardes his kinge, for the which he, his wife and children have endured all the miserye this longe tyme. Wherefore he deservith to be succored of all the worlde, seinge that God hath shewed so many miracles of his fortune, whereof you [...] maye see parte in this litell booke.[28]

The first parallel between *Las Relaciones* and *The Spanish Tragedy* occurs in the use of Pérez's pseudonym 'Peregrino' and Bel-imperia's servant Pedringano. Pérez claims that the Peregrini brothers, Raphael and Azarias, have written the first two parts and edited the text, but they are his means of writing about himself in the third person. Also, he revels in his persona as the wandering and hunted pilgrim, whom he describes in his prefatory letter to Essex: 'the Protector of all Pilgrims of Fortune'.[29] Pedringano is a wanderer or errant one in the moral sense. He is a double agent, being Bel-imperia's trusted servant who, however, is suborned by Lorenzo and betrays her assignation with Horatio in the bower. Pedringano participates in the murder of Horatio and later carries out Lorenzo's order to murder his accomplice Serberine, servant to Balthazar, but is apprehended in the act by the guard sent by Lorenzo.

Pérez relates a similar tale of multiple betrayals and political murder set against the dynastic ambitions of Philip II and Don John of Austria. As Philip's trusted Secretary of State and favourite, Pérez was privy to many political secrets and plots. Philip II was fearful of the power and ambitions of Don John, who was the leader of the Spanish occupation of the Netherlands. In order to discover his plans, Philip placed Pérez's counterpart, Juan de Escobedo, as a spy in Don

John's employ. Escobedo reported in letters to Pérez that Don John was contemplating the conquest of England and then, perhaps, Spain. Intent on exacerbating Philip's suspicions, Pérez revised Escobedo's letters to increase the certainty of Don John's dynastic ambitions. When Escobedo came to Madrid for an extended stay, his attempts to solicit aid for his master Don John, whose ambitions he now supported, infuriated Philip II, who told Pérez to arrange for the murder of Escobedo on 31 March 1578.

This chapter of the story is marked by complex schemes of political subterfuge as one conspirator is called upon by the most powerful figure to kill another conspirator who has gone over to the enemy, who represents the principal dynastic threat to the King's power. After Escobedo was killed, Philip did not imprison or prosecute Pérez, until a public hue and cry raised by Escobedo's family forced him to do so. Pérez and his supposed paramour, Ana de Mendoza, the Princess of Éboli, were arrested, she to die in prison thirteen years later. As Atey explained:

> Phillippe of Spayne, upon stronge presumptions, grewe into certaine conceipt that his brother Don John de Austria ment ambitiouslye some perillous matter [...] against his person and Estate. The speciall Counsaylor and feeder of him in this humor he knewe to be his saide principall secretorye John de Escovedo. [...] [When] Don John [...] sent Escovedo into Spayne, abowt affayres [...] it was [...] resolved that Escovedo should secretlye be made awaye. [...] After Escovedo his deathe, his wyfe [...] suspected the princesse of Ebolye to be author thereof as enemye to Escovedo, and Senor Antonio Perez to have bene the instrument procured by her, for the great friendshippe between the[m]: [...] thoughe he [Philip] knewe the Princesse to be utterly ignorant of the case, and [...] Perez to have procured it to be done by his comaundement [...] yet suffred he them bothe to be imprisoned (her to dye in prison) him to be removed from prison to prison in Castile.³⁰

The Machiavellian activities in both play and text are set against the backdrop of dynastic ambitions. Lorenzo wants to marry his sister Bel-imperia to Balthazar in order to solidify his future hold on both countries. The historical subtext to this marriage concerns the foreign Catholic marriages contemplated by Elizabeth, which were attacked by the anti-Catholic faction, and the Spanish enterprise for England in which Don John would conquer England, marry Elizabeth and reclaim the country for Catholicism. Similarly, Pérez's *Las Relaciones* concerns the period of Spanish history when Philip annexed Portugal, defeated attempts by Don Antonio, the Portuguese claimant who lived with Pérez in England, to regain Portugal and sent the Armada against England in 1588. Just as Pérez became the embodiment of political resistance to Spanish hegemony by means of his written revelations about Philip's Machiavellian hypocrisy in the Escobedo murder, so, too, Pedringano undermines Lorenzo's dynastic ambitions with his posthumous epistolary revelation about the murder of Horatio.

The pattern of secrecy and revelation is essential to both works in the form of incriminating letters.[31] Lorenzo enjoins Pedringano to secrecy about the murder of Horatio and imprisonment of Bel-imperia, and to ensure his silence Lorenzo promises him a pardon, which the duped henchman expects to be delivered when he is on the scaffold. After he is hanged, however, his letter is delivered to Hieronimo, who thus learns of Lorenzo's guilt. Pedringano says in his posthumous confession: 'in my death I shall reveal the troth' (III.vii.35). Armed with this truth, Hieronimo destroys Lorenzo's dynastic ambitions in the revenge playlet.

As the Secretary of State, Pérez knew many of the secrets which Philip did not want revealed. Throughout his imprisonment, he was commanded to turn over his cache of state papers and letters. Philip, as Anthony Froude pointed out, was in a double bind.[32] By prosecuting Pérez for Escobedo's murder, he was attempting to silence his accuser, but at the same time Philip was, of course, encouraging Pérez to reveal more than the King wanted to be made public. To resolve his dilemma, Philip encouraged Pérez through his intermediaries to confess to the murder but to remain silent about Philip's role. As reward for his partial confession, Pérez would be pardoned.

However, Pérez never agreed to this arrangement, fearing that a public confession would lead to his doom. Despite torture and the continued imprisonment of himself and his family, he wisely did not deliver all of his letters to Philip, keeping them with him throughout his years of exile. As Gregorio Marañón pointed out, these letters, some of which were printed in the third part of *Las Relaciones*, produced a series of tumultuous effects throughout Europe:

> They hastened the death of Don John of Austria. They caused the death of Escobedo and all those deaths which derived from his assassination. They were responsible for [...] Pérez's undergoing years of imprisonment and dying in exile. [...] They brought unrest, crimes and war to Spain. [...] They embittered the last years of Philip II's reign and cast a shadow no one can dissipate over the memory of Philip as a man and as a King.[33]

Pedringano's posthumous letter provides the proof of Lorenzo's guilt in Horatio's murder, and Pérez, although condemned and exiled, furnishes proof in the incriminating letters published in his *Las Relaciones* that Philip ordered the assassination of Escobedo. Concerning Pérez's cache of invaluable state papers and letters a legend has developed, which is related to the 'bloody writ' motif in *The Spanish Tragedy*. When Pérez was imprisoned in the fortress in Turégano, he agreed to provide his torturers his hoard of incriminating papers. Deprived of ink by his captors, he was forced to write the letter to his wife, who was to gather and deliver the papers, in 'his owne bloode [...] being bereft of all meanes of conversacion with any'.[34] Fortunately for Pérez, his wife was not able to find all of his diverse papers, and he later used them in his *Relaciones* and maintained them as a continuing threat against Philip II.

As Marañón pointed out, the account of the letter in blood represents Pérez's attempt to create a legend, because it is obvious that, if his captors wanted the papers, they would have provided him with the proper writing materials.[35] Pérez's letter in blood is related to the tradition of the Protestant martyrs who wrote letters in their own blood while in prison. Catharine Coats has explained that the martyrs in Jean Crespin's *Historie des Martyrs* (1554–97) used such letters to validate their lives as transmitters of God's truth: 'Blood is the medium of the martyrs' statements of faith; it writes God's truths. [...] Blood is the guarantor of veracity.'[36] By writing a letter with his blood, Pérez related the sufferings of his body to the text, epitomising his unjust punishment from the political oppression of Philip II.

In *The Spanish Tragedy*, Kyd uses Bel-imperia's letter in a similar fashion. When Hieronimo, imploring the heavens for some clue to his son's murder, walks under the room where she has been imprisoned by Lorenzo, Bel-imperia drops a letter written in her blood revealing Lorenzo's guilt (III.ii.26). At this time, Hieronimo distrusts the letter as a plot 'to entrap thy life' (III.ii.38), but, after receiving Pedringano's posthumous confession, he is able to place credence in both letters and plan his revenge against Lorenzo. Pérez's legendary letter in blood concerned his cache of letters which conveyed the truth about Philip's guilt. Bel-imperia's 'bloody writ' similarly revealed to Hieronimo the truth about Lorenzo and led to his punishment in the revenge playlet.

The final link between the two works is the depiction of the romantic entanglements which in some measure cause the crimes. In the case of Pérez, there was the infamous *leyenda de los amores* involving the triangle of Philip II, the Princess of Éboli and Pérez. Pérez did not create the legend directly in his *Relaciones*, although he referred to Philip's discontent 'with the auncient and continuall perseveraunce of the continent constancye of the princesse of Ebolye, accountinge it as contempt'.[37] Pérez implied that Philip was so upset at his continual rejection by the Princess of Éboli and, as Atey put it, by 'the great friendshippe between the said Princesse and him [Pérez]' that he prosecuted them for the murder which he had ordered.[38]

The legend was embellished in Italy as different salacious elements were introduced. Philip and Éboli had been lovers with the approbation of her husband Ruy Gómez, Secretary of State until 1573 and Pérez's benefactor. In this affair Pérez served as a go-between, but, when he and Éboli, now a widow, became secret lovers, she rejected Philip's love. To further complicate the plot, Escobedo supposedly caught the lovers *in flagrante delicto* and it was the fear that Don John's secretary would reveal their amour that prompted their determination to have Escobedo murdered.[39]

Once the *leyenda de los amores* was established, Pérez capitalised on it, depicting himself as the victim of the King's base jealousy, and the lover and pawn of the beautiful and dominant princess, to whom he attributed much of the motivation for the murder of Escobedo. Through this self-presentation, Pérez further darkened the reputation of Philip II and, to some extent, exonerated himself, because he claimed he was persecuted for reasons of love rather than felony and subversion.[40]

In his adaptation of the *leyenda de los amores*, Kyd was not interested in furnishing consistent historical parallels with the Pérez material, but rather he creates characters that are composites of the various historical personages, and he places them in dramatic action that provides repeated images of betrayal, sexual intrigue, political murder and legal punishment.[41] Lorenzo is the Machiavellian counterpart to Philip II in carrying out the murder of Horatio and Serberine, and in arranging the execution of Pedringano, but he is not directly involved in a romantic entanglement. However, he does attempt to have his sister Bel-imperia marry Prince Balthazar despite her love for Horatio, the successor to her late secret lover Andrea. Her trusted servant Pedringano betrays their love by revealing them *in flagrante delicto* in the bower. Lorenzo and Balthazar enter disguised and, after crude sexual taunts, dispatch Horatio. The manner in which Kyd constructs the murder scene as a macabre *coitus interruptus* demonstrates the sexual – alongside the class – jealousy at the heart of Lorenzo's relationship with his sister.

After betrayal, murder and Bel-imperia's imprisonment, Lorenzo silences his confederates Serberine and Pedringano. Serberine becomes a type of Escobedo killed by Pérez/Pedringano, who has carried out the orders of Lorenzo/Philip II and is then arrested and executed.

Escobedo saw Pérez and Éboli making love, both of whom then feared he would reveal their amour to Philip II. Pedringano, as a type of Escobedo who fulfils that fear, betrays the lovers to his master, Lorenzo, who kills Horatio, the rival lover to the royal Balthazar. As a type of Pérez, Pedringano is then prosecuted by the legal system which Lorenzo/Philip has activated. In sum, Kyd develops sensational images of romantic rivalries, betrayals of secrecy and political murder depicted in the anti-Leicester tradition and the Spanish Black Legend of Pérez's *Las Relaciones* in order to create a play which depicts the fall of Babylon/Spain in the last decade of the sixteenth century.

NOTES

1. Johnson, 'The Spanish Tragedy, or Babylon Revisited', pp. 24–5, 36.
2. See Broude, 'Time, truth, and right'; '*Vindicta Filia Temporis*'; 'Revenge and revenge tragedy'.
3. Hill, 'Senecan and Vergilian perspectives', pp. 159–60, 163–4.
4. Justice, 'Spain, tragedy, and *The Spanish Tragedy*', p. 287.
5. On the mythological and philosophical elements in the Pedringano hanging episode, see Ardolino, 'The hangman's noose', and Baines, 'Kyd's Silenus box'.
6. Maltby, *The Black Legend in England*, pp. 89–90.
7. *Leicester's Commonwealth*, ed. D. C. Peck, p. 45.
8. Quoted in E. Rosenberg, *Leicester: Patron of Letters*, p. 289.
9. Sidney, *Defence of the Earl of Leicester*, vol. 3, pp. 61–2.
10. Gentili, *De Legationibus Libri Tres*, vol. 2, p. v.
11. *The Phoenix Nest*, ed. H. Rollins, pp. 5–6.
12. Bowers, 'Kyd's Pedringano', p. 248.
13. Rogers. *Leicester's Ghost*, p. 35.
14. Baldwin, *On the Literary Genetics of Shakespeare's Plays*, pp. 185–91.
15. Peck, '"The Letter of Estate"', p. 34.
16. Baldwin, *On the Literary Genetics of Shakespeare's Plays*, p. 192.
17. *Leicester's Commonwealth*, p. 101.
18. Peck, '"The Letter of Estate"', p. 22.
19. Freeman, *Thomas Kyd*, p. 73.
20. Reed, 'Fortune's Monster', p. 169.
21. Pérez, *A Spaniard in Elizabethan England*, vol. 1, p. 213.
22. Pérez, 'Pieces of the Storye', p. 3.
23. Ibid., pp. 4v–5.
24. Foakes (ed.), *Henslowe's Diary*.
25. Quoted in Pérez, *A Spaniard*, vol. 1, p. 10n.
26. Reed, 'Fortune's Monster', p. 170.
27. Quoted in Pérez, *A Spaniard*, vol. 2, pp. 373–4.
28. Pérez, *A Spaniard*, vol. 1, p. 38.
29. Quoted in Ungerer, *Anglo-Spanish Relations in Tudor Literature*, p. 103.

30 Pérez, 'Pieces of the Storye', pp. 3–3v.
31 Ardolino, *Thomas Kyd's Mystery Play*, pp. 29–47.
32 Froude, *The Spanish Story of the Armada*, pp. 134–5.
33 Marañón, *Antonio Pérez: 'Spanish Traitor'*, p. 354.
34 Pérez, 'Pieces of the Storye', p. 26 (also numbered 39).
35 Marañón, *Antonio Pérez: 'Spanish Traitor'*, p. 159.
36 Coats, 'Reconstituting the textual body', p. 81.
37 Pérez, 'Pieces of the Storye', p. 19.
38 Ibid., p. 3v.
39 Marañón, *Antonio Pérez: 'Spanish Traitor'*, pp. 83–4.
40 Pérez, *A Spaniard*, vol.1, pp. 43, 197.
41 Unlike Kyd, the anonymous author of *The Star of Seville* (c. 1630–50) provides a thinly disguised version of the Pérez–Philip II controversy and the *leyenda de los amores*.

REFERENCES

Anon., *Leicester's Commonwealth: The Copy of a Letter Written by a Master of Art of Cambridge (1584) and Related Documents*, ed. D. C. Peck (Athens, OH: Ohio University Press, 1985).
Ardolino, F., 'The hangman's noose and the empty box: Kyd's use of dramatic and mythological sources in *The Spanish Tragedy* (3.4–8)', *Renaissance Quarterly* 30:3 (1977): 334–40.
Ardolino, F., 'Detection and allegory in *The Spanish Tragedy*', *Allegorica* 5:2 (1980): 168–75.
Ardolino, F., *Thomas Kyd's Mystery Play: Myth and Ritual in The Spanish Tragedy* (New York: Peter Lang, 1985).
Ardolino, F., '"In Paris? Mass, and well remembered": Kyd's *The Spanish Tragedy* and the English reaction to the St. Bartholomew's Day massacre', *Sixteenth Century Journal* 21:3 (1990): 401–9.
Ardolino, F., *Apocalypse and Armada in Kyd's Spanish Tragedy* (Kirksville: Sixteenth Century Journal Publishers, Northeast Missouri State University, 1995).
Baines, B., 'Kyd's Silenus box and the limits of perception', *Journal of Medieval and Renaissance Studies* 10:1 (1980): 41–51.
Baldwin, T. W., *On the Literary Genetics of Shakespeare's Plays, 1592–1594* (Urbana: University of Chicago Press, 1959).
Bauckman, R., *Tudor Apocalypse: Sixteenth Century Apocalypticism, Millenarianism and the English Reformation from John Bale to John Foxe and Thomas Brightman* (Appleford: Sutton Courtenay Press, 1978).
Bowers, F., 'Kyd's Pedringano: Sources and parallels', *Harvard Studies and Notes in Philology and Literature* 13 (1931): 241–9.
Broude, R., 'Time, truth, and right in *The Spanish Tragedy*', *Studies in Philology* 68:1 (1971): 130–45.
Broude, R., '*Vindicta Filia Temporis*: Three English forerunners of the Elizabethan revenge play', *Journal of English and Germanic Philology* 72:4

(1973): 489–502.
Broude, R., 'Revenge and revenge tragedy in Renaissance England', *Renaissance Quarterly* 28:1 (1975): 38–58.
Coats, C. R., 'Reconstituting the textual body in Jean Crespin's *Histoire des Martyrs* (1564)', *Renaissance Quarterly* 44:1 (1991): 62–85.
Foakes, R. A. (ed.), *Henslowe's Diary*, 2nd edn (Cambridge: Cambridge University Press, 2002).
Freeman, A., *Thomas Kyd, Facts and Problems* (Oxford: Clarendon Press, 1967).
Froude, A., *The Spanish Story of the Armada* (New York: Charles Scribner's Sons, 1892; rpt 1905).
Gentili, A., *De Legationibus Libri Tres*, trans. G. J. Laing, 2 vols (New York: Oxford University Press, 1924).
Hill, E., 'Senecan and Vergilian perspectives in *The Spanish Tragedy*', *English Literary Renaissance* 15:2 (1985): 143–65.
Johnson, S. F., '*The Spanish Tragedy*, or Babylon revisited', in R. Hosley (ed.), *Essays on Shakespeare and Elizabethan Drama in Honor of Hardin Craig* (Columbia: University of Missouri Press, 1962), pp. 23–36.
Justice, S., 'Spain, tragedy, and *The Spanish Tragedy*', *Studies in English Literature* 25:1 (1985): 271–88.
Maltby, W., *The Black Legend in England: The Development of Anti-Spanish Sentiment 1558–1660* (Durham, NC: Duke University Press, 1971).
Marañón, G., *Antonio Pérez: 'Spanish Traitor'*, trans. Charles Ley (New York: Roy, 1953).
Peck, D. C., '"News from Heaven and Hell": A defamatory narrative of the Earl of Leicester', *English Literary Renaissance* 8:2 (1978): 141–58.
Peck, D. C., '"The Letter of Estate": An Elizabethan libel', *Notes and Queries* 28:1 (1981): 21–35.
Pérez, A., 'Pieces of the Storye or Relaciones so called (by the) Peregrini their Authors', trans. A. Atey. Bodleian MS, c.239, 1595.
Pérez, A., *A Spaniard in Elizabethan England. The Correspondence of Antonio Pérez's Exile*, ed. G. Ungerer, 2 vols (London: Tamesis Books, 1974–76).
Reed, H., 'Fortune's monster and the monarchy in *Las Relaciones* de Antonio Pérez', in N. Spadaccini and J. Jalens (eds), *Autobiography in Early Modern Spain* (Minneapolis: The Prisma Institute, 1988), 163–90.
Rogers, T., *Leicester's Ghost*, ed. F. Williams (Chicago: University of Chicago Press, 1972).
Rollins, H. (ed.), *The Phoenix Nest* (Cambridge, MA: Harvard University Press, 1931).
Rosenberg, E., *Leicester: Patron of Letters* (New York: Columbia University Press, 1955).
Sidney, Sir P., *Defence of the Earl of Leicester*, in *Complete Works*, ed. A. Feuillerat, vol. 3 (London: Cambridge University Press, 1912–26).
Ungerer, G., *Anglo-Spanish Relations in Tudor Literature* (Bern: Francke Verlag, 1956).

CHAPTER 9

The Spanish Tragedy and revenge tragedy in seventeenth-century Britain and the Low Countries

Ton Hoenselaars and Helmer Helmers

In his introduction to *The Works of Thomas Kyd*, Frederick Boas remarks that the popularity of *The Spanish Tragedy* was nowhere more enduring than on the continent of Europe, and that in Holland 'Kyd's drama gained a popularity even greater than in Germany'.[1] This chapter traces the career of the play in the Low Countries. It places the work of Kyd in the context of the various political and cultural contacts between England, the Netherlands and Flanders, and looks at *The Spanish Tragedy* as one of a range of specifically English revenge plays that crossed the Channel during the early modern period. In doing so, we argue that the theatrical exchange between England and the Low Countries has for too long been studied as a one-way process and that, as a consequence, on a pure textual or bibliographical level, English editors have so far failed to appreciate the merits of the existing Dutch versions of Kyd's tragedy for their own labours. We also argue that the lasting position of *The Spanish Tragedy* in the Low Countries is of interest from a politico-religious perspective. Beyond the crisis years of the mid-century, the revenge drama of English origin continued to be popular in the Low Countries and inspired royalist appropriations of the genre that justified Charles II's revenge of his father's death. This new genre of justified royal revenge was to affect the English stage as well, but in Restoration England it never existed alongside the traditional revenge tragedy since this had gone out of fashion. The dual tradition of revenge tragedy in the Netherlands may be seen as a typical feature of the Dutch Republic in its early modern European context.

TRAVELLING THEATRE

Few conditions were more conducive to establishing contacts between the early modern stages of London and the Low Countries than the Anglo-Dutch struggle against Spain. The war brought George Gascoigne to the Low Countries, where he served from March 1573 until October 1576. George Chapman, too, was on the continent some time after 1585, joining the Dutch wars in the company of Captain Robert Sidney.[2] Christopher Marlowe was in the Low Countries at around the same time, as well as Fulke Greville, Cyril Tourneur and Ben Jonson. But the political alliance between Elizabeth I and the Low Countries not only accounts for the travels of these English poets and playwrights; it also furthered the export of acting talent to the continent. Succeeding Sir John Norris as commander of the British troops in the Netherlands, Robert Dudley crossed the North Sea with his company of players – Lord Leicester's Men – including Will Kempe. It is they who were responsible for the earliest recorded instance of an English theatre production on Dutch soil, namely at Utrecht. On 23 April 1586, in the presence of Dutch diplomats, but also of Sir Philip Sidney, the company performed the *Labours of Hercules*, a classical display of force and strength and a welcome alternative to a dramatisation of the (banned) life of St George on what used to be his name day.[3]

In the following years, English players visited the Low Countries in increasing numbers. They introduced new plays (several of which were translated by German and Dutch cooperators) and new acting styles, and significantly affected both the canon and acting practices of the rhetoricians' theatre, which developed from an amateur theatre of literary burgher societies into a professional stage in the early seventeenth century.[4] At the same time, the political and economic contacts between the two countries also led Dutch citizens to visit England; among these were Johannes de Witt, who drew the interior of the Swan playhouse; Constantijn Huygens, the translator of John Donne's poetry who is also known to have owned a copy of the folio edition of Shakespeare's plays; and Theodore Rodenburgh, who was for several years a resident agent in London on behalf of the imperial Hanseatic towns and of Emden, and who displayed a serious interest in the country's literary culture.[5]

Interestingly, on first impact, the Dutch rhetoricians' theatre – still working mainly with classical material pursuing restraints in the representation of retaliation and violence – soon developed a marked taste for English plays with exciting revenge plots, cloak and dagger situations, torn limbs, included in the repertory of the English players who were to people the continent in ever larger numbers after Leicester's premiere of 1586.

As early as 1615, the Brussels translator Everaert Syceram translated the first part of Ariosto's *Orlando Furioso* and, 'since this family [was] unknown in the Netherlands', as Syceram explained in his 'Afterword to the Reader', he replaced the story of the Este family with generous excerpts from Kyd's *The Spanish Tragedy*.⁶ It is not certain how Syceram became acquainted with the Kyd materials, which he took over quite faithfully. He may have had access to an early text or have seen a performance of the play in Brussels where, as we know from Thomas Heywood's *Apology for Actors*, a company of players from England gave a public performance.

The earliest Dutch rendering of an English revenge tragedy on stage was Theodore Rodenburgh's translation-cum-adaptation of Thomas Middleton's *Revenger's Tragedy* (1607), published in Amsterdam as *Wraeckgierighers Treurspel* (1618), without mentioning the English playwright. It is likely that Rodenburgh came across Middleton's play in the course of his protracted residence in London during the first decade of the seventeenth century, even though it was only when Rodenburgh returned to the Low Countries during the early 1610s that he started an active career as a poet and dramatist for one of the rhetoricians' chambers in the capital. In addition to producing the first Dutch translation of Guarini's *Il pastor fido* using John Dymock's *Faithfull Shepheard* of 1602, and translating into Dutch Sidney's *Defence of Poetry* as *Eglentiers Poëtens Borst-weringh*, Rodenburgh produced a host of plays for the Amsterdam stage of The White Lavender, including *The Revenger's Tragedy*.⁷ Perhaps better than any other revenge tragedy on Dutch soil during the first half of the seventeenth century, Rodenburgh's near-contemporary rendering of Middleton's tragedy – one wonders if there is any comment available on the play that is more contemporary than Rodenburgh's adaptation – brings into focus the rather drastic way in which such drama could or should be made morally acceptable.⁸ In order to achieve a safe equilibrium between the sensational and the educational, a Sidneyan balance of delight and instruction, Rodenburgh wrote a memorable Induction to the play, in which a wronged and raving Horatius seeks out Mr Adolf, his fencing instructor, before challenging his enemy to a duel. Mr Adolf, however, tries to dissuade him:

> Injustice is not righted by revenge. Revenge breeds further misery and accidents. Horatius, do not let wild anger lead you astray. It blinds all reason, intoxicates and numbs your common sense by heating of the blood. It smothers reason. For he who gains most by revenge also loses most.⁹

Eventually, Mr Adolf takes Horatius to see *The Revenger's Tragedy*, which exemplifies the destructive nature of revenge, in accordance with the play's motto, also featuring on the title page of the Dutch adaptation: 'The angry man who seeks to be avenged for every wrong will end up miserably, since acting on the devil's promptings will yield precisely this'.[10]

The far from classical genre introduced by Rodenburgh, including the safety-net advice against revenge conducted by mortals, caught on. In 1621, Adriaen van den Bergh – a charismatic Utrecht poet and theatre enthusiast, as well as the father of the first Dutch actress, Ariana van den Bergh – produced his own version of *The Spanish Tragedy*, predictably, perhaps, devoid of the original justificatory Induction featuring Revenge and the Ghost of Andrea. Van den Bergh's *Ieronimo*, played on the stage of the Utrecht rhetoricians' chamber The Rosemary (whose motto, punning on the city's name, was 'Uut rechter liefde', i.e., 'With true love'), on 6 May 1621 and published later that year (by Jan Amelisz of Utrecht), reads like a free adaptation of the English original. Van den Bergh is likely to have seen *The Spanish Tragedy* performed around the end of July 1620, when the touring company of players led by John Green gave several performances in Utrecht. We are not certain if the company played *The Spanish Tragedy* – perhaps including parts of *The First Part of Hieronimo* whose traces are present in the Utrecht play – but we know that it was part of their repertory, and that Green and his men put on *The Spanish Tragedy* at the court of Dresden on 28 June 1626.[11] The memory of an existing play would also explain why Van den Bergh was accused of plagiarism and, perhaps, why he defended himself in terms that do suggest his acquaintance with an earlier text of *The Spanish Tragedy*: 'As soon as [the smart critics] find one word from another poet, / They assume that it must all have been stolen'.[12]

The Spanish Tragedy remained popular also in the 1630s. In the early months of 1637 a revised version of Van den Bergh's translation spliced with another version of the play was performed at the Dutch Academy in Amsterdam.[13] In 1638, on the occasion of its premiere at the Municipal Theatre of Amsterdam, this play was published as *Don Jeronimo, Marschalk van Spanjens. Treur-spel*. In this new form, *The Spanish Tragedy* acquired exceptional success in the Low Countries and beyond, in Germany, Denmark and Sweden.[14]

Interestingly, Van den Bergh continued to have close ties with the theatre and may be associated also with the new version of Kyd's play (although his active involvement in the new 1637 version is highly questionable)[15] as well as with *Aran and Titus*: the 1652 poem entitled *Geest van Tengnagel* spoke of Van den Bergh as a distinguished actor in his youth, who had had the honour of bringing to life on the Dutch stage 'Jeronimo of Spain [...] the young Polidoor and Andronicus'.[16] Since Van den Bergh was definitely the author of *Jeronimo* and of a play entitled *Polidoor* (which has survived), it seemed likely that he had also written a version of *Andronicus*, possibly used also by Jan Vos. This would account for the assertion, also in *Geest van Tengnagel*, that Van den Bergh was openly angry and cursed someone more gifted to deck out plays for stealing his material. However, no version of this particular *Andronicus* (if ever there was one) has survived, and the mystery – fed by intriguing parallels between Van den Bergh's *Ieronimo* and Vos's *Aran and Titus* – lives on.[17]

By a twist of dramatic fate, the stage manager in the 'Induction' to Ben Jonson's *Bartholomew Fair* (1614) also referred to *Titus Andronicus* and *The Spanish Tragedy* together: 'Hee that will sweare, *Ieronimo*, or *Andronicus* are the best playes, yet, shall passe vnexcepted at, heere, as a man whose Iudgement shewes it is constant, and hath stood still, these fiue and twentie, or thirtie yeeres. Though it be an *Ignorance*, it is a vertuous and stay'd Ignorance; and next to *truth*, a confirm'd errour does well'.[18] In *Bartholomew Fair* it concerns a matter of taste: both *Titus Andronicus* and *The Spanish Tragedy* are considered dated, out of fashion. It foreshadows what Frederick Boas has noted as well, namely that 'with the triumph of Puritanism in the middle of the seventeenth century, and the closing of the theatres, came a sudden total eclipse of Kyd's fame; and the Restoration, with its new dramatic methods and ideals, knew not him nor his brethren of the "race before the flood"'.[19] In the Low Countries, which had started to appropriate *The Spanish Tragedy* in 1615, the traditional English revenge play was to remain popular for almost a century. Even though with its sensational representation of unbridled passion, *The Spanish Tragedy* provided a drastic alternative to the morality of restraint characteristic of Vondel's high art, *Don Jeronimo* continued to be performed at least once a year until the early eighteenth century, and printed editions of this second Kyd adaptation appeared in 1638, 1644, 1662, 1665, 1669, 1678, 1683 and 1729. No less lasting was the popularity of Jan Vos's Shakespearean adaptation entitled *Aran en Titus*, with a hundred performances before 1665 and some twenty-eight editions by 1726.

TEXTUAL TRACES

It is often difficult to establish how the printed or manuscript text of the plays in question travelled, but close scrutiny of the published translations – which still needs to be conducted systematically – does occasionally offer valuable insights for scholars interested in both Dutch and English Renaissance drama. In the case of *The Spanish*

Tragedy, elements included in the 1615 *Ariosto* translation by Everaert Syceram, for example, we learn that the Brussels translator reproduces an error found in the 1594 quarto of Kyd's play. Where the English Ghost of Andrea – with obvious reference to the sixth book of the *Aeneid* – speaks of a passage 'through the gates of horn' (I.i.82), Syceram follows Kyd rather than Virgil when he conveys the notion of sailing 'door de gaten van Hor'.[20] Ironically, the presumed availability on the continent of the 1594 copy has led Schoneveld to suggest that this was also the source of later adaptations of *The Spanish Tragedy*.[21] However, the introduction of the Painter scene in Van den Bergh's 1621 adaptation of the play suggests a later version of the play, even though we cannot exactly pinpoint which. A similar hybridity appears in the 1638 Dutch version of *The Spanish Tragedy* regarding the following stage direction: *'Jeronimo in a state of undress, with a torch and a dagger in his hand'*.[22] It takes over the first part of the stage direction from the original English edition: *'Enter* Hieronimo *in his shirt'* (II.v). However, the depiction of Hieronimo and his props is new, and, given the fact that this Dutch stage direction so closely resembles the woodcut used for the cover of the first 'illustrated' edition of *The Spanish Tragedy* in the 1615 quarto, this seems the likeliest source of *Don Jeronimo*.

Reading the extant Dutch play texts against the English originals may also raise questions which sometimes usefully interrogate or challenge the stability of the English text that is considered sacrosanct by most editors and critics. A case in point is the opening of Theodore Rodenburgh's translation of *The Revenger's Tragedy*. The opening stage direction of the English play offers itself as a useful point of departure: *'Enter* Vendici, *the* Duke, Dutchesse, Lussurioso *her sonne,* Spurio *the bastard, with a traine, passe ouer the Stage with Torch-light'*.[23] In Rodenburgh's 1618 translation this reads, back-translated into English: 'Duke, Duchess, Lussurioso, Ambitioso, Supervacuo, Spurio, Hippolito, Vendici *with their train going across the stage, with torches before them, and exit again.* Vendici *remains on stage.*'[24] There are a number of striking differences between the original and the rendering by Rodenburgh, who could have seen the play in London. One of the more telling differences is that the English quarto has the characters *'passe ouer the Stage with Torch-light'*, whereas the Dutch rendering (retranslated here) has *'going across the stage with torches before them'*. The Rodenburgh stage direction suggests that the Italian royalty on the Dutch stage did not carry their own torches; the aristocratic Italian characters were preceded by torch bearers. Certainly the Middleton original – which reads 'with torches' – could describe the same situation, but we cannot be certain. Nor can we be certain whether Rodenburgh, who could have seen the play in London, translated 'with torches' into 'with torches before them' on the basis of his personal memories. The very likelihood of the latter invites a reappraisal of stage directions in English Renaissance drama, which may lead to the conclusion that there were, on occasion, perhaps more stage personnel than critics have assumed so far. To further the argument, the *dramatis personae* provided in the printed version of the Dutch translation, though absent from Middleton's text of 1607/8, could be of help.[25]

One final example of Dutch translations creating cross-Channel challenges, and also the most complex one, is provided by a comparison between *The Spanish Tragedy* and its 1638 rendering as *Don Jeronimo*. In particular, it is worth looking at the dialogue between Lorenzo and Pedringano in II.i which, in the Dutch version, is a dialogue between Don Pedro and Pedrongano. In this particular dialogue, Lorenzo is trying to get the simpleton servant and criminal Pedringano to work for him. In order to threaten him, the 1602 English stage direction in the margin across from Lorenzo's speech reads: '*Draws his sword.*' (II.i.67). Several lines later, we read: '*Offers to kill him*' (II.i.77). Lorenzo threatens to kill Pedringano and achieves his goal.

This all looks simple and straightforward, but it is not. Looking at the stage direction from the perspective of, say, a director, one is entitled to ask the question: whose sword is to be drawn to threaten Pedringano? As a random check reveals, most English editors of the play recognise a problem here and silently produce the following emendations: 'Draw his sword' of the 1602 quarto is changed to 'Draws his sword', and 'Offer to kill him' of the 1602 quarto is changed to 'Offers to kill him' (see the editions by Neilson (1939): II.i.66–7; Mulryne (1970): II.i.67–8; Maus (1995): II.i.67–8). No one seems to object to this silent emendation of the stage directions from what is really a *prescriptive* stance to a *descriptive* one, from stage directions addressed to the player, stating what is to be done by him on stage at a particular moment, to stage directions which describe to the reader, or to an imagined audience, what may be seen on stage in a production at a particular moment.

However, the 1638 Dutch version of the play – with the touring company around Adriaen van den Bergh in its line of transmission – suggests that the stage directions that appeared from 1602 onwards may well be interpreted differently, but also more consistently than it is generally done by editors these days. The anonymous 1638 version of *The Spanish Tragedy* (with Lorenzo's name replaced by Don Pedro) has: '*Don Pedro pulls Pedrongano's sword*'.[26] It further translates the stage direction 'Offer to kill him' into a graphic line of verse – 'Speak the truth or I will chop off your head'[27] – and then interestingly rounds off the sequence with a new stage direction later in the text: 'He gives him his sword again'.[28] This detailed information changes the situation. Lorenzo (or, rather the Dutch Don Pedro) draws not his own sword but the sword of the servant, in a gesture, it would seem, of humiliation. Moreover, Pedringano is even threatened with his own sword before receiving it back after swearing full allegiance to Don Pedro. Is it the 1638 Dutch adaptor of the play who has Don Pedro draw Pedringano's sword, or is it the modern English editor who decides to have Don Pedro (alias Lorenzo) draw his own? If we agree that the question is unanswerable, we must admit that the 1638 translator-cum-adaptor – using the Van den Bergh text and the 1615 quarto – is the only consistent mediator.[29]

Naturally, the next step to take would be to study the other stage directions in the editions of the English play and the Dutch play. Although this is not the focus of the present study, it is worth noting already that descriptive and prescriptive stage directions occur side by side throughout the two versions of *The Spanish Tragedy*, yet modern editions tend to favour the descriptive stage directions. It is too early for a conclusion on this matter, but it seems that, with the recognition of the interesting contemporary interpretation of this problem in the Dutch text, no new English edition can remain silent about it any longer (like Edwards's or Cairncross's), or silently emend the problem (like the other editors'). The matter is slight, but not without interest, and goes some way towards showing how the extant material by early seventeenth-century Dutch translators may still, on occasion, break the silence and initiate a dialogue with contemporary practitioners in the English-speaking world.

REVENGE IN THE DUTCH REPUBLIC

Another way of initiating such a dialogue is to focus on the recontextualisation of *The Spanish Tragedy* and the genre of revenge tragedy in the Dutch Republic. For, besides offering unexpected insights in obscurities of the English source texts, early Dutch translations also took on new shapes and acquired new meanings and associations that are of interest to readers of the English originals.

In the majority of cases, historicising the translations of Kyd and others seems relevant only to readers of the target culture. Van den Bergh's *Ieronimo* – a case of anti-Spanish propaganda, like Kyd's original – can be properly understood only in the context of the so-called

Truce Conflicts that tore the Dutch Republic apart during the Twelve Years' Truce between the United Provinces and Spain (1609–21). Van den Bergh, a soldier who had a stake in the renewal of the war, wrote an Orangeist play that clearly distinguished itself from other revenge tragedies such as Coster's *Iphigenia* (1617) and Vondel's *Palamedes* (1625).[30] And Van den Bergh's life motto, also printed in his *Ieronimo*, is as evocative as it is telling: 'From one war to the next'.[31] If we interpret Rodenburgh's denunciation of revenge as a warning against civil war, the Dutch *Revengers' Tragedy*, too, participated in this debate. Such contexts, however, are not likely to enhance our appreciation of the English originals; the political significance of the earlier English revenge tragedies abroad largely remains confined to the Dutch sphere.

In the 1650s, however – even as the more traditional plays of English origin, like *The Spanish Tragedy* and *Aran en Titus*, continued to enjoy great popularity in the Low Countries – new Dutch revenge tragedy absorbed a marked Anglo-Dutch discourse about the Puritan revolution and English regicide. In part, this was due to Dutch anxiety about the momentous events across the North Sea, since they were of great consequence to the domestic and international politics of the Dutch Republic.[32] In part, however, it was also due to the physical closeness of the two worlds of drama, something which is perhaps best symbolised by the fact that, during his exile in the Dutch Republic, the future Charles II visited the Amsterdam Theatre on 20 October 1648 and saw a play by Isaac Vos, entitled *Beklagelijke Dwang* (*Lamentable Coercion*).[33] Englishmen came in contact with Dutch drama, but English drama also continued to enter the Dutch Republic.[34] As John Denham pointed out to the restored Charles II in 1660:

This truth we can to our advantage say,
They that would have no KING, would have no *Play*,
The *Laurel* and the *Crown* together went,
Had the same *Foes*, and the same *Banishment*.[35]

The intensified cultural exchange between both cultures significantly affected the development of the genre in the Dutch Republic in a way that has repercussions for our perception of English revenge tragedy during the Restoration as well.

In part, the presence of English drama in the Dutch Republic was a matter of English dramatists writing and publishing their works in Holland. William Lower and Christopher Wase, for instance, both resided in the Low Countries in the 1650s, and their works were published in The Hague.[36] Wase's allegorical translation of Sophocles' *Electra*, one of the paradigms of political revenge tragedy, was performed for Elizabeth Stuart in The Hague, and printed in Samuel Browne's office.[37] Several of Lower's works were printed at Adrian Vlack's.[38] Both these printing houses represented important centres of Anglo-Dutch exchange.[39] But royalist households, too, functioned as such centres of exchange, even having English plays performed, like, for example, Beaumont and Fletcher's *A King and No King* at the court of Charles II's sister, the Princess Royal, in 1654.[40] Royalists also commissioned works to be written by Dutch translators that were frequently based on English examples. Some of these were destined for the stage. It is likely that Lambert van den Bosch's adaptation of Shakespeare's *Richard III* was commissioned by a royalist Englishman. It explains why his *Roode en Witte Roos* (*The Red and the White Rose*, 1652) reads like a political revenge tragedy with Shakespeare's Machiavel as a close analogy to Oliver Cromwell.[41] In this respect, the fact that Van den Bosch also had very good contacts with the royalist community, and dedicated the Dutch edition of his history of the kings of England (*Florus Anglicus*, 1652) to the royalist merchant John Webster, deserves closer investigation.[42]

Whether encouraged by English exiles or not, it is without question that a number of Dutch poets were actively engaged in the royalist effort. The Dutch translation of Salmasius's *Defensio Regia* (1650), for example, allegedly financed by Charles II, contained prefatory poems of some of the major Dutch poets.[43] And the main objectives of these Dutch royalist poets were to gain Dutch support for the Stuart cause and to promote a Stuart invasion of parliamentary England. They sought to legitimate the retaliation of Charles II and, as we shall illustrate, did so by appropriating both the language and the conventions of the traditional English brand of revenge tragedy, though with a vengeance.[44]

Prominent among the Dutch royalists was Jan Vos, the adapter of *Titus Andronicus*, who made full use of the language he had learned from Shakespearian revenge tragedy. In his poem *Olivier Kromwel*, for instance, Vos echoes York's famous description of Queen Margaret in *3 Henry VI*, 'O tiger's heart wrapp'd in a woman's hide!' (1.4.138):

> This is he, who Nature as a Tiger tried to breed;
> A monster, that defies the cruelest beasts
> She lacked the pow'r, though not in every part
> For in a human form she bred a Tiger's heart.[45]

The tiger's cruelty may have been a commonplace, and the Shakespearian echo here could be coincidental, but it is no coincidence that the man who translated the 'ravenous tiger' Aran for the Dutch stage produced a similar kind of language to attack a political enemy. In other political poems, Vos's mastery of revenge tragedy resurfaces. In the twenty sestets comprising 'Britain to Europe' – a poem first published in the Salmasius translation financed by Charles II – Vos introduced Britain as a Senecan character rousing Europe to be avenged for Charles I.[46] Dressed in black, Europe was told to mourn no more, but to rise to action and punish the regicides (lines 1–6). The blood is already dripping in the first few lines, but Vos further enhances the horror of his poem in the fifth sestet, where he has Britain describe the continental army she envisages:

> With tendons tightly stretch Lord Strafford's skin
> About his skull; scare the cruel tyrants
> And use his shins to strike the fearful drum
> You'll blow the hollow bones as you march on,
> Fairfax will be surprised by such a sound
> Of war, which sure will make his army fly.[47]

Political retaliation is here cast in the language of revenge tragedy, the genre that earned Vos his reputation, and it is difficult to read this passage and its imaginative use of body parts without being reminded of Titus's revenge – 'Hark, villains, I will grind your bones to dust, / And with your blood and it I'll make a paste, / And of the paste a coffin I will rear' (*Titus Andronicus*, 5.2.185–7).[48] Through this kind of verse, the English genre of revenge tragedy was recycled on the political stage and reapplied within the (native) English context.

While Vos portrayed Britain as a vindictive Senecan woman, several Dutch poems written in 1649–50 turned Charles I into a revenge ghost. In the prefatory sonnet to Joan Dullaert's martyr play *Charles Stuart: or Disastrous Majesty* (written in 1649 and printed in 1652), the ghost of Charles I appears before the court that sentenced him to death.[49] Other poems have the ghost of Charles I rouse either his son, Charles II, or his son-in-law, the Dutch Stadholder William II, to avenge him.[50] The purpose of these horrifying poems was to make the Dutch support the royalist cause. The obvious problem with this rhetoric, however, was the doubtful moral nature of revenge. As we have seen, especially in Holland, revenge tragedies tended unambiguously to emphasise the fact that revenge belonged to God. Vos recognised this problem and the speaker in his 'Britain to Europe' therefore emphasises that the moral reservations about revenge – familiar from Theodore Rodenburgh's *The Revenger's Tragedy* and the Dutch renderings of Kyd's *The Spanish Tragedy* – should be temporarily put aside. Thus, divine revenge became the privilege of his English royals:

THE SPANISH TRAGEDY AND REVENGE TRAGEDY 155

Vindictiveness, which long was libelled devilish
Shall now be divine; for they who corrupt the law
And shed the royal blood, deserve high punishment.⁵¹

If Dutch audiences were to be convinced that they should ally with Charles II, vengefulness had to be revaluated. Hence, the image of the ghost of Charles I was complemented with images of his son as a just avenger. In the elaborate allegorical engraving on the broadsheet pamphlet called *The Stage of English Miseries (Het Toneel der Engelsche Ellenden)* in Figure 9.1, the idea that Charles II was part of a divine revenge plot is pointedly illustrated.⁵² Charles is shown as a personification of St George who fights the seven-headed dragon of revolution with a sword labelled 'Crown Right'. Ireland and Scotland kneel before him, and, while Ireland appears to strap on his armour, Scotland hands him a gun that has two barely legible words written on it: 'geterghde wraeck' ('provoked revenge').⁵³ Charles II's revenge is justified by the depiction of the execution of his father in the background. Dark clouds hang over the scaffold, yet it is lit up by four beams that testify God's anger, his grief and his pending revenge. Two read: 'Ire of God' ('Gramschap Gods'), the other two 'Woe, Woe' ('Wee-wee')

Figure 9.1 Toneel der Engelsche Ellenden – The Stage of English Miseries (Amsterdam: Hugo Allard, 1650)

and: 'Revenge, Revenge' ('Wraak-wraak'). Above the armies fighting in heaven (a reference to the reported sightings in England of battles in heaven during the Civil War), small but central, is God's shining sword of wrath. Charles II has become the chosen scourge of God.

Such divine support for royal revenge may also be found in one of the most outspoken political appropriations of Senecan revenge tragedy in seventeenth-century Dutch drama, Jan Bara's *Herstelde Vorst, ofte geluckigh ongeluck* (*Restored Prince, or Fortunate Misfortune*, 1650).[54] Bara presents Rasimo, a British prince in mythical times, who is visited by the ghost of his murdered father. In a passage akin to *Hamlet*, the ghost rouses Rasimo to be avenged on his father's death: 'Satisfy my plea, go! Revenge! Revenge! O, melancholy son!'[55] Like Hamlet, Rasimo is hesitant to execute the revenge throughout the play and, in the end, Ferrugo, a captain prefiguring Fairfax or Cromwell, has caused a 'terrible pestilence' to nestle itself 'in the country's marrow'.[56] Only when Rasimo is encouraged by a voice from heaven – like Charles II in the *Stage of English Miseries* – does he finally execute his much awaited revenge. Another ghost then appears with a prophecy before the diminished British court:

> Here shall the axe be crimsoned by the Vice-Roy's blood
> The Archbishop's head, and the King's, shall be cut off
> On this scaffold. Cold steel will run through their necks
> To Holland's great dismay, and France's bitter grief;
> Live long in peace, but mind the godforgotten heirs
> Of this cruel captain.[57]

In the ghost's account, the entire action of the play is really a prefiguration of the English Civil Wars, which implies that an avenger to punish the 'godforgotten heirs' is at hand.

In his essay on revenge tragedy between 1649 and 1683, John Kerrigan has argued that 'the recurrent tension in early modern drama between the rightness of what Neville calls "God's horryble vengeance for Sin" and the questionable claim of individuals to be acting as his scourge and minister was cross-cut [...] with political argument about tyranny and the limits of just rebellion'.[58] In Bara's *Hamlet*-like revenge tragedy this tension is fully resolved, as it expresses, like Wase's *Electra* (performed for Elizabeth Stuart in The Hague), the conviction that God will eventually avenge his anointed through his instrument, Charles II. Yet Bara's *Restored Prince* adds an element to the royalist hope apparent in Wase's *Electra* and to the triumph that was implicit in a Restoration *Hamlet*. Like *The Stage of English Miseries*, it is above all an attempt to move its Dutch audience into supporting the justified royalist revenge. We find the tension signalled by Kerrigan here not so much within the play itself as within Dutch culture, as the earlier form of the same genre that was politically appropriated by Bara unambiguously denounced revenge. Rodenburgh's *Wraeck-gierigers Treur-spel* and *Don Jeronimo*, which were still frequently performed in the 1650s, were only two of the plays with which Bara's *Restored Prince* was in dialogue.

A similar strategy of appropriating revenge tragedy for the royalist cause was employed by Lodewijk Meyer. The dramatist's *Verloofde Koningksbruidt* (*The Royal Bride*) also tells the story of a mythical regicide in Britain, followed by a complex revenge plot. *The Royal Bride* is vintage Senecan revenge tragedy gone into overdrive. Besides a *Hamlet*-like plot in which the ghost of the father is actually a disguised cousin of the avenger, it contains a cannibalistic scene in which the tyrant of Britain unwittingly drinks the blood of his murdered sons for wine – an obvious borrowing from Jan Vos's *Aran en Titus*.[59] Despite the onslaught at the British court, however, all ends well when one of the remaining noblemen introduces the rightful king, Atelstan, as a *deus ex machina* in the last act of *The Royal Bride*:

> My Lords, do not doubt that this is the Royal son
> Our firstborn Prince, and the lawful heir to the throne.
> Having the Tyrant's sword escaped, he kept himself
> With this dear Queen concealed in Caledonia
> All the while he patiently intelligenced with me
> To force, with violence or craft, this raging tyrant
> From his throne, and avenge his noble family.[60]

In 1652, when Meyer wrote his play, there was only one king of Britain who had recently found shelter in Caledonia. And if Atelstan is, like Rasimo, a type of Charles II, it is likely as well as understandable that Meyer foregrounded the Queen of Caledonia as the 'royal bride' of the play's title. Meyer's choice to emphasise the only Scottish character in the play's unwavering love and loyalty to the lawful heir to the throne served to celebrate the 'marriage' between Charles II and Scotland that had been engineered by the Orange court in 1650. As in *The Stage of English Miseries* (Figure 9.1), this Scottish alliance offered hope for a happy ending.

The concerns that are central to the plays of Bara and Meyer may also be found in that other Dutch rendition of an English revenge tragedy, Dirk Kalbergen's translation of John Mason's *The Turke* (1610, 1632) as *Muliassus de Turk* (1652).[61] Kalbergen's Muliassus first appears on stage as he fashions himself as a regicide: 'I'll feed the slimy earth with human brains / And drink the Princes' blood, to found my State'.[62] Like Van den Bosch's Richard III, and the tyrants in *The Royal Bride* and *Restored Prince*, Muliassus is a Machiavel who, in order to maintain his power, is prepared to murder princes. At the beginning of the Anglo-Dutch War (1652–54), this invited a comparison with Cromwell, who was frequently represented as a Turk or a Moor.[63] The arrival of the legitimate ruler of Florence, Fenizio, at the end of Kalbergen's play, may be read as the realisation of a royalist's dream: 'Those who have escaped their Deaths with us, take comfort. / Hate has left this court, nothing harbours here but rest.'[64]

Kalbergen follows the pattern of Bara and Meyer: his revenge plot, which includes the killing of princes, is followed by a happy ending with the rightful ruler restored to the throne. The ending represents the restoration of order after a period of civil war – a scheme also adopted by Lambert van den Bosch in his appropriation of *Richard III*. This is an essential element of the royalist revenge tragedy, as it underscores the divine justification for the modern avenger, Charles II. In the Dutch context of the 1650s, these endings and the other manifestations of Providence, promoted the 'magical aura of kingship' and justified Charles II's cause for a Dutch audience whose good opinion was essential for a royalist invasion in England.[65]

The close relations between the British and continental theatrical cultures during the Civil War and the Interregnum suggest that these royalist versions of revenge tragedy are to be appreciated as Anglo-Dutch rather than Dutch products. Although the echoes of *Hamlet* in Bara and Meyer do not necessarily derive from Shakespeare, the fact that Dutch poets who were working in very close proximity to royalist exiles echo Shakespeare's play does seem to bolster Nancy Klein Maguire's claim that, during performances of *Hamlet*, in 1661, 'the ghost of Hamlet's father resonated with the "ghost" of Charles I'.[66] *Titus Andronicus* and *The Turke*, on the other hand, primarily offered a negative image for the horrors of civil war and unwarranted ambition. Although political readings of Mason's source, *Lust's Dominion* (printed in London, 1657), exist, *The Turke* has not yet been discussed as a possible royalist play.[67] Kalbergen's adaptation, however, shows that Mason's original revenge tragedy, too, may have come to be seen as a caveat against the unbridled ambition of Oliver Cromwell.

Revenge tragedy was transformed by a royalist mode of interpretation that belonged to the Anglo-Dutch sphere. For this reason, Dutch revenge tragedy of the period may help us appreciate the transformations undergone also by English revenge tragedy as it was in exile during the 1640s and the 1650s. Nancy Maguire has shown that, by 'reenacting regicide and restoration' in tragicomedies after the Restoration, English playwrights were 'exonerating themselves of the execution of Charles I, while celebrating the restoration of his son'.[68] Kerrigan has rightly added to this the observation that 'of all tragic scenarios, those which turn on vengeance – using recapitulative acts to extirpate evil – most resemble, and are most compatible with, tragicomedy'.[69] It is our contention that both the Dutch plays discussed in this section and the Restoration revenge tragicomedies represent a near-simultaneous royalist attempt on either side of the North Sea to appropriate and redefine the genre of revenge tragedy. English Restoration playwrights were really continuing a propagandistic device developed abroad where royalist Dutch poets during the 1650s effectively promoted that very same Restoration in Britain.

Revenge tragedy changed during the royalist exile experience, and, when it returned to Restoration England, Kyd's fame had been, to borrow Boas's word, 'eclipsed'.[70] Our investigation suggests that the English demise of Kyd after 1660 was partly caused by changing appreciation of revenge due to political developments. Unlike *Hamlet*, *The Spanish Tragedy* could not so easily be made to fit into the royalist scheme of things. In the United Provinces, however, the theatre never became exclusively royalist. Hence, *The Spanish Tragedy* remained popular throughout the Civil Wars and the Interregnum, representing a powerful counter-discourse of revenge that royalist revenge tragedy attempted to challenge and contradict. Even though Kyd's original may be infinitely more ambiguous than the seventeenth-century Dutch adaptations, it still represents Revenge as a creature of the underworld, a threat to rather than a preserver of divine order.

CONCLUSION

In the first part of this study, we have sought to illustrate that, despite the fact that the English Renaissance plays appropriated in the Low Countries during the seventeenth century have received considerable attention, important work may still be done. With reference to *The Spanish Tragedy* and Rodenburgh's *The Revenger's Tragedy*, we have tried to show that these texts may hold an – as yet – unappreciated bibliographical interest, suggesting that the near-contemporary Dutch versions of the English play-texts should be considered more seriously than has been the case so far within the context of current English editorial practice. To arrive at a proper appreciation of the closely interconnected theatre scenes of England and the Low Countries, one is therefore inclined to call on intercultural translation studies specialists, and invite a reappraisal of the Dutch versions of the anonymous *Nobody and Some-body* (1645), Thomas Tomkis's *Lingua* (1648), Christopher Marlowe's *The Jew of Malta* (translated twice, in 1645 and 1676) and *Doctor Faustus* (before 1689), Thomas Randolph's *Amyntas* (1666) and James Shirley's *Love's Cruelty* (1668), as well as the Dutch version of William Prynne's *Histrio-Mastyx* (1639).[71]

In the second part of this study we have concentrated on the broader cultural contexts of *The Spanish Tragedy* and the revenge genre during the seventeenth century on either side of the North Sea. We have argued that revenge tragedies, like the adaptations of *The Spanish Tragedy*, became incompatible with the royalist frame of mind during the mid-seventeenth century. In royalist hands, revenge tragedy served to foreground the divine right of the protagonist to be avenged on a (regicide) tyrant, and this tended to favour the happy ending that became so prominent in Restoration tragedy. Further investigation of the religious and political gravity of the revenge genre could shed valuable new light on the interrelations between literary genre and political ideology, revenge and religious denomination, which make up only some of the immense complexities of Anglo-Dutch or Hollando-English relations during the period.

NOTES

1 Boas (ed.), *The Works of Thomas Kyd*, p. ci.
2 The records suggest that Chapman was hospitalised in the Zealand town of Middelburg in October 1586, but it is not certain if he was wounded, or was in need of medical treatment for any other reasons. See Schrickx, 'George Chapman in Middelburg in 1586', p. 165.
3 The suggestion made by Sorgen (*De Toneelkunst*), namely that the 'Will' in the correspondence referred to Shakespeare's presence in Utrecht, never had much following.
4 See Bachrach, 'Bredero en de Engelse Toneelspelers'.
5 For a biographical sketch of Johannes de Witt, see Hoenselaars, 'Johannes de Witt (c.1566–1622)'; Leek, *Shakespeare in Nederland*, p. 24. For a biographical sketch of Rodenburgh and his English connections, see Hoenselaars and Abrahamse, 'Theodore Rodenburgh and English studies', pp. 324–39.
6 Quoted in Worp, 'Die Fabel der *Spanish Tragedy*', p. 183. See also Boas, *The Works of Thomas Kyd*, pp. ci–cii. An English translation of the Kyd materials is in progress.
7 See Hoenselaars and Abrahamse, '*Chi sara sara*: Theodore Rodenburgh (1574–1644) en Italië'; and Abrahamse, *Het toneel van Theodore Rodenburgh, 1574–1644*.
8 For further information, see Groote, '*The Revenger's Tragedy* and an early

Dutch version by Theodore Rodenburg', and Schrickx, 'The Revenger's Tragedy and its contemporary Dutch adaption by Theodore Rodenburg'.
9 The Revenger's Tragedy (1618), 'Induction'. Unless otherwise specified, all translations are ours. 'Het ongelijck en rechtmen door het wreken niet: / De wraeck verweckt noch meerder ramp, en onghelucken; / Horatius en laet u zelven niet verrucken / Door woeste toorens tocht, die reden gatsch vermomt, / En maeckt verstandts vernunft benevelt en bedomt, / Door hetten van het bloedt, die reden doet versmooren. Ia die in wraeck 't meest wint die heeft het meest verlooren.'
10 In the original: 'De dulle woeste mensch / die al zijn leed wil wreken, / Blijft inde nickers wensch / ellendelijcke steken'. (See title page and 'Induction', sig. A4).
11 Limon, Gentlemen of a Company, pp. 21–3; and Verlaan, 'Adriaen van den Bergh', vol. I, p. 57.
12 'Vinnense so een woort van andere Poëten, / So moetet in haer sin alt'mael ghestoolen heeten'. Verlaan, 'Adriaen van den Bergh', vol. 1, p. 20.
13 Vita and Geesink, Academie en Schouwburg, p. 43.
14 See Fleming (ed.), Jeronimo Marschalck in Hispanien.
15 With regard to the money that Van den Bergh received from the theatre at the time the text of Don Jeronimo was produced, Verlaan suggests that he may have received an indemnity, 'Adriaen van den Bergh', vol. 1, pp. 25–6. The theatre wanted a proper version of The Spanish Tragedy and bought Van den Bergh out.
16 Quoted in Verlaan: 'die hooggeachte / Speelder in zijn jonge tijt. / Die Jeronimo van Spanje, / En de jonge Polidoor; En Andronicus [...] Eerst op 't Duyts toneel dee leven,' 'Adriaen van den Bergh', vol. 1, pp. 198–9.
17 On the career of Jan Vos as it intersects with the afterlife of Shakespeare, see Hoenselaars, 'Translation futures'.
18 Jonson, Bartholomew Fair, p. 16, lines 106–11.
19 Boas, p. xiii.
20 The Spanish Tragedy, Induction, p. 82; and Worp, 'Die Fabel der Spanish Tragedy', p. 185.
21 Schoneveld's standard checklist suggests the 1594 version of The Spanish Tragedy and 1605 text of The First Part of Ieronimo as the basis of the text. See his Intertraffic of the Mind, pp. 167–245 (p. 212, sv 369–70).
22 In the original: 'Jeronimo ontkleedt, met eene toorts ende degen in sijn handt.' Don Jeronimo, Marschalck van Spanjens Trevr-spel. Vertoont Op d'Amsterdamsche Schouwburgh, Den 12. October 1638 (Amsterdam: Ioost Hartgersz,1638), sig. B2r.
23 Jackson, The Revenger's Tragedy, sig. A2r.
24 Wraeck-gierigers treur-spel (Amsterdam, 1618), sig. A1r. The quotation derives from the retranslation into English of Rodenburgh's revenge play, currently being prepared by Hoenselaars. This new edition of the play will be accompanied by a full survey in English of Rodenburgh's contacts with England. Before the new English version of the play, however, an old-spelling edition will be produced.

25 DUKE, DUCHESS, LUSSURIOSO, AMBITIOSO, SUPERVACUO AND JUNIOR *true sons of the Duke*, SPURIO *the Duke's bastard son*, VENDICI AND HIPPOLITO *noblemen and brothers*, ELIZA *mother*, CASTIZA *her daughter*, DONDOLO *servant*, ANTONIO AND PIRENIO *noblemen of standing*, ALIAGA, FIRST NOBLEMAN, SECOND NOBLEMAN, THIRD NOBLEMAN (added 1634), FOURTH NOBLEMAN (added 1634), FIRST JUDGE, SECOND JUDGE, PRISON OFFICERS, *two Servants to* SPURIO.

26 In the original: '*D. Pedro trect Pedron ganos Deghen uyt*' (sig. A4v).

27 In the original: '*En spreeckt de waerheydt / of ick schend dy voort den kop*' (sig. A4r).

28 In the original: '*Hy geeft hem sijn degen weer*' (sig. B1r).

29 Edwards (1959) and Cairncross (1967) are consistent in a different way by simply conveying the quarto's change here from descriptive to prescriptive stage directions, without any further editorial intervention, but also without remarking on the unusual quality in any way. The touring player manuscript of 1662 adopts the first stage direction, and incorporates the second into the speech of Don Pedro. See Fleming, *Jeronimo Marschalck in Hispanien*, p. 214.

30 See Smits-Veldt, *Samuel Coster, Ethicus-Didacticus*, p. 74.

31 In the original: 'Wt d'een in d'ander Crygh', Verlaan, 'Adriaen van den Bergh', vol. 1, p. 215.

32 On the impact of the English Civil Wars and the execution of Charles I in the Dutch Republic, see Helmers, *The Royalist Republic*.

33 See Vita and Geesink, *Academie en Schouwburg*, p. 248.

34 Shakespeare's *The Taming of the Shrew* was one of the plays which travelled to the Dutch Republic in this period. See Helmers, 'Unknown shrews'.

35 Denham, *The Prologue to His Majesty* (1660). Broadsheet pamphlet.

36 See Kathman, 'Lower, Sir William (c.1610–1662)', and Hodges, 'Wase, Christopher (1627–1690)'.

37 Wase, *Electra of Sophocles* (1649). See Maguire, 'The theatrical mask/masque of politics', p. 8; and Kerrigan, 'Revenge tragedy revisited, 1649-1683', pp. 230–1.

38 Lower's *The Enchanted Lovers: a Pastoral* (1658), *The Amorous Fantasme: a Tragi-comedy* (1659) and *The Noble Ingratitude a Pastoral Comedy* (1659) were all printed in The Hague.

39 See Keblusek, *Boeken in de Hofstad*.

40 Cited in Geyl, *Orange and Stuart*, p. 129. See also Lesser, 'Mixed government and mixed marriage in *A King and No King*'.

41 Hoenselaars, 'Shakespeare and the early modern history play'.

42 Bosch, *Engelsche Florus* (1652).

43 See Sellin, 'Royalist propaganda'.

44 The argument presented in the second part is based partly on Helmers, 'The cry of the royal blood'. See also Helmers, *The Royalist Republic*, 172–97.

45 In the original: 'Dit is hy daar Natuur een tiger van wou teelen; / Een schrikdier, dat het wreedst der wilde dieren tart: / Maar 't is haar macht gemist;

doch niet in alle deelen: / Want in een menschenschyn schiep zy een tygers hart.' Vos, *Olivier Kromwel, &c*, in *Alle de Gedichten*, vol. I (1662), p. 161.

46 Vos, 'Brittanje aan Euroope, toen Koning KAREL D'EERSTE vermoordt, &c', in Salmasius, *Koninklijkke verdediging, voor Kaarel den I* (Rotterdam: Naeranus, 1650), **5r-**8r. The poem also appeared in *Verscheyde Nededuytsche gedichten* (Amsterdam: Lodewyck Spillebout, 1651), pp. 79-82; and in J. Vos, *Alle de Gedichten van den poëet Jan Vos* (Amsterdam: Jacob Lescaille, 1662), pp. 463-7.

47 In the original: 'Gy zult mijn Straffortshuit, tot schrik der wreê tirannen, / Op Strafforts bekkeneel met taie peezen spannen, / En slaan met zijn gebeent op zulk een trom voor't volk; / In't trekken zult gy op zijn holle schonken blaazen; / Want zulk een krijgsgerucht zal Fairfax zelf verbaazen; / En 't leeger wegh doen vliên, als eertijdts voor zijn dolk.' Vos, 'Brittanje aan Euroope', lines 31-6.

48 See Vos's rendering of this passage in *Aran en Titus*: 'Dies zal ik u de neus flux uit uw' aanzicht bijten, / En al wat manlijk is van uwe lichaam rijten, / En stroopen u de huidt, al leevendig van 't lijf, / En steeken u aan 't spit; en schaffen 't helsche wijf, / Uw' godvergete moêr, de gaargebraaden schinken: / En geeven haar uw' bloedt, met wijn doormengt, te drinken' (lines 1887-92).

49 Dullaert, 'Voorzangk', in *Karel Stuart of Rampzalige Majesteit: Treurspel* (1652). In his discussion of Dullaert's sonnet, Duits mentions both *Hamlet* and Hooft's *Geeraerd van Velsen* as possible sources for the ghost. See Duits, 'Horror als voorafje (1652)'.

50 See also Knuttel 6363, *De geest van Karolus Stuart* (n.p. 1649) and Knuttel 6328, *Wonderlijcke Geest des Conincx* (n.p. 1649). The ghost of Charles I also appears to Charles II in Vos's poem *Zeekrijgh* ('Naval War', 1653).

51 In the original: 'De Wraakzucht die altijdt voor duivelsch is gelastert, / Die zal nu godtlijk zijn; want die de wet verbastert, / En 's Koninx bloedt vergiet, verdient de zwaarste straf.' Vos, 'Brittanje aan Euroope', lines 103-5.

52 Zoet, *Het Tooneel der Engelsche elende*. British Library, Thomason 669f12 (88). EEBO 122153. Stolk Atlas nr. 2157. Van Kuijk mentions the pamphlet in Kuyk, *Oude politieke spotprenten*, pp. 17, 152. See also *The Abraham Cowley Text and Image Archive*.

53 The presence of Ireland in a role facilitating revenge suggests that the engraving was made before October 1649, by which time Cromwell had subdued Ireland. More likely, however, the pamphlet dates from early in 1650, when Charles agreed to the Scottish Covenanters' demands and became King of Scotland, which finally enabled him to come to action after having been stuck in Jersey for months. The battle of Worcester, in September 1651, posits the latest possible date. Kuyk, in *Oude politieke spotprenten*, erroneously dates the broadside 1652 (p. 152); the *Atlas van Stolk* (1976) has 1651.

54 Bara, *Herstelde Vorst, ofte Geluckigh Ongeluck* (1650), sig. 760 E 69.

55 In the original: 'Voldoe mijn beê, op! wraeck! wraeck! ô bedruckte Soon!', Bara, *Herstelde Vorst, ofte Geluckigh Ongeluck*, sig. A4r.
56 In the original: 'Ghy voed, helaes! in't merch, een binnelandsche pest / Wiens kole sal soo diep door uwe lenden woeden', Bara, *Herstelde Vorst, ofte Geluckigh Ongeluck*, sig. I2r.
57 In the original: 'hier de Vice-Roy [Strafford] de bijle sal bebloeden, / Daer 't hooft van Cantelbergh [Laud], en 's Konings [Charles I] sijn geknot / Het stael door strot en neck gedreven op't schavot, / Ten rou in Hollandstuyn, en druck in't Hof der Vrancken; / Leef lang in vreê, maer straft de god-vergete rancken / Van dese Capiteyn.' Bara, *Herstelde Vorst, ofte Geluckigh Ongeluck*, sig. I3v.
58 Kerrigan, 'Revenge tragedy revisited', p. 232.
59 Meyer's editors offer evidence of several traces of *Aran en Titus* in Meyer's play and prefer it to Seneca's *Thyestes* as the source for the cannibalistic scene. Meyer, *Verloofde Koninksbruidt*, pp. 45–7.
60 In the original: 'Ghy Heeren, twijffelt niet; deeze is de Koningszoon, / Onze erffelijke Vorst, en wettigh oir der kroon, / Die, 't zwaerdt van den Tiran ontvlucht, zich by Mêvrouwe, / In Kaledonien, bedekt'lijk heeft ghehouwen, / En onderwijl met my staâgh onderling verstandt / Om met gheweldt, óft list, den woeden Dwingelandt / Te bonzen van den troon, en zijn gheslacht te wreeken.' Meyer, *Verloofde Koningksbruidt*, pp. 153–4, lines 1817–23.
61 Kalbergen, *Muliassus de Turk. Treurspel* (1652). We used the copy of the Royal Library in The Hague, 448 J 193. The most probable source text is not the first, but the second, 1632 edition of Mason's play.
62 In the original: 'Ik zal de slijmige aard met menschen brein vet mesten, / En zuipen Princen bloedt, om zoo mijn Staat te vesten.' Kalbergen, *Muliassus de Turk. Treurspel*, sig. C1v.
63 Vondel called Cromwell 'The Turk of English Barbary', who 'with his Janizaries' feared the Dutch war effort because his 'bloody' rule was unjustified. See Vondel, 'Uitvaert van Wylen den Doorluchtigen Zeehelt, Marten Harpertsz. Tromp' ('Funeral of the late illustrious naval hero, Marten Harpertsz. Tromp'), (1653).
64 In the original: 'Gy die met ons de dood ontsprongen zijt, schept luste / De haat is uit dit Hof, hier huisvest niet dan ruste.' Kalbergen, *Muliassus de Turk. Treurspel*, sig. F4r. Retranslated from the Dutch.
65 Hill, *Some Intellectual Consequences of the English Revolution*, pp. 13, 27.
66 Maguire, *Regicide and Restoration: English Tragicomedy 1660–1671*, p. 121.
67 See also Jowitt, 'Political allegory'.
68 Maguire, *Regicide and Restoration*, p. 3.
69 Kerrigan, 'Revenge tragedy revisited', p. 237.
70 Boas, *The Works of Thomas Kyd*, p. xiv.
71 The existing checklist of relevant materials still contains a veritable multitude of research opportunities in English Renaissance drama. See Schoneveld, *Intertraffic of the Mind*, pp. 167–245.

REFERENCES

Abrahamse, W., *Het toneel van Theodore Rodenburgh, 1574–1644* (Amsterdam: AD & L, 1997).
Atlas van Stolk (Rotterdam: Atlas van Stolk, 1976).
Bachrach, A. G. H., 'Bredero en de Engelse Toneelspelers', in *Rondom Bredero* (Culemborg: Tjeenk Willink-Noorduijn, 1970), pp. 71–89.
Bara, J., *Herstelde Vorst, ofte Geluckigh Ongeluck* (Amsterdam: L. Spillebout, 1650). Royal Library in The Hague, 760 E 69.
Boas, F. (ed.), *The Works of Thomas Kyd* (Oxford: Clarendon Press, 1901).
Bosch, L. van den, *Engelsche Florus, of Kort begryp der Engelsche geschiedenissen van de eerste tyden af tot de doodt van Karel I. Eerst in 't Latijn beschreven door L. v. Bos en nu door den selven in 't Nêerduytsch vertaelt* (Amsterdam: Nicolaes van Ravesteyn, 1652).
Denham, J., *The Prologue to His Majesty at the First Play Presented at the Cockpit in Whitehall* (London: G. Bedell and T. Collins, 1660). http://gateway.proquest.com/openurl?ctx_ver=Z39.882003&res_id=xri:eebo&rft_id=xri:eebo:citation:99869591 [last accessed 30 January 2014].
Duits, H., 'Horror als voorafje: De "Voorzangk" bij Joan Dullaarts *Karel Stuart* (1652)', in H. Duit, A. J. Gelderblom and M. B. Smits-Veldt (eds), *Klinkend boeket: Studies over renaissancesonnetten voor Marijke Spies* (Hilversum: Verloren, 1994), pp. 113–19.
Dullaert, J., 'Voorzangk', in *Karel Stuart of Rampzalige Majesteit: Treurspel* (Amsterdam: Gerrit van Goedesberg, 1652).
Fleming, W. (ed.), *Jeronimo Marschalck in Hispanien: Das deutsche Wandertruppen-Manuskript der 'Spanish Tragedy'* (Hildesheim and New York: Georg Olms Verlag, 1973).
Geyl, P., *Orange and Stuart* (London: Phoenix Press, 2001).
Groote, B. de, '*The Revenger's Tragedy* and an early Dutch version by Theodore Rodenburg', unpublished MA dissertation, University of Ghent, 1973.
Helmers, H. J., 'Unknown shrews. Three Dutch adaptations of The/A Shrew', in G. Holderness and D. Wootton (eds), *Gender and Power in Shrew-Taming Narratives, 1500–1700* (Basingstoke: Palgrave Macmillan, 2010), pp. 123–44.
Helmers, H. J., 'The cry of the royal blood. Revenge tragedy and the Stuart cause in the Dutch republic', in A. van Dixhoorn, E. Strietman and J. Bloemendal (eds), *Literary Cultures and Public Opinion in the Low Countries, 1450-1650* (Leiden: Brill, 2011), pp. 219–50.
Helmers, H. J. *The Royalist Republic. Literature, Politics and Religion in the Anglo-Dutch Public Sphere, 1639-1660* (Cambridge: Cambridge University Press, 2015).
Hill, C., *Some Intellectual Consequences of the English Revolution* (London: Weidenfeld and Nicolson, 1980).
Hoenselaars, A. J., 'Shakespeare and the early modern history play', in M. Hattaway (ed.), *The Cambridge Companion to Shakespeare's History Plays* (Cambridge: Cambridge University Press, 2002), pp. 25–40.
Hoenselaars, A. J., 'Johannes de Witt (c.1566–1622), humanist and visitor to

London', in *Oxford Dictionary of National Biography* www.oxforddnb. com/index/68/101068056/ [last accessed 30 January 2014].
Hoenselaars, A. J., 'Translation futures: Shakespearians and the foreign text', *Shakespeare Survey* 62 (2009): 273–82.
Hoenselaars, T. and W. Abrahamse, '*Chi sara sara*: Theodore Rodenburgh (1574–1644) en Italië', *Incontri: Rivista europea di studi italiani* 10:2 (1995): 57–64.
Hoenselaars, T. and W. Abrahamse, 'Theodore Rodenburgh and English studies', in J. Roding and L. H. van Voss (eds), *The North Sea and Culture 1550–1800* (Hilversum: Verloren, 1996), pp. 324–39.
Hodges, R. E., 'Wase, Christopher (1627–1690)', in *Oxford Dictionary of National Biography*, www.oxforddnb.com/view/article/28802 [last accessed 30 January 2014].
Jackson, M. P. (ed.), *The Revenger's Tragedy: Attributed to Thomas Middleton. A Facsimile of the 1607/8 Quarto* (Rutherford, NJ: Fairleigh Dickinson Unversity Press, 1983).
Jonson, B., *Bartholomew Fair*, in *Ben Jonson*, ed. C. H. Herford and P. and E. Simpson, 11 vols. (Oxford: Clarendon Press, 1925–52), vol. 6 (1938), pp. 1–141.
Jowitt, C., 'Political allegory in late Elizabethan and early Jacobean "Turk" plays: The case of Dekker and Marston's *Lust's Dominion* (1599–1600) and John Mason's *The Turke* (1606-8)', *Comparative Drama* 37 (2003): 411–43.
Kalbergen, D., *Muliassus de Turk: Treurspel. Gerijmt door Dirk Kalbergen. Gespeelt op d'Amsterdamsche Schouwburg* (Amsterdam: Dirk Cornelisz. Houthaeck, 1652). Royal Library in The Hague, 448 J 193.
Kathman, D., 'Lower, Sir William (*c.*1610–1662)', *Oxford Dictionary of National Biography*, www.oxforddnb.com/view/article/17094 [last accessed 30 January 2014].
Keblusek, M., *Boeken in de Hofstad: Haagse boekcultuur in de Gouden Eeuw* (Hilversum: Verloren, 1997).
Kerrigan, J., 'Revenge tragedy revisited, 1649–1683', in *On Shakespeare and Early Modern Culture* (Oxford: Oxford University Press, 2001), pp. 230–54.
Knuttel 6363, *De geest van Karolus Stuart verscheenen aan de Nederlanden* (n.p., 1649).
Knuttel 6328, *Wonderlijcke Geest des Conincx, Coninck over Engelandt, Schotlandt, en Eyrlandt, wraeck begerende over eenen Jan Coke Advocaet, ende soliciteur voor den Republijcke van Engelandt* (n.p., 1649).
Kuyk, J. van, *Oude politieke spotprenten* (Den Haag: M. Nijhoff, 1940).
Leek, R. H., *Shakespeare in Nederland: Kroniek van vier eeuwen Shakespeare in Nederlandse vertalingen en op het Nederlands toneel* (Zutphen: De Walburg Pers, 1988).
Lesser, Z., 'Mixed government and mixed marriage in *A King and No King*: Sir Henry Neville reads Beaumont and Fletcher', *ELH* 69 (2002): 947–77.
Limon, J., *Gentlemen of a Company: English Players in Central and Eastern Europe, 1590–1660* (Cambridge: Cambridge University Press, 1985).

Maguire, N. K., 'The theatrical mask/masque of politics: The case of Charles I', *Journal of British Studies* 28:1 (1989): 1–22.
Maguire, N. K., *Regicide and Restoration: English Tragicomedy 1660–1671* (Cambridge: Cambridge University Press, 1992).
Meyer, L., *Verloofde Koninksbruidt*, ed. M. A. Schenkeveld-van der Dussen (Utrecht: Instituut De Vooys, 1978).
Rodenburg, T., *Wraeck-gierigers treur-spel* (Amsterdam: Paulus van Ravesteyn, 1618).
Schoneveld, C. W., *Intertraffic of the Mind: Studies in Seventeenth-century Anglo-Dutch Translation with a Checklist of Books translated from English into Dutch, 1600–1700* (Leiden: Brill, 1983).
Schrickx, W., '*The Revenger's Tragedy* and its contemporary Dutch adaption by Theodore Rodenburg', in P. Bilton (ed.), *Essays in Honour of Kristian Smidt* (Oslo: University of Oslo, 1986), pp. 104–9.
Schrickx, W., 'George Chapman in Middelburg in 1586', *Notes and Queries* 40:2 (1993): 165.
Sellin, P., 'Royalist propaganda and the Dutch poets on the execution of Charles I', *Dutch Crossing* 24 (2000): 241–64.
Smits-Veldt, M. B., *Samuel Coster, Ethicus-Didacticus* (Groningen: Wolters-Noordhoff, 1985).
Sorgen, W. G. F. A. van, *De toneelkunst te Utrecht en de Utrechtse Schouwburg* (Den Haag, 1885).
The Abraham Cowley Text and Image Archive. http://etext.virginia.edu/kinney/small/turning worm.htm [last accessed 30 January 2014].
Verlaan, T., 'Adriaen van den Bergh: Het leven van een rederijker in de eerste helft van de zeventiende eeuw; zijn betrekkingen met het zwerftoneel, en met Jeronimo, een "Spanish Tragedy" van die naam', unpublished MA thesis, Groningen University, 3 vols, 1983.
Vita, E. O. de and M. Geesink, *Academie en Schouwburg: Amsterdams toneelrepertoire 1617–1665* (Amsterdam: Huis aan de Drie Grachten, 1983).
Vondel, 'Uitvaert van Wylen den Doorluchtigen Zeehelt, Marten Harpertsz. Tromp' ('Funeral of the Late Illustrious Naval Hero, Marten Harpertsz. Tromp') (Amsterdam, 1653).
Vos, J., 'Brittanje aan Euroope, toen Koning KAREL D'EERSTE vermoordt, &c,' in Salmasius, *Koninklijkke verdediging, voor Kaarel den I* (Rotterdam: Naeranus, 1650).
Vos, J., *Alle de Gedichten van den poëet Jan Vos* (Amsterdam: Jacob Lescaille, 1662).
Vos, J., 'Aran en Titus', in *Toneelwerken*, ed. W. J. C. Buitendijk (Assen: Van Gorcum, 1975), pp. 99–210.
Wase, C., *Electra of Sophocles: Presented to Her Highnesse the Lady Elizabeth* (The Hague: Samuel Browne, 1649).
Worp, J. A., 'Die Fabel der *Spanish Tragedy* in einer nierderländischen Uebersetzung des *Orlando Furioso* (1915)', *Shakespeare-Jahrbuch* 29–30 (1894): 183–91.
Zoet, J., *Het tooneel der Engelsche elende* (Amsterdam: Hugo Allard, n.d.).

PART IV
Doing Kyd

CHAPTER 10

Staging Babel:
The Spanish Tragedy IV.iv. in performance

Tony Howard

There's a play I've been longing to do for years ... There's an English writer who goes by the name of Thomas Kyd. They say Shakespeare stole *Hamlet* from him. I've discovered another injustice, too, a forgotten play by Kyd called *The Spanish Tragedy*. It's a blood feud, a tragedy that ends in suicide. [...] We want our people to enjoy this play, to be uplifted by it, and towards this end, I've simplified the plot.

Orhan Pamuk[1]

Kyd's overdue re-emergence on to the stage faces recurring practical challenges. Modern directors preparing an acting text of *The Spanish Tragedy* must somehow 'simplify' a play whose immense popularity meant that the accumulating texts – 1594, the 1602 Additions, the mysterious *First Part of Hieronimo* (1605) – pose unique problems. And not only must Kyd's directors confront fundamental editorial questions; unlike editors they have to *resolve* them, without footnotes or equivocations. This chapter examines the four major twentieth-century revivals – Robert David MacDonald's at Glasgow Citizens Theatre (1978); Michael Bogdanov's for the National Theatre (Cottesloe 1982; Lyttelton transfer 1984); Alan Drury's BBC Radio 3 version (1994); Michael Boyd's at the RSC's Swan Theatre (1997) – and touches on the play's surprising reappearances since then, from an actual performance in a disused factory in London's main Turkish district to a fictional performance in a Turkish border town. Should Kyd's directors use the Additions which – whoever wrote them – contain some of the most magnificent language in English Renaissance drama? (Drury did.) Or will the production be based on the 1594 text (as with Bogdanov and Boyd)? Or will it be freely adapted, perhaps following the 1967 Regents edition and using *The First Part of Hieronimo* to motivate the later events? (MacDonald did.) Next, how should the play's rhetorical formality be dealt with? (All made major cuts but on different principles.) Would Kyd's long passages in Latin be retained? (All cut drastically.) Then directors must decide whether Hieronimo's revenge-play *Soliman and Perseda* (IV.iv) was originally acted in 'sundry languages'. If it was, would 'fidelity' paradoxically involve *new writing* – commissioning translations of eighteen speeches into Latin, Greek, Italian and French? And what are the challenges for modern actors and audiences if *The Spanish Tragedy* does climax in a multilingual cacophony, echoing Babel? In short, how creatively has contemporary theatre handled a great but problematic Elizabethan text? Its initial impact of course is visual.

SEEING KYD

Space
Several productions have equated Kyd's world with a torture chamber, a bare box within which to study suffering. In 1982 the Cottesloe studio became an off-white bloody cell, with a high rear wall decked with instruments of torture (Figure 10.1). A metal throne like an electric chair snared victims and a central girdered unit framed the executions; a looming fretwork canopy turned it into a bower for Horatio to die in. For Act IV's court celebrations a festive tent was dropped in; but it contained a giant skull-faced figure of Revenge which, opened up, revealed itself as a kind of monstrous iron-maiden (Figure 10.2): inside hung Horatio's blue-grey corpse.

In 1997 at the Swan – which is inspired by seventeenth-century thrust stages and inevitably suggests a *Theatrum Mundi* – blank wooden surfaces created an unforgiving austerity. The ruling elite sat rigidly in a line against the back wall in constricting costumes that for

Figures 10.1 and 10.2 The Spanish/Portuguese throne and the iron-maiden in Michael Bogdanov's production of *The Spanish Tragedy*

all their opulence had been dirtied and degraded by war. Hieronimo, grieving, would stand exposed and alone on the long thrust stage; his 'garden' was a mockery of Nature, a row of swaying suspended planks. Bogdanov had located the play in a timeless abattoir of crude power politics; Boyd, as in his later *Hamlet* (2004), evoked a dark, specifically Renaissance world of haunted ambition and religious fear – what one newspaper called 'A Chamber in Hell'.[2] But in Glasgow, Robert David MacDonald firmly located Hieronimo's tragedy in the *modern* world. A ruined brick building was backed by a twisted metal sky. In the middle stood a scaffold where prisoners were executed at the end of a civil war which evoked both 1930s Spain and the recent coup in Chile. Andrea's helpless Ghost would be chained to it.[3] Drury's radio version, of course, took place inside our heads, where imagination and madness had free rein. Thomas Kyd's universe proved ubiquitous.

Bodies
Glasgow's Revenge was a bored pageboy in white who spoke the servants' lines and flipped in each fatal letter. He shone a torch in Hieronimo's eyes to examine his pain. He was the Boy with the Box. At the National, Revenge became a workmanlike, unseen, crop-haired executioner who supplied the key props, or just slouched and watched. At the RSC, and more in line with early modern iconography, it was a masked figure, constantly circling the theatre, never clearly seen, and the fact that Revenge roamed the whole auditorium expanded the play's Chinese-box structure. In the bloody climax of IV.iv, murderers were murdered, watched by the royal audience, who were watched by the Ghost, who was watched by us – and any one of us might at any moment be in the eye line of Revenge. Hieronimo aches to know 'the author' of his sufferings: in these productions fate could seem all-controlling (Boyd) or merely a lesser force that ensures human viciousness is given scope (Bogdanov). Revenge could personify cynicism (Bogdanov) or a frightening acceptance that horror is built into the natural order of things: in the Arcola Theatre's *Spanish Tragedy* of 2009, Revenge was a sweet little girl with pigtails, a pink dress – and the axe with which Horatio's mother would kill herself. Alan Drury's radio version explored these extremes, working purely with sound and the listener's imagination; he supported the Ghost and Revenge with angelic singing *and* apocalyptic radiophonic noise, suggesting an endless metaphysical conflict between light and darkness, pity and terror.

Speech

As soon as Kyd's actors speak – 'When this eternal substance of my soul / Did live imprison'd in my wanton flesh' (I.i.1–2) – the barriers between life and death become destabilised. MacDonald and Boyd spotlit the process. At the Citizens, wretched dead Andrea could remember nothing of his life: touched by Revenge, the corpse jerked upright and rattled off its first words; but it kept halting, its speeches broke up. Revenge prompted it. Michael Boyd developed this idea, so that Andrea's mind remained in hell. There was a soundtrack of distorted voices overlaid with screams; then Andrea, shrieking and inarticulate, had to be *taught* by Revenge to speak:

> When this eternal ...
> When this eternal ...
> When this eternal substance of my soul ...

A curtain opened to reveal a frozen Court of 'the living dead' who became animate as they were named.[4] Thus from the very beginning MacDonald and Boyd both connected consciousness with language, and – like Kyd – linked suffering and cruelty to linguistic collapse: 'Where words prevail not, violence prevails' (II.i.108).

WHICH TEXTS?

MacDonald in Glasgow was the one director to use *The First Part of Hieronimo* to delve into the origins of revenge, presenting the naive chivalry of Andrea (in braided scarlet), Bel-imperia's first passion and Lorenzo's rage. Andrea was murdered in an adaptation of the Alcario scene (*Hieronimo*, scene vii). Next, MacDonald drew on the Additions. His first half ended with the Painter scene, or rather with a dreamlike response to it – because he made the Portuguese Viceroy a blinded Francis Bacon Pope. Spain kept him prisoner and ignorant of his son's survival. He was wretched enough to accept any role imposed on him and became an artist in Hieronimo's sick imagination, in an absurdist scene evoking Lear and Gloucester. Insanely, Hieronimo slashed his own groin in a version of Isabella's tree/womb speech, and Revenge watched impatiently, waiting for self-harm to turn to slaughter.[5] Tormented helplessness was the human condition. Like MacDonald, Alan Drury was a dramatist in his own right, and equally inventive in his treatment of Kyd; his Radio 3 production aimed to provide a swift, listenable version containing the best of all the writing, including the Additions. So he, too, used the 1602 Painter scene, but his Hieronimo also imagined old Bazulto was Horatio's ghost (as in 1594: III.xiii).

Oliver Cotton's Hieronimo tried to be *objective* about the agonies he asked the artist to depict; he made 'I do brave things' confessional. Drury, that is, showed how the Additions allow Hieronimo to investigate his own madness.

The NT and RSC, however, preferred Kyd's original structure. In both cases the repertoire situation was significant. Under Peter Hall the National was pursuing a 'library' policy of staging major European classics with minimal directorial intervention, and just the previous year Bogdanov and Michael Bryant (Hieronimo) had collaborated on Calderon's honour drama *The Mayor of Zalamea*. The RSC scheduled Kyd in repertoire with Matthew Warchus's modern-dress *Hamlet*, and in these quasi-scholarly contexts it was logical to use the earliest editions. However, whatever versions were used, sooner or later the actors had to face the practical problem: how should Kyd's notorious rhetoric – dismissed by T. S. Eliot as 'bombast'[6] – be edited and spoken? Here the modern theatre had to learn how to deal directly with Kyd.

SPEAKING KYD

In the play's first major staging for centuries, Glasgow's approach to language was exploratory. MacDonald broke up many long speeches (Lorenzo joined in Balthazar's 'Yet might she love me' refrain (II.i.19)), but John Somerville as Hieronimo had to carry the middle of the production with a long collage of 'mad' passages from both 1594 and 1602. At first he seemed nervous of the most hyperbolic writing, speaking slowly and straining for pathos – but gradually his speaking became full-voiced and thrilling. Somerville was a striking figure, immensely tall and far too young to be Horatio's father; this gave his scenes a Brechtian quality. But in Radio 3's version, the intimacy of the medium helped *naturalise* the language – which, I will argue, has been the aim of most of Kyd's British directors. Alan Drury used microphone close-ups to emphasise asides; he drew attention to the ways in which revenge drama splits the world into private versus public discourses, malcontents and victims. And as Cotton whispered to us, his listener-confidants, even *The Spanish Tragedy* became intimate and plausible.

Michael Bogdanov's approach was to accept the text's formality but, wherever possible, energise it. Generally his cast played for pace, effectively re-establishing *The Spanish Tragedy* as great *popular* theatre. The tone was defined at the National by three characters: Bryant's Hieronimo, Lorenzo (Greg Hicks) and – unexpectedly – the would-be street-smart Pedringano.[7] Bryant opted for a dignified poetic realism, easing the tragic laments into his own understated style; Hicks made Lorenzo supple, clever and metal-voiced, revelling in plots and couplets. Buckley's Pedringano emerged as a crowd-pleasing murderer-clown who established black comedy as a keynote of the play; and it was outrageous farce that would topple this Lorenzo in the end. Bogdanov handled the Lorenzo–Balthazar duologues superbly. He used them to establish the play's literary style but invested them with a sense of angry frustration which the villains' rhetoric tried to hide – until, that is, Hicks's Lorenzo relaxed and seduced the audience by demonstrating how to control social inferiors (with threats, flattery and cash). In contrast, Boyd sliced through the plotters' speeches, cutting five of Balthazar's opening eight lines in II.i and even those 'Yet might she love me' rhymes that tie him in self-destructive knots.[8] If the Cottesloe's first scenes were dominated by Lorenzo the Machiavel, at the Swan he was merely a rich man enraged by the upstart Horatio; instead, the tone of Michael Boyd's production was set by the Ghost (Patrice Naiambana). Andrea's tormented description of Hades was terrified and appalling. But as he recounted his life-story, his arrogance was revealed; he claimed he 'possessed' Bel-imperia and raged at the 'divorce betwixt my love and ME!' (I.i.14).[9] As she spoke to her brother and suitors, the Ghost moved in on her unseen – an incubus trying to reclaim her (Figure 10.3).

Figure 10.3 Siobhan Redmond (Bel-imperia) and Patrice Naiambana (the Ghost of Don Andrea) in Michael Boyd's production of *The Spanish Tragedy*

Bel-imperia in fact provided one of the clearest contrasts between the NT and RSC, as if Bogdanov and Boyd prioritised the different halves of her name. At the National, Patti Love's Bel-imperia was the wooer (Roger Gartland's Horatio was prosaic). In the garden at night, with birdsong in the air, Bogdanov evoked the love-play of *A Midsummer Night's Dream*; the actors relished their Venus/Mars allusions and Ovidian tropes. So the violence was shocking: the first physical horror came when Horatio's blood watered the ground and Hicks's Lorenzo capped the murder with a joke: 'these are the fruits of love' (II.iv.55).[10] At the Swan, however, Bel-imperia was ashen, tense – and imperious. Siobahn Redmond explored her erotic language precisely and stressed her political intelligence. She never loved Horatio. She calculated

Figure 10.4 Michael Bryant (Hieronimo) in Michael Bogdanov's production of *The Spanish Tragedy*

Figure 10.5 Peter Wight (Hieronimo) in Michael Boyd's production of *The Spanish Tragedy*

that an affair could 'further my revenge' (I.iv.66). The word 'murder' beat through her premeditated speeches like a pulse. In the bower she *rebuffed* Horatio's 'hand' with her 'foot' (a sensually charged moment at the National); like her brother, she was in control and, whereas Bogdanov accepted II.iv as a love scene, Boyd made it about sexual manipulation. He backed it with menacing piano chords, not nightingales.

Michael Bryant as Hieronimo was the soul of the National's *The Spanish Tragedy*. Dapper and genial in the first peace-seeking scenes (Figure 10.4), he was transformed by Horatio's death, 'swirling seamlessly from emotion to emotion. Within two lines, he can say "revenge" in dark guttural tones and turn grieved and broken on the word "wounded".'[11] His laments were slightly trimmed to prevent audience laughter but Bryant made 'Sweet lovely rose' (II.v.46), for example, simple and moving – the tragic metamorphosis of the scene's opening poetry.[12] He humanised the text by *finding* it, making the rhetoric the inevitable expression of his pain; this Hieronimo spoke with astonishing formality so as not to scream. Boyd, however, concentrated on the play's ensemble qualities. Peter Wight (well-known as a character actor from Mike Leigh to *The Bill*) quietly downplayed the text's stylisation. He was an Everyman, a stocky lower-middle-class functionary lost in a maze of corruption (Figure 10.5).

At the climax of the great discovery scene, Hieronimo contemplates suicide and breaks into fourteen lines of Latin. Bryant made this an outburst of anguish from the depths; Wight gave it a liturgical quality and, suppressing his emotion, tried to comfort his wife with a conventional 'dirge'. Latin returns in III.xiii, with:

[*Enter* Hieronimo, *with a book in his hand.*]
HIERONIMO. *Vindicta mihi!*

Here Boyd adjusted the text to suit an audience without Latin, and clarified Hieronimo's Christian dilemma. Peter Wight's book was the King James Bible: 'For it is written, "Vengeance is mine, saith the Lord."'[13] And instead of quoting Seneca, he consulted and quoted Exodus to justify revenge: 'Thou shalt take life for life, eye for eye, tooth for tooth, foot for foot, hand for hand, burning for burning, wound for wound, stripe for stripe.'[14]

For most of the play Hieronimo's family are the puppets of unseen forces. Isabella cries: 'O where's the author of this endless woe?' (II.v.39), and so in Act IV Hieronimo determines to become both '[a]uthor and actor' of his own revenge, 'Bearing his latest fortune in his fist' (IV.iv.147–8).[15] Metaphorically and literally he will strike back through theatre, trapping his foes in a fiction that takes away their identity, their language and their lives.

BABEL

And the Lord said Behold, the people is one, they have all one language, and this they begin to do; and now nothing will be restrained from them, which they imagined to do.

Go to, let us go down, and there confound their language, that they may not understand one another's speech.

So the Lord scattered them abroad from thence upon the face of all the earth. (Genesis 11:6–8)

Drury and Bogdanov made the preparations for *Soliman and Perseda* amusing. On the radio Hieronimo pretended to be a harmless eccentric, Lorenzo was prim and not too clever – 'The prince but asked a question' (IV.i.91) – and their acceptance that Hieronimo just happened to have an old student drama in his pocket was very funny. Bogdanov's interpretation was similar: the old man reversed the play's genres, turning assassins into clowns. But Boyd's approach was far more analytical. He asked *why* Lorenzo put himself into Hieronimo's power, and also why Hieronimo murders the only person who apparently shows him sympathy – Lorenzo's father, the Duke of Castile.

Boyd made Castile a dangerous politician, the force behind the throne and the man whose line will rule two nations if Bel-imperia weds Balthazar. He *browbeat* his son into humouring Hieronimo: nothing must disturb the diplomatic harmony. So the RSC production made IV.i nervous and hesitant, driven on by Hieronimo's increasingly hysterical laughter. As he outlined his play there was general unease. His tone became delirious and alarming in his delivery of 'stirr'd with an exceeding HATE' (IV.i.123), and there was a grim pause broken by Lorenzo: 'O excellent' (127). This cast mined the scene for subtext – competitors eyeing each other on the brink of an abyss – and Boyd cut the last lines to make the end starkly ominous: 'Now shall I see the fall of Babylon' (195).[16]

When Philip Edwards edited his great Revels *Spanish Tragedy* in 1959, he queried whether an audience – especially an 'unlettered audience' – would really have been 'asked to endure sixty lines in languages they could not understand'.[17] Yet the printer's note is explicit: *'Gentlemen, this play of* Hieronimo *in sundry languages, was thought good to be set down in English more largely, for the easier understanding to every public reader'* (IV.iv, between 10 and 11). Hieronimo's ploy of trapping his enemies in different languages is fundamental to Kyd's dramatic and intellectual structure: scholars like Philip Edwards had had no chance to experience this in the professional theatre, but in performance the act of revenge becomes biblical and apocalyptic, fusing Babylon and Babel. First Babel: Hieronimo turns hubris into chaos at the very moment when, as in Genesis, 'the people is one, and they have all one language': 'Spain is Portugal / And Portugal is Spain' (I.iv.132–3). Bereaved, mocked and maddened, having failed literally to dig down to Hades to find Justice, Hieronimo uses his play to create a cacophony that isolates his enemies – 'confounds their language' – and so he mimics God. He assumes control over life, death and, indeed, damnation; not only would Francis Bacon later describe revenge as a kind of 'wild' justice, he specifically condemned the revenge that denies the victim the chance to repent.[18] Lorenzo and Balthazar can have no speeches of recognition or repentance – they die 'in character', slaughtered like dumb beasts. In this most linguistically elaborate of tragedies, communication, agency and life perish together.

'But this will be a mere confusion, / And hardly shall we all be understood,' protests Balthazar (IV.i.180–1). With responsibility to their broader audiences in mind, both the BBC and Glasgow Citizens – a people's theatre in the Gorbals with tickets costing 50p or nothing – used the English text for the play-within-the-play. The National Theatre and the RSC, with their agenda of staging a classic in its 'original' form, made Hieronimo's actors speak in foreign languages. To achieve this, the National commissioned translations into Latin and Greek (credited to Eric Pratt), and Italian and French. The RSC borrowed this text fifteen years later.

SUNDRY TONGUES

In 1978 Robert David MacDonald chose the English text but provided compensating stylisation. He staged *Soliman and Perseda* with the utmost formal simplicity as a shadow-play behind a white curtain. Gradually the gauze turned red, soaked through with blood, and thus the Citizens established the modern tradition that the play should descend (or rise?) into *Grand Guignol*. On radio, Drury took a different road and made *Soliman and Perseda* a slice of amateur dramatics; the overt incompetence of the royal performers was contrasted to the secret intimacy of their deaths (a soft sigh only we and Hieronimo could hear). Balthazar-as-Soliman exposed his smugness with '*our princely eye*' (IV.iv.46), Lorenzo mouthed clichés like a Tory politician at the dispatch box – as in '*Rhodes' loss is nothing*' (37) – and the King of Spain was equally bored by the play and the diplomacy with Portugal. Drury set maddened tragic knowledge against crass power.

It was Michael Bogdanov's production that first dared to use the 'sundry languages'. He proved the nightmarish force of the device. These actor-aristocrats were bewildered by the concept of polyglot theatre, and their 'confusion' was transferred to the audience in an increasingly surreal scene. Hieronimo became a lord of misrule. Lorenzo and Balthazar wore oversized stock costumes, like children raiding the grown-ups' wardrobe, Balthazar put up a sign saying 'TROY' instead of 'RHODES', and the murderers proved very poor actors indeed. Balthazar was ludicrously overconfident and Lorenzo was hammy. In contrast, Bel-imperia played with passion and Hieronimo became increasingly savage. The dramatic force of these specific languages also became clear. Poor Balthazar recited Latin like a schoolboy; Lorenzo savoured his Machiavellian Italian – but was ironically silenced after just three lines. Bel-imperia, we are told, is fluent in French and her pent-up fury exploded in a Racinian tirade: '*Tyran! Tes demandes, no solicite pas en vain! Les oreilles sont bouches contre toutes les plaintes*', and through it all pounded Hieronimo's Aeschylean Greek, a primal call to revenge: '*Tou d'Erastonos aphanisthentos*'. Balthazar/ Soliman switched instantly from operatic loyalty ('*Carissimus tamen est mihi Erasto!*') to homicide ('*Erastonem sic moriturum!*') because Hieronimo scared him into it, in a cartoon replay of his earlier corruption by Lorenzo.[19] The courtiers clapped everything, especially the coup of Horatio's discovery, 'until Hieronimo's tongue slapped on the floor. Trickles, spurts and finally showers of stage blood added to the chaos (even reaching the front row of the paying public) in which black comedy and horror were inextricable.'[20] The Cottesloe audience seemed astonished; Bogdanov's comedy had allowed them to feel detached superiority to the characters, but then the genres reversed again.

Fifteen years later, Boyd additionally proved we could understand emotional complexities within this scene despite its language barriers. While Peter Wight's Hieronimo spoke the Bashaw's lines prosaically, manoeuvring his enemies towards death, these well-educated aristocrats relished their roles. Lorenzo (Robert Glenister) loved the sound of his own voice, gave the Italian a vicious flourish, and Bel-imperia (Siobhan Redmond) toyed mock-incestuously with her brother (*'Mon Erasto!'*), then unleashed her contempt. Intriguingly, the play-within-the-play allowed Balthazar (Darrell D'Silva) to discover more humanity than in 'real' life: he shouted out his adoration of Bel-imperia and there was a long pause as his Soliman considered whether to betray his friend. Lorenzo seemed to laugh as he realised that a trick had killed him; everyone joined in: Balthazar choked in agony, and they applauded; Bel-imperia died in pain, but with a gasp of achievement.

Bogdanov's and Boyd's very different approaches proved the scene's rich possibilities: the National Theatre production climaxed in hysteria and outrageous excess; the RSC conveyed an immense amount about the characters through their 'confounded' language. At the Swan it was *this* part of IV.iv that mattered most, as the play-within-the-play brought the bitter intrigues to their conclusion. But at the National, the climax was yet to come – the 'oration' of Hieronimo focused everything on *his* personal tragedy.

BABYLON

The second half of the scene also has a Biblical model. Hieronimo now assumes the role of Daniel, who alone could 'make the matter known' (IV.i.187) in Babylon when incomprehensible words appeared on Belshazzar's wall and disrupted the feast: '*Mene, Mene, Tekel, Upharsin*' ('I will read the writing unto the king, and make known to him the interpretation'). The meaning of Babylon's 'unknown language' is: '"Thy kingdom is divided" [...] In that night was Belshazzar the king of the Chaldeans slain.'[21] Now Hieronimo, too, steps forward to translate, and he divides Portugal from Spain for ever.

But then the scene takes an astonishing turn. Hieronimo delivers his 'oration' and rushes to hang himself, mirroring his son's death; but he is pulled from the noose, and a long interrogation begins – 'Why hast thou murdered my Balthazar? / [...] / But who were thy confederates in this? / [...] / [...] Why speak'st thou not? (IV.iv.167, 176, 179) – as if he had never even spoken. After the classical balance and poetic 'justice' of the Senecan death scene he contrived, Hieronimo is literally dragged back into a world of moral deafness, where now *his* are the words no one can understand. Threatened with 'tortures' to make him say what he has already said, Hieronimo pre-empts whatever torture can do to him, like the philosopher Anaxarchus 'who, when put to the torture [...] bit off his tongue and spit it in the face of the tyrant'.[22] But then they tell him to write his confession, and then give him a pen, and then a knife... Editors long ago deduced that two versions of the scene were wrongly printed together in 1594, one in which Hieronimo explained everything in an eighty-line monologue, one where he didn't. Readers, however – including future directors – first encounter this strange conflated text, a nightmare of non-communication, which takes the chaos of the Babel scene even further and indeed seems prepared for, in the 1602 Painter scene:

PAINTER: And is this the end?
HIERONIMO: O no, there is no end: the end is death and madness.[23]
('Fourth Addition', 162–3)

Directors must cut their own paths through the text here, and 'simplify' to make their own statements. Boyd simply cut *all* Hieronimo's explanations. Wight never justified his acts, he was exultant, crazed and isolated in a world beyond discourse. The BBC and NT versions, however, focused on Hieronimo's last mental journey: as the kings scrabbled after written evidence, Cotton and Bryant both dwarfed them. Bogdanov scarcely shortened the 'oration' and Bryant was remarkable as he narrated – indeed *relived* – the entire play. Hesitant at first, he meditated on life and theatre ('To die today [...] / [...] And in a minute starting up again' (IV.iv.79, 81)), and put intense emotional pressure on key phrases: '*This spectacle*' (89) was a snarl. Despite almost imperceptible hesitations, however, he maintained Kyd's rhythms:

Here lay my [...] *hope*, and here my hope hath end:
Here lay my [...] *heart*, and here my heart was slain: [...]
From forth these wounds [*sob*] came breath that gave ME life.
(IV.iv.90–1, 96)[24]

After so many words, the last – 'First, take my tongue, and afterwards my *HEART*' (IV.iv.191) – were his escape into silence. But neither those words nor his bloody gestures meant a thing to the politicians.

Hieronimo's frantic struggle to make the state understand the truth behind the spectacle had special meaning for audiences in 1982. Only six months earlier, Michael Bogdanov had been on trial in the Old Bailey facing three years' imprisonment for directing members of this *Spanish Tragedy* company, including Bryant and Hicks, in Howard Brenton's anti-imperialist *The Romans in Britain*. Hicks had played the victim of an attempted rape, and Bogdanov was charged with 'procuring persons for acts of gross indecency in a public place'.[25] 'All theatre is illusion,' he said years later, 'The play was a metaphor for any country that is raped culturally and militarily.' But when a judge ruled that stage 'illusions' *are* 'reality', 'I was committed for trial.' It was a 'nightmare'.[26] Hieronimo would understand.

BEYOND SILENCE

Alan Drury's final focus was psychological. The Additions version made Oliver Cotton's Hieronimo disturbingly eloquent. He was almost benign as he explained the logic of the killings; then he strayed into a landscape of madness where right and wrong were meaningless and he revelled vocally in the other fathers' pain. But his self-mutilation was rational: he sacrificed his tongue 'to express the rupture of my part' ('Fifth Addition', 48) – even, in Cotton's performance, the *rapture*.[27] He died triumphant. There was uproar, a massive electronic noise suggesting a massacre, and then the angelic voice and Andrea's revenge. But Drury cut the details of the characters' 'just' rewards; louder than ever, the apocalyptic roar returned. In Glasgow, in total contrast, the ending was anti-cathartic: the dead rose and slunk off in all directions to haunt the world. Andrea remained shackled to the gallows. Unbothered soldiers cleaned the stage. Differently again, at the National, Revenge's last words became a black-comic punchline – 'Now begins their *lasting* tragedy' – and audiences roared. But the most elaborate coda came from Michael Boyd, whose reading of *The Spanish Tragedy* now became clear. Boyd was fascinated by the concept of speech itself and, despite the elite's showy eloquence, the failure of human discourse. Evoking the *'Mene, Mene, Tekel'* on Belshazzar's wall, he projected key phrases from the play on to the set, including 'Hieronimo's desperate last speech'.[28] Here, Boyd implied, was more than the extinction of a Renaissance clique. At the beginning, wrenched from mere death into the hell of self-consciousness,

Andrea had shrieked out Artaudian sounds. Boyd had explored the terror of language's collapse, and his end repeated his beginning. Andrea's laughter overlapped with new sounds of torment, and then the Ghost of Horatio attempted to speak:

HORATIO: When this eternal ...
When this eternal ...
When this eternal ...
REVENGE: Substance of my soul.
HORATIO: Substance of my soul ...

Horatio was drowned out by triumphant chords. This ending was not logical – Horatio's enemies are already dead – but there was one last revelation: Revenge removed its mask – and was Hieronimo. His humanity was for ever lost.

The Spanish Tragedy's three shows-within-the-play chart the collapse of art, from Act I's celebratory dumb-show of knights and crowns, to Revenge's auto-destructive marriage masque, to the final bloodbath. They reflect the degeneration of an idea, the *topos* of Life as Theatre. In I Corinthians 4:9, St Paul compared the early Christians to the condemned in the Roman arena: 'For we are made a spectacle unto the world, and to angels, and to men'. The reward for their integrity and endurance, watched by the heavenly audience of the blessed, would be salvation. This became a common Christian conceit, and Hieronimo refers to it in Act IV. But by then his imagination is so clouded that he claims 'all the saints do sit soliciting' not for the souls of the virtuous but 'For vengeance on those cursed murderers' (IV.i.33–4). And, of course, Kyd ultimately presents human life as a theatre of cruelty, staged for the hungry satisfaction of the dead. Revisiting Kyd therefore – and especially Hieronimo's nightmare spectacle of aphasia and death – we are asked if tragedy can only perpetuate degeneration, the 'scattering' of humanity into alienated fragments, or if it can point however minimally towards renewal. Few plays pose the problem so starkly.

At the end of Peter Brook's 2001 production of *Hamlet*, Brook seemed to be in dialogue with Kyd and *The Spanish Tragedy*. When Adrian Lester's dying Hamlet said: 'The rest is silence' (*Hamlet*, 5.2.300), he was wrong: suddenly the dead arose, and the play began again: 'Who's there?' (1.1.1). But whereas Kyd's characters – especially in Boyd's cyclic, even nihilistic, version – are resurrected to suffer an 'endless tragedy', Brook's *Hamlet* argued that tragedy deals with more than extinction, that Hamlet's journey towards knowledge is an endless one, and communal, and could be conducted through art. When the Players arrived in Elsinore in this production – multilingual, multi-racial and trans-cultural, like almost all Brook's late work – Hamlet asked for a speech he'd heard about the death of Priam: 'It was in ancient Greek'. The First Player (the Japanese actor Yoshi Oida) obliged; he chanted the dead language passionately, to a musical accompaniment that moved from African percussion to a piercing Noh flute as the emotion heightened. And – this is the point – Polonius was deeply moved: 'Look whe'er he has not turned his colour, and has / tears in 's eyes' (*Hamlet*, 2.2.499–500), he whispered. Brook reversed Kyd's use of theatre as a metaphor for savage non-communication; this polemical scene demonstrated art's power to communicate on a level 'deeper' than vocabulary, syntax, prejudice or culture. Brook's international company was founded in the belief that theatre can create a space for contact and epiphany – can indeed, perhaps, undo Babel: 'The prevailing thrust of modern literary and cultural criticism has demonstrated the untrustworthiness of language as a stable means of communication. Brook flies in the face of this and asserts language's transparency.'[29] Yet he has often been accused of political naivety. Michael Bogdanov, who had been the Assistant Director of Brook's legendary *A Midsummer Night's Dream*, criticised him for a lack of political engagement and, indeed, parodied his experiments with language in the Cottesloe *Soliman and Perseda*. Brook's visionary *Hamlet*, with its black Prince, white Queen, Muslim Ghost, Jewish Polonius and Indian Ophelia, closed in London three days before the 9/11 attack on the Twin Towers.

> Perhaps we are far closer to our ancestors now than we have ever been. Perhaps Kyd's *Spanish Tragedy* is a manifestation of our own taste for bloody revenge in a world where death and mutilation have become sanitized by the digitized news report or the internet YouTube image.[30]

STRANGE AND FRIGHTFUL DREAMS OF REVENGE

Repeated endlessly on television and inspiring countless books, essays and websites ('War, terrorism and spectacle'; '9/11, Spectacles of terror and media manipulation'; 'The Babel conspiracy' ...), 9/11 redefined Hieronimo's words: 'See here my show, look on this spectacle' (IV.iv.89). One result was that revenge drama in general and Hieronimo's 'show' in particular took on new force as a political metaphor. For example, Alex Cox's filmscript for *The Revengers Tragedy* (2002) ended with shots of the Towers collapsing while Vindice murmured 'Revenge'. In 2003, as the Anglo-American-led invasion of Iraq loomed closer and Bush and Blair ignored the international protests, Alex Cox's team workshopped their next planned film, *The Spanish*

Tragedy, and made IV.iv a ferocious satire on the ruling elite. 'It doesn't take place in Spain,' Cox commented, 'they speak English.'[31] In this screenplay Lorenzo 'declaims in Italian', Hieronimo 'plots in Greek', and Bel-imperia responds to Balthazar 'flattering her in Latin' by cutting his throat. The camera makes clear the difference between fiction and truth: 'Up close, we see the stabbing is real, as red blood flows'. But in this version the power-brokers *simply did not listen* to Hieronimo's oration: they were distracted by their own celebrations, 'keen to get down to the bar'.[32] They understood the consequences of their politicking only when they examined their children's corpses and Hieronimo tormented them by reciting 'Is your heart filled with pain? They won't come back again ...', his version of Elvis's 'Are you lonesome tonight?' Black comedy seemed one of the few logical responses to escalating wars of retaliation.

In 2002 Orhan Pamuk's novel *Snow* was published in Turkey. Seeking a metaphor for the violent complexity of political, ethnic and religious relations in the twenty-first century, he, too, turned to the last scene of *The Spanish Tragedy*. In an essay 'The anger of the damned', Pamuk described watching the live images of 9/11 on an Istanbul street and reflected on the reactions of the accidental audience around him, the clamour of weeping, anger – and satisfaction. 'What,' he asked, 'prompts an impoverished old man in Istanbul to condone the terror in New York?' The answer, he argued, 'is not Islam or what is idiotically described as the clash between East and West or poverty itself. It is the feeling of impotence deriving from degradation, the failure to be understood, and the inability of such people to make their voices heard.'[33] In *Snow*, published a few months later, viewers are again watching television when the screen erupts into violence, but this time it happens at the end of a live broadcast of *The Spanish Tragedy*.

KYD BETWEEN EAST AND WEST

Snow is set in Kars, an isolated Turkish border town riven by political and religious tensions which are worsened, the state media claim, by insurgents, militants and artists:

> Although the people of Kars once lived side by side in happy harmony, in recent years outside forces have turned brother against brother. Disputes between Islamists, Secularists, Kurds, Turks and Azeris drive us asunder for specious reasons. (*Snow*, p. 301)

It's a mixed society haunted by 'strange and frightful dreams of revenge' (p. 214). A coup takes place during a theatrical performance, briefly bringing to power Sunay Zaim, an actor who has dedicated his career to supporting Turkey's secularist state; he decides that what the people now need most is *The Spanish Tragedy*. Sunay's belief in Kyd's local significance leads him to outdo the seventeenth century with new Additions 'to make it more relevant'. He begins 'with some alterations inspired by Brecht's *The Good Person of Szechuan*', but 'most of the changes are the fruits of my own imagination' (p. 341). As a result the novel's narrator, watching and rewinding a videotape of the show, says, 'The first half is almost impossible to summarise. I could make out a blood feud in some "backward, impoverished and benighted" town, but when its inhabitants started killing one another I had no notion of why: neither the murderers nor their victims offered any explanation for the copious bloodshed.' Sunay adds jokes, folk-dance, 'erudite discussions about the meaning of life', plus 'scenes from Shakespeare, Victor Hugo and Brecht' and

> an assortment of short soliloquies on such matters as city traffic, table manners, the special traits Turks and Muslims will never lose, the glories of the French Revolution, the virtues of cooking, condoms and raki, and the way prostitutes belly-dance ... As one outburst followed another, it became increasingly hard to believe they conformed to any logic at all. (pp. 399–400)

Yet this *is* a logical development given *The Spanish Tragedy*'s history as a play in constant transition, always accreting new material and inviting writers from Ben Jonson to Robert David MacDonald to collaborate with Kyd (or interfere). Indeed, Sunay believes the play is so 'relevant' that it must be completely transformed: 'It was very late that Sunay decided to change the title of the drama [...] to *A Tragedy in Kars*' (p. 399).

One of *Snow*'s main characters is Kadife, the leader of a group of young Muslim women protesting against the secularist authorities' ban on the wearing of headscarves. Some take their militancy further, to the point of suicide. Kadife is blackmailed into appearing in an act of political theatre which will seem to signal her rejection of their beliefs. Sunay wants her to play Bel-imperia: 'You're a proper Spanish lady with a covered head, but then you tire of the blood feud and in a burst of anger you pull off your scarf to become the rebel heroine' (p. 314). Rumours run through the city, blurring fact and fiction ('She'll bare her head', 'A play in which Kadife bares her head for all in Kars to see will [...] have profound political consequences'), and state television announces a live relay that will free 'the nation':

> the people of Kars would be delivered from the religious prejudices that for too long had excluded them from modern life and prevented women

from enjoying equality with men. Once again life and art were to merge in a bewitching historical tale of unparalleled beauty. (pp. 372–3)

In this tense situation *The Spanish Tragedy* provokes complex debates about art and the state; the relative powers of language and spectacle – 'The only script we have this evening is Kadife's hair. [...] Let your hair speak for itself, and let the men go mad!' (pp. 347, 352) – and on spiritual and gender issues which British Kyd productions had marginalised as of scarce historical interest: 'If you commit suicide, you'll go to hell'; 'The main reason for suicide, obviously, is pride'; 'The moment of suicide is the time when they understand best how lonely it is to be a woman, and what it really means to be a woman' (pp. 412–13). Pirandellian arguments about free will, illusion and reality blur into issues of media distortion and propaganda, and the climax of the *Tragedy* actually comes when Kadife fires an apparently empty gun at Sunay's character – and he's killed:

> They were ready for him to sit up at any moment and deliver a long, instructive tirade on death; but at the uncommonly realistic sight of his bloodied face, they lost hope. [...] Everyone in the hall, and everyone else in Kars, was forced to accept the reality of what they had just seen. (pp. 419–20)

In Pamuk's recreation of Kyd's play there's no oration, no final statement from the protagonist at all. The state press pretend there *was*. They claim the audience 'had no trouble understanding the actor's last words, and they will never forget that he sacrificed his life for art' (p. 344). What happened? Perhaps Sunay stage-managed his own suicide, giving Kadife a loaded gun to make himself a secular martyr and outdo the spectacle of Muslim radicals dying in the streets. ('What I am trying to do is push the truths of art to their outer limits; to become one with myth.') But his show dissolves into postmodern uncertainty and post-9/11 conspiracy theories. Some believe they witnessed an accident; others are certain Kadife murdered him in revenge; others think there was an unseen army sniper. The courts fudge history with a meaningless verdict: 'Negligent homicide' (pp. 416–17). Meanwhile Pamuk also politicises the fate of Kyd's Isabella: the actor's widow suffers 'a mental breakdown' – that is, she goes 'on the rampage' and is confined in a military mental institution to stop her naming names. *Snow* quickly sold a hundred thousand copies in Turkey. In 2006 Pamuk won the Nobel Prize for Literature – particularly for discovering 'new symbols for the clash and interlacing of cultures'.[34]

Elements of *The Spanish Tragedy* which had long been invisible now seemed crucial in Britain, too. An internet reviewer of Mitchell Moreno's 2009 production (Arcola Theatre) thought it just as well that 'dangerous references to Islam' in IV.iv were hidden by the foreign languages.[35] These 'references' amount to nothing but the name of 'Holy Mahomet, our sacred prophet', but the comment revealed the play's new immediacy; Moreno's *Tragedy* existed in a substantially changed theatrical universe where extreme onstage violence had become common – post-Sarah Kane, post-Tarantino, post-Abu Ghraib. This time the action took place in an exposed and claustrophobic concrete space. At one end of the cramped room a metal garage door clattered up and down; at the other end, through a glass-panelled door, the audience half-heard offstage arguments, half-glimpsed meathook torture chambers. Reviewers described 'a stygian corridor' with the audience sat in rows facing one another, only inches from the violence: 'There's nowhere to hide'.[36] Everything located Kyd in the present. There were video conferencing links with Portugal, whose ruler spoke on the news channel PNN; conversations were bugged; Lorenzo rewarded loyalty with car keys. Diplomats and murderers all wore Paul Smith suits – which were ominously replaced for the play-within-the-play by disposable white overalls. They were soon blood-soaked.

When the final scene came, reviewers were still astonished by its 'screech inducing' violence and registered the 'unnerved'[37] audience's 'yelps of nervous laughter and horrified gasps'.[38] But Moreno's play-within-the-play did more. It became a ghoulish, bravura parody of avant-garde performance idioms from Brook to the Wooster Group; and the effect was exactly appropriate, suggesting that Hieronimo's play still pushes us towards the very limits of rationality – and of our art. Decadent twenty-first-century 'actors' recited incomprehensible speeches at microphone stands, surrounded by video projections of violence but blind to their importance. The new Hieronimo (Dominic Rowan) created stylistic incompatibility and chaos: 'a Katie Mitchell-style layering of sound effects' clashed with 'streamers of red ribbon' (as in Brook's *Titus Andronicus*) and the very literal 'spreading stain of stage blood'.[39] Hieronimo's Babel was postmodern now.

THE PLAY TO END ALL PLAYS?

Slowly *The Spanish Tragedy* and that last cacophonic scene have become iconic. Orhan Pamuk's *Snow* calls *The Spanish Tragedy / The Tragedy in Kars* 'The Play to End All Plays'; and in his novel it literally heralds the destruction of Theatre, or at least of the provincial theatre where it's performed: soon 'half the building had been torn down, the other half had been turned into a warehouse' (p. 417). But if Hieronimo's play has become emblematic of an era of violence and failed communication, its recent performance history offers us positive images too – images of what the Nobel Committee called the *'interlacing* of cultures' rather than the *'clash'*. Though *Snow* ends with a Turkish theatre turned into a warehouse, it's intriguing that Mitchell Moreno's *Spanish Tragedy* was staged in a factory turned into a theatre – the Arcola in Dalston, which serves London's largest Turkish and Kurdish communities. Since 2000 the Arcola has played a key role in regenerating – through culture – one of the most deprived boroughs in Britain. The Arcola specialises in rediscovering European classics; it is also home to youth theatres, writers' groups, a local oral history project and Ala-Turka: this is a Turkish-speaking and Kurdish-speaking theatre that brings the communities together. Kyd himself can be inspirational: in 2005 a documentary team followed the RSC's voice expert Cicely Berry from New York to Seoul to Moscow to the favelas of Rio de Janeiro, where she works with teenagers threatened by poverty and drugs gangs, and uses poetry and voice-work to help them express their identity. The film's title came from *The Spanish Tragedy*. Berry saw Lorenzo's statement, 'When words prevail not, violence prevails' as profoundly important – but she reshaped it: *When Words Prevail*.

NOTES

1 Pamuk, *Snow*, p. 314. All subsequent quotations from this source will be referenced parenthetically in the text.
2 Hemming, 'A sparkling evening in hell'.
3 See Howard, 'Renaissance drama productions', pp. 64–6. My comments in this chapter are based on my contemporary notes on the stage productions and on a study of the records of the National Theatre, Royal Shakespeare Company and BBC versions of *The Spanish Tragedy* in the Sound Archive of the British Library. Bogdanov: Cottesloe Theatre, 6 December 1982; Drury: BBC Radio 3, 8 November 1994; Boyd: Barbican Pit, 5 January 1998.
4 Billen, 'The week in reviews'.
5 Howard, 'Renaissance drama productions', pp. 64–6. Isabella was cut; Bel-imperia was a solitary woman dominating a male world, with fashion-plate elegance.
6 Eliot, *The Sacred Wood*, p. 46.
7 Pedringano was played by Joss Buckley (1982) and Bev Willis (1984).
8 The RSC cut his lines from 119 to 129, and most of his 'Both well and ill' speech. The NT cast created a good sense of formal balance between Balthazar and Lorenzo (e.g. in II.ii.18– 23: 'O sleep mine eyes ...', 'Watch still, mine eyes ...') while using it to establish Lorenzo's power over the Prince.
9 Throughout the quotations italicised words indicate performance emphases.

10 In 1982 Patti Love – recently praised as the schizophrenic Mary Barnes in David Edgar's play – was miscast; for the Lyttelton transfer Miranda Foster, a decade younger, played Bel-imperia.
11 Hill, 'The Spanish Tragedy – Lyttelton'.
12 The cuts from Hieronimo's speech (II.v.15–33) included the 'dark and deathful shades', some apostrophes ('O poor Horatio!', 'O wicked butcher!') and lines mocked in Pyramus and Thisbe: 'my sweet son, / O no, but he that whilom was my son'.
13 Romans 12:19.
14 Exodus 32:23–5. For clarity's sake, the RSC slightly misquoted here, inserting 'take life' for 'give life'.
15 Boyd cut Isabella's line and Hieronimo's response.
16 Boyd cut the line which is, via Hamlet's parody, probably the most recognisable in Kyd: 'And if the world like not this tragedy' (IV.i.197).
17 Edwards, 'Introduction', The Spanish Tragedy, p. xxxvii.
18 'Some, when they take revenge, are desirous the party should know whence it cometh. This is the more generous.' Bacon, The Essays, p. 72.
19 Promptbook, The Spanish Tragedy directed by Michael Bogdanov (1982).
20 Howard, 'The Spanish Tragedy – Lyttelton 1984', pp. 127–42.
21 Daniel 6:5–30.
22 Natural History of Pliny, p. 164.
23 Edwards, The Spanish Tragedy, p. 133.
24 The National kept only his lines concerning the shrieks in the night and the details of the play (up to 'the bashaw I became', IV.iv.130). The latter was crucial: Hieronimo never explicitly stated that Bel-imperia was part of the plot, and this motivated the hunt for his accomplices. His promise not to speak again ('I have no more to say') was fulfilled because Bogdanov cut almost all his lines between his suicide attempt and his last speech.
25 'Best of times, worst of times',' Sunday Times, 30 March 2003.
26 Ibid.
27 Edwards, The Spanish Tragedy, Fifth Addition, line 48, p. 135.
28 Hemming, 'A sparkling evening in hell'.
29 Lavender, Hamlet in Pieces, p. 84.
30 'The Spanish Tragedy,', www.britishtheatreguide.info.
31 Le Cain, 'Interview with Alex Cox and Tod Davies',' http://sensesofcinema.com.
32 Quoted from The Spanish Tragedy video recording, 2003.
33 Pamuk, 'The Anger of the Damned'.
34 See the 'Nobel Prize Committee commendation' in The Guardian, 13 October 2006.
35 'The Spanish Tragedy at the Arcola',' http://intervaldrinks.blogspot.co.uk, 16 October 2009.
36 See Bassett's review in the Independent on Sunday, 25 October 2009, and the review on http://oughttobeclowns.blogspot.com, 16 October 2009.
37 Tripney, 'The Spanish Tragedy,', www.thestage.co.uk/reviews, 21 October 2009.

38 Bassett, review in the *Independent on Sunday*, 25 October 2009.
39 Review on http://intervaldrinks.blogspot.co.uk, 16 October 2009.

REFERENCES

Bacon, F., *The Essays*, ed. J. Pitcher (Harmondsworth: Penguin, 1985).
Bassett, K., '*The Spanish Tragedy*, Arcola, London, *Annie Get Your Gun*, Young Vic, London, *Twelfth Night*, Courtyard, Stratford-upon-Avon', *Independent on Sunday*, 25 October 2009.
'Best of times, worst of times: Michael Bogdanov', *Sunday Times*, 30 March 2003.
The Bible: Authorised King James Version with Apocrypha, ed. R. Carroll and S. Prickett (Oxford: Oxford University Press, 1997).
Billen, A., 'The week in reviews: Theatre: So *Hamlet* drops the bullets from the gun. Then he gets the giggles', *Observer*, 11 May 1997.
Edwards, P. (ed.), *The Spanish Tragedy*, The Revels Plays (London: Methuen, 1959).
Eliot, T. S., *The Sacred Wood and Major Early Essays* (New York: Dover Publications, 1998).
Hemming, S., 'A sparkling evening in hell', *Financial Times*, 10 December 1997.
Hill, H., '*The Spanish Tragedy* – Lyttelton', *The Times*, 25 June 1984.
Howard, T., 'Renaissance drama productions: Kyd – *The Spanish Tragedy* 1978', *Research Opportunities in Renaissance Drama* 21 (1978): 64–6.
Howard, T., '*The Spanish Tragedy* – Lyttelton 1984; Census of Renaissance drama productions (1984)', *Research Opportunities in Renaissance Drama* 27 (1984): 127–42.
Kyd, T., *The First Part of Hieronimo and The Spanish Tragedy*, ed. A. S. Cairncross (London: Arnold, 1967).
Lavender, A., *Hamlet in Pieces* (London: Nick Hern Books 2001).
Le Cain, M., 'Interview with Alex Cox and Tod Davies', *Senses of Cinema* 24 (2003). http://sensesofcinema.com/2003/24/alex-cox/cox_davies/ [last accessed 30 January 2014].
'Nobel Prize Committee commendation', *Guardian*, 13 October 2006.
Pamuk, O., 'The anger of the damned', trans. M. Isin, *New York Review of Books*, 15 November 2001.
Pamuk. O., *Snow*, trans. M. Freely (London: Faber and Faber, 2004).
Pliny, *Natural History of Pliny*, trans. J. Bostock and H. T. Riley, vol. 2 (London: Henry C. Bohn 1855).
Promptbook, The Spanish Tragedy directed by Michael Bogdanov, National Theatre, London, 1982.
'Review: *The Spanish Tragedy*', http://oughttobeclowns.blogspot.com/2009/10/review-spanish-tragedy.html, 16 October 2009 [last accessed 30 January 2014].
The Spanish Tragedy, video recording, 2003. Courtesy of director Alex Cox.

'*The Spanish Tragedy* at the Arcola', http://intervaldrinks.blogspot.co.uk/2009/10/spanish-tragedy-at-arcola.html, 23 October 2009 [last accessed 30 January 2014].

'*The Spanish Tragedy*', www.britishtheatreguide.info/reviews/spanishtragedy-rev.htm [last accessed 30 January 2014].

The Spanish Tragedy: Scenes from a Reading of Thomas Kyd's Play, Adapted for the Cinema by Tod Davies. Uploaded to YouTube from alexcoxfilms, 2 September 2008.

Tripney, N., '*The Spanish Tragedy*', www.thestage.co.uk/reviews/review.php/25956/the-spanish-tragedy, 21 October 2009 [last accessed 30 January].

CHAPTER 11

Hieronimo still mad: why adapt *The Spanish Tragedy* today?

Tod Davies

Thomas Kyd wrote *The Spanish Tragedy* some time in the late 1500s, in an Elizabethan London that was busy reinventing English culture. The legitimate and regionally oriented Plantagenets had been defeated by Henry VII, who quickly moved to establish a centralised, grandiose, imperial state, which his descendants, Henry VIII and Elizabeth I, expanded and consolidated. The commons suffered, as the commons always do under these circumstances. They lost many a right, and many a space that had been public became part of some lord's domain. What they got in return was the chance for some of their sons – some, mind you, and certainly very few of their daughters – to climb up the social ladder and partake of crumbs from the imperial table.

Kyd, the son of a scrivener, was one of those crumb takers. And *The Spanish Tragedy* is the tragedy of a naive and hardworking man at the table of the rich, who is robbed of everything he loves – including justice. If that isn't a reason to adapt the play for a modern audience, I don't know what is.

The usual reason to adapt an older play is that it is of historical interest or, more importantly, of artistic relevance to a modern audience. By artistic relevance, I mean that it has something to offer to the endless debate about who we are and why we are here that is at the root of all art.

When considering the problems of adapting any play, that is, how to prune the action so that everything left goes to point out the theme, the main issue is to decide which theme is the dominant one. In *Fear and Loathing in Las Vegas*, for example, the book's main theme was obviously the impossibility of being anything but brutalised in a brutal world; it was not how much fun two wacky guys on drugs could have in Las Vegas. And in adapting that book to the screen, I pruned the action and dialogue to fit the theme that had emerged as the dominant one in the book.

In *The Spanish Tragedy*, the biggest technical problem in the adaptation is pruning away all the extraneous bits and, perhaps, leaving in some of the play's Additions, if they go to pointing out the theme the adaptor has determined has the most relevance for the audience. In my case, *The Spanish Tragedy* is the tragedy of a well-intentioned, honourable man who believes in the justice of an unjust society – until it takes away the thing he loves most in the world. In talking this over informally, a modern history don of my acquaintance protested: 'But surely, to adapt *The Spanish Tragedy* – it's just a waste of time for a modern audience!'

But the adaptor is drawn to certain pieces of work just because they are not a waste of time for the modern audience – just because they are strangely relevant to the present-day discourse, and have something to add – and this is the case with *The Spanish Tragedy*. For me this play is the story of Hieronimo, a hard worker at the table of the King. His son, Horatio, a war hero, has the guts to fall in love with the King's niece. This infuriates her perverse brother, Lorenzo, who wants her to marry a prince he has a particular (political) crush on, and he and the prince kill Hieronimo's son. Being rich kids, they get off, of course. And then Hieronimo takes his revenge.

While I was working on the adaptation, two speeches immediately stuck out at me from the first read of the play – two speeches that are filled brim-full of feelings I can directly understand as relevant: one poignantly so, and one in a depressingly familiar base sort of way. The first is Hieronimo's speech after finding Horatio's body, when he is so overcome with shock that he denies it is his son at all. He remembers how favoured Horatio was by the higher-ups and seems to see no irony in the fact that this was shown by Horatio being allowed to wait on them at table, when he says:

> Besides, he is so generally belov'd,
> His Majesty the other day did grace him
> With waiting on his cup: these be favours
> Which do assure he cannot be short-liv'd.
>
> (First Addition, 10–13)[1]

And then the speech made by Lorenzo, the King's nephew: dissolute, selfish, perverse, a recognisable type to me; in my youth we called his type a 'messed-up rich kid', and we all knew enough to stay away from them. He says, when he decides it is better to betray one of his underlings to keep his own skin safe:

And better it's that base companions die,
Than by their life to hazard our good haps.
Nor shall they live, for me to fear their faith:
I'll trust myself; myself shall be my friend,
For die they shall, slaves are ordain'd to no other end.
(III.ii.115–19)

This is the messed-up rich kid *par excellence*. His perverse desire to control his sister, his weird relationship with the prince, Balthazar, his spoiled assurance that, no matter what evil thing he does, he'll be protected, kept reminding me of a kid I knew in high school: a hugely rich kid, who murdered his sister by battering her with a typewriter. He sells real estate now, in San Francisco, though they mention his jail term now and again when he shows up in the business section of the local newspapers. He is the modern Lorenzo *par excellence*.

But to get back to the play, when looking at it closely, I saw in it much about the world depicted that is easily understood in the context of today – and therefore it takes very easily to a modern adaptation that places the action in a modern setting.

First off, all the characters speak in languages that no one understands. Everywhere in the play there is cacophony: too many stimuli, too much politicking, not enough calm or everyday life. Does this sound familiar? Moreover, in the play globalisation is a feature. As John Ralston Saul has pointed out, today's elites are tied more by loyalty to each other than to their own countries – the rich in one country can relate to the rich in another more than they can to the poor or the middle class in their own. They do, too, in Kyd's *Spanish Tragedy*: Balthazar is given more honour at the Spanish court than Horatio, a soldier who has worked, along with his family, for the country's interests. The whole court reminds me of what the New York art critic Robert Hughes calls the 'International White Trash' set.[2] Read the court scenes. Can't you just see Castile having Andy Warhol to paint Bel-imperia's portrait?

And then there is the character of Hieronimo himself, a character who is immediately recognisable as contemporary: the decent man betrayed by an indecent society. Kyd obviously related to Hieronimo. I don't stress this in my own adaptation, but Hieronimo is the director of plays for the King's banquets and, later in the play, he is the author of a tragedy. And, finally, he is the director of the final play, *Soliman and Perseda*, and the author of the whole of the Spanish tragedy. Just like Thomas Kyd. And it is Hieronimo's anguish – the madness produced by the frustrations of the world around him – that, I believe, is behind the incredible popularity of the piece in its own time, as well as accounting for its extreme relevance in ours. It is a universal sorrow that everyone can relate to – the unjust loss of an only child. Cindy Sheehan, in our own day, could tell us much about that kind of anguish.[3]

But the play gets its special charge from the circumstances, its special force from the shared experience of the author and the audience in a world that was becoming increasingly polarised in terms of class, and increasingly – indeed, terrifyingly so, if you were without protection – authoritarian. This is very modern. And it was easily adapted to a modern setting, with a modern actor. The perfect actor, in fact, to play Hieronimo, is Derek Jacobi,[4] whose best performances are of the sane man in the insane society – his Claudius in *I, Claudius* is but one such example.[5] Hieronimo is driven mad by unjust authority. He hates this authority, and goes from considering authority to be the top, and himself its loyal agent, to believing all its offspring should be slaughtered. And I believe Kyd felt this deeply himself, and that the audience, even if unconsciously, felt it deeply, too.

Perhaps the special torture for Hieronimo – and I think for Hieronimo we can read Kyd, as well – is being put in a position of thinking that society has been changed so that merit can make a good man or woman rise to the top. No holds barred! Good behaviour will bring justice and an inevitable rise, and then to discover that it is not so, it is the same old slavery but with a happy face on it, that what it really means is being put down ruthlessly if one is in any way inconvenient to one's betters. Those who are underneath in this world are given the illusion that they can rise, which keeps them in service to those above. But, as Kyd's play shows, they can't. They are invisible, mute, ghostlike. Even after Hieronimo has explained in great detail why he has killed Lorenzo and Balthazar, he is still asked to explain himself. No one hears. This is why he bites out his own tongue. But in Kyd's play, no one understands anyone else anyway – they are constantly speaking in different languages.

As to why Hieronimo kills Castile (Drew Scofield in the clips), brother of the King and father of Lorenzo (Marc Warren), while this has always been a problem for scholars, the reason for it would be particularly clear to a modern audience – it certainly was, anyway, to a modern adaptor: Castile has a glimmer of understanding that Lorenzo has wronged Hieronimo, but he tamps it down as too inconvenient for himself. He chooses class loyalty and family convenience over justice, and so comes in for his share of the revenge.

Hieronimo shows the hatred of the author for an unjust authority and the rage that comes with the understanding that the same old shell game is still in place – and the hatred of the audience that suffered under this same system but felt powerless to do something about it. This rage is a powerful thing. And don't let anybody think it is not still with us. I felt some of it a while ago when I read in *The Guardian* an article by a woman whose son had died in Iraq. She pointed out that the troops don't have adequate body armour to deal with the kind of mines they encounter there – too pricey – but that the Prime Minister's wife drives around London in an armoured car. This two-tiered protection isn't even in favour of a king, but the wife of a 'public servant'. And why is his family more important, of more worth, than the family of that woman who lost a son in Iraq? That is a real question Kyd's play asks. There is nothing even cynical about it. Why is one person's child considered to be worth more than another? Why should one person's child have safety and security that another's lacks? Why should there be one standard of justice for the rich and elite, and another for the rest? Hieronimo asked that question in the sixteenth century. He's still waiting for an answer. That frustration is still very much around.

And so to answer the Oxford modern history don's question, 'isn't the study of these old plays just a waste of time?', I have to say: it is important that we do not lose sight of the fact that culture is not just about entertainment, not just about providing a haven from an overly complex, unjust world. It is about explaining that complexity, that injustice. Culture is about knowing who we are – not just as individuals but as a society as well. And we can't know who we are unless we know where we come from. If a regime denies people the access to the knowledge of their past, it has cut off all knowledge at the root – just like Isabella cuts down the arbour in which Horatio is murdered. And the knowledge that Hieronimo was driven mad, in the late sixteenth century, by circumstances that could easily drive a loving father mad today – that is knowledge that people need to have in order to understand their own lives and the world around them. To highlight that knowledge from the past is the adaptor's art. And it is what makes working on a play like *The Spanish Tragedy*, and on a character like Hieronimo, so deeply satisfying.

NOTES

1 Edwards, p. 122.
2 Hughes, 'The rise of Andy Warhol'.
3 See her memoirs, *Peace Mom: A Mother's Journey through Heartache to Activism*, published in 2006.

4 Several scenes from a 2003 script reading of Thomas Kyd's *The Spanish Tragedy* I adapted for the cinema are available on alexcoxfilms's channel, youtube.com. They were impromptu filmed by Len Gowing, who shot Alex Cox's earlier Jacobean.Net project, *Revengers Tragedy* (2002).
5 This is a BBC Television adaptation of Robert Graves's *I, Claudius* and *Claudius the God* (1976).

REFERENCES

Fear and Loathing in Las Vegas, dir. Terry Gilliam, Universal Pictures UK, 2005.
Hughes, R., 'The rise of Andy Warhol', *The New York Review of Books*, 18 February 1982.
I, Claudius, dir. Herbert Wise, BBC Television series, 1976.
Revenger's Tragedy, dir. Alex Cox, Palisades Tartan, 2003.
Sheehan, C., *Peace Mom: A Mother's Journey through Heartache to Activism* (New York and London: Atria Books, 2006).
Spanish Tragedy – Script Reading. Adapted for cinema by Tod Davies. Soho Theatre, 12 February 2003. http://www.youtube.com/user/alexcoxfilms/videos?query=spanish+Tragedy [last accessed 30 January 2014].

CHAPTER 12

'For what's a play without a woman in it?'

Carol Chillington Rutter

The woodblock illustration below the title to the 1615 quarto of *The Spanish Tragedy* captures a sequence of actions that happen across two of the play's scenes but freezes them into a single nightmare image of horror (Figure 12.1). At the left of the frame, Horatio, in Elizabethan doublet, hose, ruff, boots and spurs, is hanging dead, 'strange fruit' trussed up in his father's arbour, the wounds that have been thrust over and over into his body ('thus, and thus') cynically mocked as 'the fruits of love'. Hieronimo, sword in one hand, presses the flame of the torch he carries in his other hand close to his son's face, discovering the murder, while over his shoulder a speech tag unravels from his mouth like a howl caught by the wind: 'Alas it is my son Horatio.' At his back, facing the other way, Bel-imperia, in farthingale, hair piled pyramid-wise on top of her head, is caught in a captor's grasp, and she's calling out, 'Murder, helpe, Hieronimo', her speech tag looping backwards over his. Her brother Lorenzo, face masked in a black stocking while, incongruously, rosettes gaily garter his hose, has her by the wrist. He's waving his sword in his other hand, his speech tag calling out, 'Stop her mouth' (II.iv.55-63). Does he intend gagging her? Or killing her?

These four figures, sensational in themselves, will turn out to leave a lasting impression upon Elizabethan theatre and a legacy, as Tony Howard has shown elsewhere in this book, into the twenty-first century. They offer what Titus Andronicus will call, in a play that's indebted to Kyd's, 'A pattern, precedent, and lively warrant' (*Titus Andronicus*, 5.3.43) to subsequent imitators: Horatio, the Romeo betrayed; Lorenzo, the ingenious Machiavel; Bel-imperia-after-Clytemnestra, a model for Tamora and every other woman who plots slaughter upon love's murder; Hieronimo, the benumbed, bereft father who goes mad weighing up, questioning justice versus revenge, then gets deadly sane

Figure 12.1 Woodcut on the title page of the 1615 Q7 edition of Thomas Kyd's *The Spanish Tragedy*

again when – 'About, my brain', as one of his stepchildren, his aptest pupil, will say – he puts on a play that is very much 'the thing' to end all questioning (*Hamlet*, 2.2.565, 582). 'Lively warrant', indeed.

But there's a fifth figure who doesn't make it into the 1615 illustration (or even, except in passing, into this book); a figure who's as much a 'precedent' as the others. She's Isabella. The wife. The mother. She bears thinking about, not least for her legacy. This chapter, then, gives her *Doing Kyd*'s last word, an epilogue that also serves as a prologue for the continuing cultural work that Isabella, and *The Spanish Tragedy*, perform sometimes incognito, sometimes in her and its own right, in subsequent theatre.

When he's casting *Soliman and Perseda*, Hieronimo asks rhetorically: 'what's a play without a woman in it?' (IV.i.97). We might alter the question: 'What's a play *with* a woman in it? What's the woman doing in this play?'

Isabella first enters *The Spanish Tragedy* behind her husband, who's been 'pluck[ed]' by 'outcries' from his 'naked bed' (II.v.1ff). By the time she arrives, Hieronimo has tracked the woman's screams he's heard, not slumbering, not dreaming, to his garden. Intending 'rescue', he encounters instead a 'murd'rous spectacle', 'A man hang'd up [...] / And in my bower, to lay the guilt on me'. It's only as he's grappling with the body, cutting it down, that he recognises 'garments [...] I oft have seen' and realises 'it is Horatio my sweet son!' There follow twenty lines of lament, framed as a series of questions ('Who?' (18), 'What?' (19), 'why?' (24), 'why?' (26), 'what?' (28), 'How?' (31)) directed at the 'savage monster', the 'vild profaner', the 'wicked butcher' who's done the killing; but also at the 'heavens' who 'made [...] night to cover sin'; at the 'earth' who declined to swallow up the spoiler of 'this sacred bower'; and, perhaps most poignantly, at the dead child himself, the reproachful father (like parents do, assuming some fault must have been the child's) wanting to know 'what hadst thou misdone, / To leese thy life ere life was new begun?' (This speech is, of course, a 'pattern' and a 'precedent'. We're going to hear it again, borrowed and rewritten, when first a Nurse then one Old Capulet finds a girl called Juliet dead; and again, when an Athenian bellows-mender playing an am-dram Thisby discovers her Pyramus not asleep but slain.)

Like her husband, Isabella has risen from bed. She's anxious. Her 'husband's absence' has made her 'heart to throb', and now, stumbling upon the 'world of grief' that's lying in his arms, she can only dumbly echo Hieronimo's bewilderment – 'O where's the author of this endless woe?' – before yielding to a torrent of grief that she imagines as transforming her body into a natural disaster, 'wretchedness' she expresses as 'outrage':

> Then is he gone? and is my son gone too?
> O gush out, tears, fountains and floods of tears,
> Blow, sighs, and raise an everlasting storm:
> For outrage fits our cursed wretchedness.
>
> (II.v.42–5)

This 'worthy son', called 'Sweet lovely rose, ill-pluck'd before [his] time' (II.v.46), is kissed, Hieronimo's words having run out. It's the mother who closes the boy's eyes; the father who takes the *memento mori* from the corpse, the handkerchief that was Bel-imperia's love token to Andrea, returned to her, post mortem, then given again, to Horatio, and now 'besmear'd with [his] blood'. 'It shall not from me till I take revenge,' Hieronimo vows. But neither will Horatio's corpse. Hieronimo won't 'entomb' it 'till I have reveng'd' (II.v.51, 52, 54). And perhaps it's that word 'revenge', repeated now by Hieronimo for the third time in fifteen lines, that prompts Isabella to counter his extremity's extravagant wildness with near monosyllabic stoic tags, with proverbial axioms that tell eternal law as she knows it, that register the moral balance of the universe, and that, reassuring, counselling patience while promising retribution, work like clutched straws to keep wronged men's grip on sanity:

> The heavens are just, murder cannot be hid,
> Time is the author both of truth and right,
> And time will bring this treachery to light.
>
> (II.v.57–9)

These are not platitudes. Not a soft option. Patience requires fortitude – not least, while it's looking like resignation. Here, Isabella is Hieronimo's anchor and best adviser. But it is advice he appears to reject, firstly retorting that she, with him, should 'dissemble' to 'learn by whom all this was brought about': that is, that they should hood their hearts, gag their 'plaints' (II.v.61, 63, 60), become Lorenzo-style Machiavels; then secondly, practising despair, rehearsing suicide, appearing on the verge of killing himself by setting *'his breast unto his sword'* as he utters Horatio's dirge, only at the last minute *'throw*[ing] *it from him'* as with Isabella he *'bears the body away'* (II.v.68, 81).

What I want to observe from this sequence is how Isabella, in just two speeches, performs an epitome of the parts Hieronimo will play out more largely across the next three acts. She is their miniature, their synopsis. She is the pattern of uncontrollable parental grief in a play that painfully, almost obsessively, re-performs this trope: her little world of tears finds sympathy in macrocosmic cataclysms, storms and floods, analogies between micro and macro that her husband will pick up and extend when he next appears on stage, his eyes 'no eyes, but fountains fraught with tears'; his life 'no life, but lively form of death'; the world 'no world, but mass of public wrongs' (III.ii.1–3). Railing, furious, Isabella is typically 'feminine' (as Kristine Steenbergh codes 'feminine fury' elsewhere in this book) and she predicts the 'feminised' emotional route Hieronimo will take, yielding to vengefulness. But that's only half her repertoire. For she is also the pattern of *vir*-tuous, manly reason, holding out for truth, for time, for justice, a precedent for a direction he *might* take. In this, she anticipates Hieronimo's swings from insane fantasising to rational calculation: 'Hieronimo beware, [...] / [...] to entrap thy life this train is laid'; 'by circumstances try / [...] to confirm this writ' (III.ii.37–8, 48–9); 'Hieronimo, beware: go by, go by' (III.xii.31); and most resolutely:

> *Vindicta mihi!*
> Ay, heaven will be reveng'd of every ill,
> Nor will they suffer murder unrepaid:
> Then stay, Hieronimo, attend their will,
> For mortal men may not appoint their time.
>
> (III.xiii.1–5)

When we next see Isabella, though, she's lost her balance. Her husband has just been handed Pedringano's letter by the Hangman who's turned him off; a letter that incriminates Lorenzo and Balthazar in Horatio's murder; a letter that proves Bel-imperia's accusation 'was not feign'd' (III.vii.50); a letter that arms Hieronimo to demand redress:

> I will go plain me to my lord the king,
> And cry aloud for justice through the court,
> Wearing the flints with these my wither'd feet,
> And either purchase justice by entreats
> Or tire them all with my revenging threats.
>
> (III.vii.69–73)

For Hieronimo, then, the torments that have led his 'tortured soul' to 'the brazen gates of hell' (while his 'broken sighs', 'hovering in the air', 'Soliciting for justice and revenge', have helplessly 'Beat at the windows of the brightest heavens' like butterflies flailing their wings against glass) appear to have found remedy (III.vii.9–14). In written evidence. In access to the King. In proof. Hieronimo exits (at one door?), mind framed to vindication – as Isabella enters (at the other?), mind blasted.

She's carrying flowers, medicinal herbs to 'purge the eye [...] / [...] the head'. But which of them, she wonders, 'will purge the heart'? There's 'no medicine' for her 'disease', she says, nor 'any physic to recure the dead'. '*She runs lunatic*', as the stage direction has it; talking to her female servant as if she were the child Horatio whom she'd promised 'gowns and goodly things [...] / [...] a whistle and a whipstalk'; then imagining her soul on 'silver wings' mounted 'unto the highest heavens' where she sees Horatio 'Back'd with a troop of fiery cherubins', miraculously restored, bizarrely jubilant, 'Dancing about his newly-healed wounds' (III.viii.1–5; 10–11; 15–16; 18–19). The irony of this choreographic cross-traffic is appalling: one parent exiting apparently saved, the other entering, unutterably lost; the void of failed communication between them bottomless.

It's an irony that's re-enacted in Isabella's third and final scene. By IV.iii, Hieronimo has retraced his steps from sanity to insanity and back again. In III.xii, shunted aside by Lorenzo who blocks his meeting with the King, he has flipped mentally, gone berserk, threatened to 'rip the bowels of the earth' with his dagger, to 'make a pickaxe of my poniard', to 'marshall up the fiends in hell' to 'Give me my son!' (III. xii.71, 75, 77, 70). In III.xiii he has met Don Bazulto, a father, like himself, seeking justice for a murdered son. '*Staring him in the face*' (SD) he has taken the old man for Horatio (III.xiii.2) and marvelled how 'Sweet boy, how art thouchang'd in death's black shade!' Then his eyes have refocused, the gears of his mind re-engaged, and the two old geezers – the 'lively image' of one another's 'grief' – have staggered off, leaning on each other (III.xiii.146, 162). It's in this fragile state of recovery that he has met Castile and patched up a (fake) reconciliation with Lorenzo (III.xiv.157), which leads directly to his access to Bel-imperia (which makes them conspirators, IV.i) and what follows, the invitation to supply some 'entertainment of the ambassador', some 'show' to grace her betrothal to Balthasar (IV.i.61).

So is set in motion *Soliman and Perseda*. A play. A distraction – to distraction? Hieronimo is diverted, 'Doctor Theatre' appearing to have cured him of frenzy, who busies himself – Peter Quince-like – passing out parts, profiling characters, ordering costumes, instructing the acting, knocking up a curtain behind which he promises to prepare 'a strange and wondrous show' that 'shall make the matter known' (IV.i.185, 187) in a sensational final revelation. Fixing the performance, Hieronimo appears fixed. Of course, the 'fix' is a fiction, dissimulation, a spectacular final flourishing of the dissembling that Hieronimo urged in II.v. It will be a cover for a true plot. So this theatre will, in ways almost no one expects, 'mind [...] true things by what their mock'ries be' (*Henry V*, 4.0.53). Still, Hieronimo, like Titus Andronicus after him (conducting an impromptu with Chiron and Demetrius feigning themselves Murder and Rapine), will never look saner than when he's directing his play.

But as he exits to see his plotted 'fall of Babylon', Isabella enters, once again their traffic crossing (IV.ii). While her husband is elsewhere ordering his world on stage, crafting artificial 'confusion' to real ends, she appears in their garden, in the arbour. Here, the natural world has been ordered, plotted, artificially crafted to tame a wilderness, to repair the original violation of the world's first garden, the ancient fall of man that Horatio's death, mockingly remembering forbidden fruit, has so grimly re-enacted. Under Isabella's direction, this order, this nature, is ruined: weapon in hand, she lays waste to the garden. That is, she anticipates Hieronimo's Babylonian 'confusion' with Edenic 'confusion':

> Down with these branches and these loathsome boughs
> [...]
> I will not leave a root, a stalk, a tree,
> A bough, a branch, a blossom, nor a leaf
> [...]
> Fruitless for ever may this garden be,
> Barren the earth
>
> (IV.ii.6, 10–11, 14–15)

And as she curses 'this tree' – the tree where Horatio hung – 'from further fruit', so she curses her 'womb [...] for his sake' 'from further fruit' by turning the hacking, slashing, cutting tool upon herself (IV. ii.35–6). Thus, the antic disposition Hieronimo has put on, the suicidal episodes he's dallied with, find true performance in Isabella. Mad, seeing her son's ghost 'solicit[ing]' her 'with his wounds' (IV.ii.24), she kills herself. As she dies, Hieronimo enters – almost, it would appear, having to step over her body, for there's no one around to clear it; IV.iii begins with the stage direction, '*He knocks up the curtain*'. (By the by, does his 'curtain' going up conceal his wife's body behind? A nice touch, since, when the curtain comes down at the end of *Soliman and Perseda*, another body will be discovered.) His play is announced – and it will end with that horrible, bizarre replay that takes us back to the garden, to what is imaged in the 1615 woodblock illustration, to the nightmare printed on Isabella's insane mind: a boy 'butcher'd', 'hanging', 'slaughter'd as you see' (IV.iv.106, 111–12). It's a spectacle to end his parents' lives.

As when she offers the epitome of Hieronimo's future action in Act II, Isabella in Act IV literalises the metaphors he has circulated. She becomes what he imagines. Theatrically, their double act sets up a kind of parallel play that permits the playwright to stage interiority, to rootle around in the human cranium, to anatomise the heart, to show mental and emotional states outside the body even as he's concentrating so relentlessly on the materiality of that body. His experiments, his achievements moving between Hieronimo and Isabella, are going to have extraordinary impact.

So what is Isabella's legacy? Who are her 'daughters'? I'll name just a few across four centuries. Most immediately, there's Shakespeare's Ophelia, who enters *Hamlet* 4.5 grief-crazed, handing out memory flowers – rosemary, rue, but not violets – that seem to remember Isabella's homoeopathic herbs, and speaking 'things in doubt / That carry but half sense' (4.5.6–7). Like Isabella's broken utterance that shifts from hallucination to clarity, from what she remembers to what she imagines, working upon the audience's imagination to make sense of it, Ophelia's 'speech is nothing, / Yet the unshapèd use of it doth move / The hearers to collection' (4.5.7–9). Ophelia, like Isabella, is equal parts horrible and pitiable – and threatening. Like Isabella, she sees the dead. Like Isabella, but different, she returns to nature.

Then there is Lady Macbeth, whose husband challenges the Physician he's ordered to attend her to produce some medicine, 'some sweet oblivious antidote' to the 'perilous stuff / Which weighs upon the heart', some concoction of homoeopathic rhubarb to 'Pluck from the memory a rooted sorrow', to 'Raze out the written troubles of the brain' (5.3.43–7). Mind-shattered, Lady Macbeth, like Isabella wakened from sleep, rises from bed, functions in the space of nightmare, *walks in her sleep* – and like Isabella, re-performs the past, talking to the unseen, the undead dead, shards of conversation cutting up her brain. The animal wail of anguish from Isabella – 'O!' – is lengthened by Lady Macbeth: 'O, O, O!' (5.1.43). The herbs that fail to purge one heart fail too to 'cleanse' the other's 'fraught bosom' (*Macbeth*, 5.3.46).

By the time we get to the mad scene in Sheridan's *The Critic* (1779), it has become the stuff of parody, cued, it appears, by Isabella's original appearance on stage in her nightgown. When English 'Tilburina', in another Spanish tragedy, this one, a 'Carry On' Armada farce (staged as a play-within-the-play), loses her mind after her beloved 'Don Ferolo Whiskerandos' is murdered, the script directs (as Puff, the playwright, reads it out): 'she comes in stark mad in white satin'. 'Why in white satin?' inquires Sneer, Puff's rival, who turns to 'the critic' Dangle for confirmation:

> PUFF: O Lord, sir, when a heroine goes mad she always goes into white satin – don't she Dangle?
> DANGLE: Always – it's a rule.
> PUFF: Yes – here it is. [Looking at the book.] 'Enter Tilburnia stark mad in white satin, and her confidant stark mad in white linen.'
>
> (p. 375)[1]

Perhaps dressed after Isabella's fashion, Tilburina certainly raves after Isabella's fashion:

> The wind whistles – the moon rises – see,
> They have killed my squirrel in his cage!
> Is this a grasshopper! – Ha! no, it is my
> Whiskerandos [...]
> An oyster may be crossed in love!
>
> (p. 376)

But the raving, so shocking in Isabella, so poignant in Ophelia, so soul-blistering in Lady Macbeth, is now, too, merely the silly stuff of parody, mocked as a lapse of poetic decorum. 'There, do you ever desire to see anybody madder than that?' asks Puff of 'Tilburina's' performance. 'You observed how she mangled the metre?' 'Yes, egad,' answers Dangle, 'it was the first thing made me suspect she was out of her senses' (p. 376).

A hundred years later, however, the flower-dealing woman in white is once again the object of horror, the tropes originating with Isabella and inherited by Ophelia now reconfigured by the gothic imagination: so Bram Stoker makes her in *Dracula* where Lucy Westenra, in a diary entry a week before her death, writes that she's lying in bed 'like Ophelia in the play' loaded 'with "virgin crants and maiden strewments"' (p. 161)[2] – the garlic wreath Van Helsing gives her for a necklace. Vampirised, undead, a wraith in white who speaks a twisted salacious love language, she walks on Hampstead Heath where, it's reported by the *Westminster Gazette*, a number of 'tiny tots' have been lured away at sunset by a 'bloofer lady'. Their 'grubby-faced' performances, pretending to be the 'bloofer lady', are, writes the *Gazette*'s correspondent, worthy of 'Ellen Terry' – the Victorian theatre's most celebrated Ophelia (p. 213).

It's as a version of Ophelia that Isabella is most recognised in the twentieth century: distantly, as mind-blown Blanche du Bois in Tennessee Williams's *A Streetcar Named Desire* (1947), wanting the music that loops recurrently through her head (and that stops with a pistol shot and the death of a boy) *to stop for ever*, asking her sister to pin violets to her suit jacket before she steps out with her last 'gentleman caller' into the kind care of strangers; more nearly, as Nora in the last scene of Sean O'Casey's *The Plough and the Stars* (1922), crazed by the double loss of husband (to the Easter Uprising) and her infant son (premature, still-born). She appears like a ghost out of the back room of Bessie's attic flat where the whole gang of tenement dwellers are holed up, waiting for the Tommies to clear off out of Dublin and the shooting to stop. She 'is clad,' says the Stage Direction,

> only in her nightdress; her hair, uncared for some days, is hanging in disorder over her shoulders. Her pale face looks paler still because of a vivid red spot on the tip of each cheek. Her eyes are glimmering with the light of incipient insanity; her hands are nervously fiddling with her nightgown

while she talks to her dead husband about a goldfinch, a place beneath a bramble tree, something she 'can't remember', a name – 'Maura, Maura [...] if th' baby's a girl' – murmurings that turn to 'Screaming' when (like Isabella seeing her dead son, and Ophelia imagining her dead father) Nora sees her dead baby: 'He's there. He's there, an' they won't give him back to me!' (204–6).[3]

Is it fanciful to see the latest manifestation of these tropes which earlier playwrights externalised – grief, loss, the fragmenting of identity, the breaking apart of logically sequenced articulation, mental meltdown, the death of love – *internalised* in Sarah Kane's *4:48 Psychosis* (2000)? 'My mind is the subject of these bewildered fragments' says the voice (or one of them) that speaks Kane's play. (p. 210).[4] The stunned fantasies this mind admits are not unlike Isabella's imaginings; neither is the 'desperation clawing and all-consuming panic drenching' it; the 'gape in horror' it fixes on the world. This is a mind that constantly sees itself (Ophelia-like) drowning: 'I will drown in dysphoria / in the cold black pond of my self / the pit of my immaterial mind'. This is a mind that 'write[s] for the dead / the unborn'; a black mind, joking with insanity, its sense of humour (not unlike Hamlet's, Titus Andronicus's, even Isabella's and Ophelia's) black: 'How can I return to form / now my formal thought has gone?' (p. 213).

Wherever human consciousness asks a question like that last one, wherever parents are woken from the dead of night to encounter what makes their 'heart to throb' in terror, to wonder, gazing on a nightmare: 'When will this fearful slumber have an end?' (*Titus Andronicus*, 3.1.251), wherever our response to loss is to wish apocalyptically 'th'estate o'th' world [...] undone' (*Macbeth*, 5.5.48), and 'nature's germens' to 'tumble all together / Even till destruction sicken' (4.1.75–6), so that vast Nature will display, will evidence, the ruin of our hearts, Thomas Kyd's Isabella is there before us. Kyd's play offers us a proxy. She runs mad so that we can stay sane.

NOTES

1 All quotations are taken from the Oxford World's Classics edition of *The Plays of Richard Brinsley Sheridan*.
2 Quotations from the novel first published in 1897 are taken from the 1984 Penguin edition.
3 Quotations are from the Macmillan edition of O'Casey's *Three Plays*.
4 Quotations are from the Methuen Drama edition, *Sarah Kane Complete Plays*.

REFERENCES

Kane, S., *Complete Plays* (London: Methuen, 2001).
O'Casey, S., *Three Plays* (London: Macmillan, 1973).

Sheridan, R. B., *The Plays of Richard Brinsley Sheridan* (London: Oxford University Press, 1970).
Stoker, B., *Dracula* (Oxford: Penguin, 1984).

PART V

Thomas Kyd bibliography, 1993–2013
Nicoleta Cinpoeş

The Bibliography is divided into subsections which differentiate between the editorial, critical, performance and digital focus, while also indicating the type of source and the presence of Thomas Kyd's *The Spanish Tragedy* within it. The range includes editions of the play, single-authored books with Kyd being the exclusive focus, chapters in single-authored books, articles in collections and journals, unpublished material (i.e., doctoral theses) and electronic resources. A wealth of other published material has not been included, however: this is mainly print and electronic material in which Thomas Kyd and *The Spanish Tragedy* feature in passing.

A number of electronic editions are available on open access websites, such as www.luminarium.org (Renascence editions database), www.bartleby.com and www.elizabethanauthors.com; others are part of educational packages for students provided by commercial enterprises, such as www.sparknotes.com/, www.gradesaver.com. Between 2003 and 2013, several editions of *The Spanish Tragedy* have appeared on open-access websites and have subsequently disappeared. Among them, two were particularly significant as they adapted the playtext – one for the stage (Ernest Ruckle's version), the other for the screen (Tod Davies's version, which was released in *Exterminating Angel Press*, issue 4, in 2006).

EDITIONS OF THE PLAY

The Spanish Tragedy (Whitefish: Kessinger Publisher, 2004).
Barker, S. and H. Hinds (eds), *The Routledge Anthology of Renaissance Drama* (2003).
Bate, J. and E. Rasmussen (eds), '*The Spanish Tragedy* (with Additions)', in *Shakespeare and Others: Collaborative Plays* (London and New York: Palgrave Macmillan, 2013).

Bevington, D. (ed.), *The Spanish Tragedy*, Revels Student Editions, based on the Revels Plays edited by Philip Edwards (Manchester and New York: Manchester University Press, 1996).
Bevington, D. and E. Rasmussen (eds), '*The Spanish Tragedy*', in D. Bevington, L. Engle, K. Eisaman Maus and E. Rasmussen (eds), *English Renaissance Drama: A Norton Anthology* (New York: W. W. Norton, 2002), pp. 3–73.
Calvo, C. and J. Tronch (eds), *The Spanish Tragedy*, Arden Early Modern Drama (London: Arden Shakespeare, 2013).
Gibson, C. (ed.), *Six Renaissance Tragedies* (Basingstoke: Macmillan Press, 1997).
Kinney, A. (ed.), *Renaissance Drama: An Anthology of Plays and Entertainment* (Oxford: Blackwell, 1999).
Manly, J. Matthews (ed.), *The Spanish Tragedy* (Dodo Press, 2005).
Maus, K. Eisaman (ed.), *Four Revenge Tragedies: The Spanish Tragedy, The Revenger's Tragedy, The Revenge of Bussy D'Ambois, The Atheist's Tragedy* (Oxford and New York: Oxford University Press, 1995).
Smith, E. (ed.), '*The Spanish Tragedie*' with '*The First Part of Jeronimo*', Renaissance Dramatists (Harmondsworth: Penguin Books, 1998).

ELECTRONIC EDITIONS

The Spanish Tragedie, www.gutenberg.org/files/6043/6043-h/6043-h.htm.
The Spanish Tragedy. A Study Guide from Gale's 'Drama for Students' (iOS device book, 2005).

CRITICAL STUDIES

Ardolino, F. R., *Apocalypse and Armada in Kyd's Spanish Tragedy* (Kirksville: Sixteenth Century Journal Publishers, Northeast Missouri State University, 1995).
  Reviews
  Carman, G., 'Review of Frank Ardolino. *Apocalypse and Armada in Kyd's Spanish Tragedy*', *Renaissance Quarterly* 50:2 (1997): 617–18.
  Nass, B., 'Review of Ardolino, Frank R. *Apocalypse and Armada in Kyd's Spanish Tragedy*', *Shakespeare Bulletin* 14:4 (1996): 42–3.
  Norland, H. B., 'Review of Ardolino, Frank. *Apocalypse & Armada in Kyd's Spanish Tragedy*', *Moreana* 33:127/128 (1996): 185–7.
Erne, L., *Beyond The Spanish Tragedy: A Study of the Works of Thomas Kyd* (Manchester: Manchester University Press, 2001).

Reviews
Gearhfart, S. S., 'Review of Erne, Lukas. *Beyond The Spanish Tragedy: A Study of the Works of Thomas Kyd*', Sixteenth-Century Journal 34:3 (2003): 877–9.
Griffin, E., 'Review of Erne, Lukas. *Beyond The Spanish Tragedy: A Study of the Works of Thomas Kyd*', Medieval and Renaissance Drama in England 18 (2005): 277–82.
Gunby, D., 'Review of Erne, Lukas. *Beyond The Spanish Tragedy: A Study of the Works of Thomas Kyd*', Modern Language Review 98:4 (2003): 956–7.
McCabe, R. A., 'Review of Erne, Lukas. *Beyond The Spanish Tragedy: A Study of the Works of Thomas Kyd*', Review of English Studies 54 (216) (2003): 525–6.
Simkin, S., 'Review of Erne, Lukas. *Beyond The Spanish Tragedy: A Study of the Works of Thomas Kyd*', Literature and History 12:2 (2003), 88–9.
Smith, E., 'Review of Erne, Lukas. *Beyond The Spanish Tragedy: A Study of the Works of Thomas Kyd*', Times Literary Supplement, 3 May 2002, 31.
Stevenson, W., *Shakespeare's Additions to Thomas Kyd's The Spanish Tragedy: A Fresh Look at the Evidence Regarding the 1602 Additions* (Lewiston, NY, and Lampeter: Edwin Mellen Press, 2008).

CHAPTERS IN SINGLE-AUTHORED BOOKS

Aebischer, P., '"Not dead? Not yet quite dead?": *Hamlet*'s unruly corpses', in *Shakespeare's Violated Bodies: Stage and Screen Productions* (Cambridge: Cambridge University Press, 2004), pp. 64–101.
Allman, E. J., 'Ch. 3. The revenge as rival author', in *Jacobean Revenge Tragedy and the Politics of Virtue* (Newark, DE: University of Delaware Press; London and Cranbury: Associated University Presses, 1999), pp. 57–85.
Burnett, A. P., 'Ch. 1. Huge frenzy and quaint malice: Seneca and the English Renaissance', in *Revenge in Attic and Later Tragedy* (Berkeley: University of California Press, 1998), pp. 1–32.
Diehl, H., 'Ch. 4. Rehearsing the Eucharistic controversies: The revenge tragedies', in *Staging Reform. Reforming the Stage. Protestantism and the Popular Theater in Early Modern England* (Ithaca, NY: Cornell University Press, 1997), pp. 94–124.
Dillon, J., 'Ch. 6. Shaping a rhetoric' and 'Ch. 7. English and alien', in *Language in Medieval and Renaissance England* (Cambridge:

Cambridge University Press, 1998), pp. 141–61 (notes 238–40) and 162–87 (notes 240–3).

Engel, W. E., 'Ch. 1. "Common places of memory": Visual regimes and charmed spaces', in *Death and Drama in Renaissance England* (Oxford and New York: Oxford University Press, 2002), pp. 37–64.

Findlay, A., 'Ch. 2. Revenge tragedy', in *A Feminist Perspective on Renaissance Drama* (Oxford: Blackwell, 1999), pp. 49–86.

Goodland, K., 'Monstrous mourning women in Kyd, Shakespeare, and Webster', in *Female Mourning and Tragedy in Medieval and Renaissance English Drama: From the Raising of Lazarus to King Lear* (Aldershot: Ashgate, 2005), pp. 155–70.

Griffin, E., 'Thomas Kyd's tragedy of "the Spains"', in *English Renaissance Drama and the Specter of Spain: Ethnopoetics and Empire* (Philadelphia: University of Pennsylvania Press, 2009), pp. 67–96.

Graham, K. J. E., 'Ch. 4. The mysterious plainness of anger: The search for justice in satire and revenge tragedy', in *The Performance of Conviction. Plainness and Rhetoric in Early English Renaissance* (Ithaca, NY: Cornell University Press, 1994), pp. 125–67.

Gurr, A., 'The evolution of tastes', in *Playgoing in Shakespeare's London* (Cambridge: Cambridge University Press, 2004), pp. 142–223.

Hamlin, W. M., 'Ch. 6. *The Spanish Tragedy*: Doom and exile of justice', in *Tragedy and Scepticism in Shakespeare's England* (London and New York: Palgrave Macmillan, 2005), pp. 155–66.

Honan, P., 'Ch. 8. Attitudes', in *Shakespeare: A Life* (Oxford: Oxford University Press, 2000), pp. 120–44.

Hunter, G. K., 'Ch. 3. The emergence of the university wits: Early tragedy – On victim tragedy', in *English Drama 1586–1642: The Age of Shakespeare* (Oxford: Clarendon Press, 1997), pp. 69–92.

Kerrigan, J., 'Ch. 7. '"Remember me!": Horestes, Hieronimo and Hamlet', in *Revenge Tragedy: Aeschylus to Armageddon* (Oxford: Clarendon Press, 1996), pp. 170–92.

Kiefer, F., 'Ch. 10. Fate on the stage', in *Writing on the Renaissance Stage: Written Words, Printed Pages, Metaphoric Books* (Newark, DE: University of Delaware Press; London: Associated University Presses, 1996), pp. 232–46.

Kiss, A., 'Ch. 5. Identity and authorship in *The Spanish Tragedy*', in *The Semiotics of Revenge: Subjectivity and Abjection in English Renaissance Tragedy* (Szeged: Department of English, Jozsef Attila University, 2012), pp. 71–106.

Lin, E. T., 'Imaginary forces: Allegory, mimesis, and audience interpretation in *The Spanish Tragedy*', in *Shakespeare and the Materiality* of Performance (New York: Palgrave Macmillan, 2012), pp. 71–106.

Macfaul, T., 'Staying fathers in early Elizabethan drama: *Gorboduc* to *The Spanish Tragedy*', in *Problem Fathers in Shakespeare and Renaissance Drama* (Cambridge: Cambridge University Press, 2012), pp. 20–63.

Maus, K. Eisaman, 'Ch. 2. Machiavels and family men', in *Inwardness and Theater in English Renaissance* (Chicago: University of Chicago Press, 1995), pp. 35–71.

Mousley, A., 'Structuralism: *King Lear*; *The Duchess of Malfi*; *Hamlet*; *The Spanish Tragedy*', in *Renaissance Drama and Contemporary Literary Theory* (Basingstoke: Macmillan, 2000), pp. 42–73.

Munro, L., '"Ieronimo in Decimo sexton": Tragedy and the text', in *Children of the Queen's Revels: A Jacobean Theatre Repertory* (Cambridge: Cambridge University Press, 2005), pp. 134–63.

Neely, C. T., 'Ch. 1. Initiating madness onstage: *Gammer Gurton's Needle* and *The Spanish Tragedy*', in *Distracted Subjects: Madness and Gender in Shakespeare's Early Modern Culture* (Ithaca, NY: Cornell University Press, 2004), pp. 27–45.

Neill, M., 'Anxieties of ending', in *Issues of Death: Mortality and Identity in English Renaissance Tragedy* (Oxford: Clarendon Press, 1997), pp. 203–15.

Richmond-Garza, E. M., 'Ch. IV. "Canst paint me a tear?" Kyd's inversion of Senecan revenge', in *Forgotten Cities/Sights: Interpretation and the Power of Classical Citation in Renaissance English Tragedy* (New York: Peter Lang, 1994), pp. 133–53.

Shaughnessy, R., '*Hamlet*' (sections: 'Revenge' and 'Mad in craft'), in *The Routledge Guide to William Shakespeare* (London and New York: Routledge, 2011), pp. 195–200.

Waldrom, J., 'Revenge, sacrifice, and post-Reformation theater: *The Spanish Tragedy*', in *Reformations of the Body: Idolatry, Sacrifice, and Early Modern Theater* (New York: Palgrave Macmillan, 2013), pp. 117–47.

Watson, R. N., 'Ch. 1. Religio Vindicis. Substitution and immortality in *The Spanish Tragedy*' and 'Ch. 2. Giving up the ghost', in *The Rest Is Silence: Death as Annihilation in the English Renaissance* (Berkeley, Los Angeles and London: University of California Press, 1999), pp. 55–73 and 74–102.

Wells, S., 'Christopher Marlowe and Shakespeare's other early contemporaries', in *Shakespeare & Co.* (London: Penguin, 2006), pp. 61–105.

White, M., 'Ch. 4. Places of pleasure. Outdoor playing spaces and theatre practice', in *Renaissance Drama in Action. An Introduction to Aspects of Theatre Practice and Performance* (London and New York: Routledge, 1998), pp. 109–43.

CRITICAL ARTICLES IN COLLECTIONS

Brown, K., 'Professional productions of early modern drama in the UK and the USA, 1960–2010', in P. Aebischer and K. Prince (eds), *Performing Early Modern Drama Today* (Cambridge: Cambridge University Press, 2012), pp. 178–217.

Calvo, C., 'Thomas Kyd and the Elizabethan Blockbuster: *The Spanish Tragedy*', in T. Hoenselaars (ed.), *The Cambridge Companion to Shakespeare and Contemporary Dramatists* (Cambridge: Cambridge University Press, 2012), pp. 19–33.

Colón Semenza, G. M., '*The Spanish Tragedy* and revenge', in G. A. Sullivan, Jr, P. Cheney and A. Hadfield (eds), *Early Modern English Drama: A Critical Companion* (Oxford and New York: Oxford University Press, 2006), pp. 50–60.

Colón Semenza, G. M., '*The Spanish Tragedy* and metatheatre', in E. Smith and G. A. Sullivan, Jr (eds), *The Cambridge Companion to English Renaissance Tragedy* (Cambridge: Cambridge University Press, 2010), pp. 153–62.

Craig, H., 'The 1602 Additions to *The Spanish Tragedy*', in H. Craig and A. F. Kinney (eds), *Shakespeare, Computers, and the Mystery of Authorship* (Cambridge: Cambridge University Press, 2009), pp. 162–80.

Empson, W., '*The Spanish Tragedy* (II)', in J. Haffenden (ed.), *Essays on Renaissance Literature*, vol. 2 (Cambridge: Cambridge University Press, 1994), pp. 41–65.

Erne, L., 'Thomas Kyd's Christian tragedy', in T. Hester (ed.), *Renaissance Papers 2001* (Cambridge: Boydell & Brewer, 2002), pp. 17–34.

Erne, L., 'Thomas Kyd's *Cornelia*,' in T. J. Schoenberg and L. J. Trudeau (eds), *Literature Criticism from 1400–1800* (Detroit: Thomson Gale, 2006), pp. 207–14 [reprint from *Beyond The Spanish Tragedy*].

Erne, L., 'Kyd, Thomas', in A. Stewart and G. Sullivan (eds), *The Encyclopedia of English Renaissance Literatre* (Oxford: Blackwell, 2011), pp. 572–6.

Feerick, J. E., 'Groveling with earth in Kyd and Shakespeare's historical tragedies', in J. E. Feerick and V. Nardizzi (eds), *The Indistinct Human in Renaissance Literature* (New York: Palgrave Macmillan, 2010), pp. 231–52.

Fuchs, B., 'Sketches of Spain: Early modern England's "Orientalizing" of Iberia', in A. J. Cruz (ed.), *Material and Symbolic Circulation between Spain and England, 1554–1604* (Aldershot: Ashgate, 2008), pp. 63–70.
Happé, P., '"Alone in the Place": Soliloquy in Magnyfycence, Apius and Virginia and *The Spanish Tragedy*'. in A. Lascombes (ed.), *Tudor Theatre: 'Let There Be Covenants ...': Convention et Theatre* (Bern: Peter Lang, 1998), pp. 27–44.
Hill, E., 'Revenge tragedy', in A. F. Kinney (ed.), *A Companion to Renaissance Drama* (Oxford: Blackwell, 2002), pp. 326–35.
Hillman, R., 'Thomas Kyd, *The Spanish Tragedy*', in T. Betteridge and G. Walker (eds), *The Oxford Handbook of Tudor Drama*, (Oxford: Oxford University Press, 2012), pp. 566–83.
Hirschfeld, H., '"Conceived of young Horatio his son": *The Spanish Tragedy* and the psychotheology of revenge', in K. Cartwright (ed.), *A Companion to Tudor Literature* (Chichester: Wiley-Blackwell, 2010), pp. 444–58.
Kline, D. T., 'The circulation of the letter in Kyd's *The Spanish Tragedy*', in L. E. Kermode, J. Scott-Warren and M. van Elk (eds), *Tudor Drama Before Shakespeare, 1485–1590: New Directions for Research, Criticism, and Pedagogy* (Basingstoke and New York: Palgrave Macmillan, 2004), pp. 229–47.
Leggatt, A., '"A Membrane as Broken": Returning from the dead in *The Spanish Tragedy*', in A. Höfele, and W. Koppenfels (eds), *Renaissance Go-Betweens: Cultural Exchange in Early Modern Europe* (Berlin: de Gruyter, 2005), pp. 214–30.
Lopez, J., 'Performances of early modern drama at academic institutions since 1909' and 'Performances of early modern drama by amateur and student groups since 1887', in P. Aebischer and K. Prince (eds), *Performing Early Modern Drama Today* (Cambridge: Cambridge University Press, 2012), pp. 218–24 and 225–7.
Masten, J., 'Ch. 20. Playwriting: Authorship and collaboration', in J. D. Cox and D. S. Kastan (eds), *A New History of Early English Drama* (New York: Columbia University Press, 1997), pp. 360–5 and 376–9.
Matheson, T., 'Shakespeare without words', in P. Kennan and M. Tempera (eds), *Shakespeare: The Tragedies* (Bologna: CLUEB, 1996), pp. 65–74.
Matuska, Á., 'Tarantino's *Kill Bill* and the Renaissance tradition of revenge plays', in P. Drábek, K. Kolinská and M. Nicholls (eds), *Shakespeare and His Collaborators Over the Centuries* (Newcastle upon Tyne: Cambridge Scholars Press, 2008), pp. 211–20.

Maus, K. Eisaman, 'The Spanish Tragedy, or, The Machiavel's Revenge', in S. Simkin (ed.), Revenge Tragedy (Basingstoke: Palgrave Macmillan, 2001), pp. 88–106.

Mulryne, J. R., 'Nationality and language in Thomas Kyd's The Spanish Tragedy', in J. P. Maquerlot and M. Willems (eds), Travel and Drama in Shakespeare's Time (Cambridge and New York: Cambridge University Press, 1996), pp. 87–105.

Norland, H. B., 'Kyd's formulation of the conventions of revenge tragedy', in A. Lascombes (ed.), Tudor Theatre: 'Let there be covenants...': Convention et Théâtre (Bern: Peter Lang, 1998), pp. 67–88.

Smith, E., 'Ghosting writing: Hamlet and the Ur-Hamlet', in A. Murphy (ed.), The Renaissance Text: Theory, Editing, Textuality (Manchester: Manchester University Press, 2000), pp. 177–90.

Smith, M., 'The theatre and the scaffold: Death as spectacle in S. Simkin (ed.), The Spanish Tragedy', in Revenge Tragedy (Basingstoke: Palgrave Macmillan, 2001), pp. 71–87. [Also in SEL: Studies in English Literature, 1500–1900 32:2 (1992): 217–32.]

Stockholder, K., 'The aristocratic woman as scapegoat: Romantic love and class antagonism in The Spanish Tragedy, The Duchess of Malfi, and The Changeling', in A. L. Magnusson and C. E. McGee (eds), The Elizabethan Theatre, XIV (Toronto: Meany, 1996), pp. 127–51.

CRITICAL ARTICLES IN JOURNALS

Ardolino, F., 'Hieronimo Agonistes: Kyd's use of Hieronimo as sanctified revenger in The Spanish Tragedy', Journal of Evolutionary Psychology 15:3–4 (1994): 161–5.

Ardolino, F., 'Contention within a little room: Marlowe, Kyd, the Dutch libel, and the Paris massacre', Journal of Evolutionary Psychology 16:3–4 (1995): 242–7.

Ardolino, F., 'The influence of Spenser's Faerie Queene on Kyd's Spanish Tragedy', Early Modern Literary Studies: A Journal of Sixteenth- and Seventeenth-Century English Literature 7:3 (2002), 70 paragraphs.

Ardolino, F., 'Thomas Dekker's use of Kyd's The Spanish Tragedy in Satiromastix', English Language Notes 41:1 (2003): 7–18.

Ardolino, F., 'The induction of Sly: The influence of The Spanish Tragedy on the two Shrews', Explorations in Renaissance Culture 31:2 (2005): 165–87.

Ardolino, F., 'Shakespeare's allusion to The Spanish Tragedy in The Merchant of Venice (2.2)', Discoveries 23:2 (2006), 10 paragraphs.

Ardolino, F., 'Staging Spenser: The influence of Spenser's Bower scenes on Kyd's *The Spanish Tragedy*', *Spenser Review* 38:3 (2007): 13–21.
Ardolino, F., 'Translating contexts: The purpose of Hieronimo's *Soliman and Perseda* playlet in *The Spanish Tragedy*', *Discoveries: Online Publications of the South-Central Renaissance Conference* 24:2 (2007), 20 paragraphs.
Ardolino, F., 'Kyd's The Spanish Tragedy', *Explicator* 67:3 (2009): 178–83.
Ardolino, F., 'Middleton's use of Kyd's *The Spanish Tragedy* in *Your Five Gallants*', *Notes and Queries* 59:4 (2012): 575–7.
Ardolino, F., 'Kyd's use of the *Axiochus* in *The Spanish Tragedy*', *Discoveries* 29:1 (2012), 11 paragraphs.
Austen, G., 'Seneca, Kyd and Shakespeare: The place of *Hamlet* in the evolution of revenge tragedy', *English Review* 10:1 (1999): 10–13.
Barrie, R., '"Unknown languages" and subversive play in *The Spanish Tragedy*', *Explorations in Renaissance Culture* 21 (1995): 63–80.
Bruster, D. 'Shakespearean spellings and handwriting in the additional passages printed in the 1602 *Spanish Tragedy*', *Notes and Queries* 60.3 (2013): 420–4.
Byron, M., 'Logic's doubt: *The Spanish Tragedy* and *Tamburlaine*', *Comitatus: A Journal of Medieval and Renaissance Studies* 30 (1999): 81–94.
Cinpoeş, N., 'Elizabethan and Jacobean Drama website', *Bulletin of the Society for Renaissance Studies* 23;2 (2007): 8–12.
Coral Escolá, J., 'Seneca, what Seneca? The chorus in *The Spanish Tragedy*', *SEDERI: Journal of the Spanish Society for English Renaissance Studies* 17 (2007): 5–26.
Coral Escolá, J., 'Vengeance is yours: Reclaiming the social bond in *The Spanish Tragedy* and *Titus Andronicus*', *Atlantis: Journal of the Spanish Association for Anglo-American Studies* 29:2 (2007): 59–74.
Crosbie, C., 'Oeconomia and the vegetative soul: Rethinking revenge in *The Spanish Tragedy*', *English Literary Renaissance* 38:1 (2008): 3–33.
Cutts, D., 'Writing and revenge: The struggle for authority in Thomas Kyd's *The Spanish Tragedy*', *Explorations in Renaissance Culture* 22 (1996): 147–59.
Dillon, J., '*The Spanish Tragedy* and staging languages in Renaissance drama', *Research Opportunities in Renaissance Drama* 34 (1995): 15–40.
Díaz-Fernández, J. R., 'Thomas Kyd: A bibliography, 1966–1992', *Bulletin of Bibliography* 52:1 (1995): 1–13.

Donaldson, I., 'The importance of dying well: Last acts in Jacobean tragedy and the brevity of the "Shakespearean moment"', *Times Literary Supplement*, 13 February 1998: 13–14.

Dunn, K., '"Action, passion, motion": The gestural politics of counsel in The Spanish Tragedy', *Renaissance Drama* 31 (2002): 27–60.

Erne, L., 'W. E. Burton's Dramatic Works of Thomas Kyd of 1848', *Notes and Queries* 44:4 (1997): 485–7.

Erne, L., '"Enter the Ghost of Andrea": Recovering Thomas Kyd's two-part play', *English Literary Renaissance* 30:3 (2000): 339–72.

Escolà, J. C., '"Vengeance is yours": Reclaiming the social bond in The Spanish Tragedy and Titus Andronicus', *Atlantis: Revista de la Asociación Española de Estudios Ingleses y Norteamericanos* 29:2 (2007): 59–74.

Freeman, A., 'Thomas Hawkins, Richard Farmer, and the authorship of The Spanish Tragedy', *Notes and Queries* 50 (248):2 (2003): 214–15.

Griffin, E., 'Ethos, empire, and the valiant acts of Thomas Kyd's tragedy of "the Spains"', *English Literary Renaissance* 31:2 (2001): 192–229.

Griffin, E., 'Nationalism, the Black Legend, and the revised *Spanish Tragedy*', *English Literary Renaissance* 39:2 (2009): 336–70.

Griffin, E., '"Spain is Portugal / And Portugal is Spain": Transnational attraction in The Stukeley Plays and The Spanish Tragedy', *Journal for Early Modern Cultural Studies* 10:1 (2010): 95–116.

Grimmett, R., '"By heaven and hell": Re-evaluating representations of women and the angel/whore dichotomy in Renaissance revenge tragedy', *Journal of International Women's Studies* 6:3 (2005): 31–9.

Hadfield, A., 'A handkerchief dipped in blood in *The Spanish Tragedy*: An anti-Catholic reference?', *Notes and Queries* 46:2 (1999): 197.

Hadfield, A., *The Spanish Tragedy*, the Alençon marriage plans, and John Stubbs's *Discoverie of a Gaping Gulf*, *Notes and Queries* 47:1 (2000): 42–3.

Hadfield, A., 'The *Ur-Hamlet* and the fable of the kid', *Notes and Queries* 53:1 (2006): 46–7.

Hagen, T., 'An English Renaissance understanding of the word "tragedy"', *Early Modern Literary Studies* Special Issue 1 (1997): 5.1–30. http://extra.shu.ac.uk/emls/si-01/si-01hagen.html [last accessed 30 January 2014].

Hamelman, S., 'Revenge tragedy and the art of the aside', *Shakespeare and Renaissance Association of West Virginia* 16 (1993): 64–87.

Han, K. M., 'From dread to mockery: The scenes of death in *The*

Spanish Tragedy and *The Revenger's Tragedy*', *Medieval and Early Modern English Studies* 18:1 (2010): 139–59.

Hartley, A. J., 'Social consciousness: Spaces for characters in *The Spanish Tragedy*', *Cahiers Élisabéthains: Late Medieval and Renaissance Studies* 58 (2000): 1–14.

Hile, R. E., '*The Spanish Tragedy* as intertext for Orhan Pamuk's *Kar (Snow)*', *Mediterranean Studies* 18 (2009): 143–67.

Hillman, R., 'Botching the soliloquies in *The Spanish Tragedy*: Revisionist collaboration and the 1602 additions', *Elizabethan Theatre* 15 (2002): 111–29.

Hodgdon, B., 'Recent studies in Tudor and Stuart drama', *Studies in English Literature, 1500–1900* 43:2 (2003): 495–544.

Hoenselaars, T., 'The seventeenth-century reception of English Renaissance drama in Europe', *SEDERI: Journal of the Spanish Society for English Renaissance Studies* 10 (1999): 69–87.

Hopkins, L., 'What's Hercules to Hamlet? The emblematic garden in *The Spanish Tragedy* and *Hamlet*', *Hamlet Studies: An International Journal of Research on The Tragedie of Hamlet, Prince of Denmarke* 21:1–2 (1999): 114–43.

Hunter, G. K., 'Tacitus and Kyd's *The Spanish Tragedy*', *Notes and Queries* 47:4 (2000), 424–5.

Hutson, L., 'Rethinking the "Spectacle of the Scaffold": Juridical epistemologies and English revenge', *Representations* 89 (2005): 30–58.

Irish, B. J., 'Vengeance, variously: Revenge before Kyd in early Elizabethan drama', *Early Theatre: A Journal Associated with the Records of Early English Drama* 12:2 (2009): 117–34.

Jackson, M. P., 'Parallels and poetry: Shakespeare, Kyd, and *Arden of Faversham*', *Medieval and Renaissance Drama in England: An Annual Gathering of Research, Criticism and Reviews* 23 (2010): 17–33.

Jakacki, D. K., '"Canst paint a doleful cry?": Promotion and performance in *The Spanish Tragedy* title-page illustration', *Early Theatre: A Journal Associated with the Records of Early English Drama* 13:1 (2010): 13–36.

Kahan, J., 'Re-evaluating Philip Edwards's argument: Could Burbage have played Hieronimo?', *Ben Jonson Journal: Literary Contexts in the Age of Elizabeth, James and Charles* 5 (1998): 253–5.

Kahan, J., 'An argument for emending Bazardo to Buzalto in the 1602 version of *The Spanish Tragedy*', *English Language Notes* 40:3 (2003): 13–19.

Kahan, J., 'The 1597 additions to *The Spanish Tragedy* and its subsequent influence on *A Warning for Faire Women*', *ANQ*:

A Quarterly Journal of Short Articles, Notes, and Reviews 17:2 (2004): 20–4.
Karam, F., 'Spanish tatters', *Theatre Crafts International* 32:2 (1998): 15–16.
Kiefer, F., 'Creating a Christian revenger: *The Spanish Tragedy* and its progeny *vs Hamlet*', *Shakespeare Yearbook* 13 (2002): 159–80.
Kietzman, M. J., 'Speaking "to All Humanity": Renaissance drama in Orhan Pamuk's *Snow*', *Texas Studies in Literature and Language* 52:3 (2010): 324–53.
Lange, J., '"Be deaf my ears": The power of silencing in Thomas Kyd's *The Spanish Tragedy*', *Shakespeare and Renaissance Association of West Virginia: Selected Papers* 17 (1994): 68–81.
Lidh, T. M., '"To Know the Author Were Some Ease of Grief": Ben Jonson's lost play', *Ben Jonson Journal: Literary Contexts in the Age of Elizabeth, James and Charles* 17:1 (2010): 60–75.
Lovascio, D., 'Julius Caesar's "Stony Heart": Thomas Kyd's *Cornelia* and *The Mirror for Magistrates*', *Notes and Queries* 59:1 (2012): 52–3.
Mazzio, C., 'Staging the vernacular: Language and nation in Thomas Kyd's *The Spanish Tragedy*', *SEL: Studies in English Literature, 1500–1900* 38:2 (1998): 207–32.
McAdam, I., '*The Spanish Tragedy* and the politico-religious unconscious', *Texas Studies in Literature and Language* 42:1 (2000): 33–60.
Mercure, M., '*The Spanish Tragedy* and the supernatural: Exploring the coexistence of patriotic and subversive interpretations in *The Spanish Tragedy*', *Undergraduate Review* 5 (2009): 140–3.
Merriam, T., 'Marlowe versus Kyd as Author of *Edward III* I.i, III, and V', *Notes and Queries* 56:4 (2009): 549–51.
Monateri, P. G., 'Sovereign ambiguity: From Hamlet to Benjamin via Eliot and Schmitt', *Anglistik* 20:2 (2009): 121–30.
Nicholl, C., 'Scribblers and assassins', *London Review of Books*, 31 October 2002: 30–3.
Owens, R., 'Thomas Kyd and the letters to Puckering', *Notes and Queries* 53:4 (2006): 459–61.
Owens, R., 'A possible candidate for "Shore" in the matter of the Dutch Church Libels', *Notes and Queries* 54:3 (2007): 253–5.
Owens, R., 'Parody and *The Spanish Tragedy*', *Cahiers Élisabéthains: A Biannual Journal of English Renaissance Studies* 71 (2007): 27–36.
Owens, R., 'Thomas Hawkins's attribution of the authorship of *The Spanish Tragedy*', *Notes and Queries* 54 (252):1 (2007): 74–5.

Owens, R., 'Lamb roasts Kyd: Charles Lamb's reaction to Thomas Kyd's *Spanish Tragedy* in Specimens', *Charles Lamb Bulletin* 142 (2008): 60–70.
Owens, R., 'The career of Thomas Kyd relating to his attendance at Merchant Taylors' School', *Notes and Queries* 56:1 (2009): 35–6.
Perry, C., 'The uneasy republicanism of Thomas Kyd's *Cornelia*', *Criticism: A Quarterly for Literature and the Arts* 48:4 (2006): 535–55.
Pollard, T., 'What's Hecuba to Shakespeare', *Renaissance Quarterly* 65:4 (2012): 1060–93.
Riemer, A. P., 'Troubled speech: The representation of madness in Renaissance drama', *Sydney Studies in English* 19 (1993): 21–30. http://openjournals.library.usyd.edu.au/index.php/SSE/article/view/487/459 [last accessed March 2015].
Rist, T., 'Memorial revenge at the Reformation(s): Kyd's *The Spanish Tragedy*', *Cahiers Élisabéthains: A Biannual Journal of English Renaissance Studies* 71 (2007): 15–25.
Salkeld, D., 'Kyd's *Absalon*', *Notes and Queries* 40:2 (1993): 177.
Salkeld, D., 'Kyd and the courtesan', *Notes and Queries* 47:1 (2000): 43–8.
Sheerin, B., 'Patronage and perverse bestowal in *The Spanish Tragedy* and *Antonio's Revenge*', *English Literary Renaissance* 41:2 (2011): 247–79.
Siemon, J. R., 'Sporting Kyd', *English Renaissance Drama* 24:3 (1994): 553–82.
Smith, E., 'Author *v.* character in early modern dramatic authorship: The example of Thomas Kyd and *The Spanish Tragedy*', *Medieval and Renaissance Drama in England* 11 (1999): 129–42.
Sofer, A., 'Absorbing interests: Kyd's bloody handkerchief as palimpsest', *Comparative Drama* 34.2 (2000): 127–53.
Tassi, M. A., 'The player's passions and the Elizabethan painting trope: A study of the Painter Addition to Kyd's *The Spanish Tragedy*', *Explorations in Renaissance Culture* 26:1 (2000): 73–100.
Thomson, P., 'Hieronomo's abstracts', *Studies in Theatre and Performance* 24:1 (2004): 63–4.
Vickers, B., 'Thomas Kyd, secret sharer', *Times Literary Supplement*, 15 April 2008: 13–15.
Vickers, B., 'Shakespeare and authorship studies in the twenty-first century', *Shakespeare Quarterly* 62:1 (2011): 106–42.
Vickers, B., 'Identifying Shakespeare's Additions to *The Spanish Tragedy* (1602): A new(er) approach', *Shakespeare* 8.1 (2012): 13–43.
Waugh, S., A. Adams and F. Tweedie, 'Computational stylistics using artificial neural networks', *Literary and Linguistic Computing*:

Journal of the Association for Literary and Linguistic Computing 15:2 (2000): 187–97.

West, W. N., '"But this will be a mere confusion": real and represented confusions on the Elizabethan stage', *Theatre Journal* 60:2 (2008): 217–33.

Williams, G., 'Being seen is believing: Spectacle, ethics, and the others of belief in Elizabethan revenge tragedy', *Theta VIII, Théâtre Tudor* (2009): 253–74. http://umr6576.cesr.univ-tours.fr/publications/theta8/fichiers/pdf/williams.pdf [last accessed 30 January 2014].

Zamir, T., 'Wooden subjects', *New Literary History: A Journal of Theory and Interpretation* 39:2 (2008): 277–300.

Zunino Garrido, C., 'Rhetoric and truth in *The Spanish Tragedy*', *SEDERI: Journal of the Spanish Society for English Renaissance Studies* 12 (2001): 341–8.

DOCTORAL DISSERTATIONS

Booth, G. A., 'Violent performance: A cultural analysis of the intersection of violence and embedded performance in Elizabethan and Jacobean tragedy', PhD dissertation, University of Toronto, 1996.

Coral, J., 'The subjectivity of revenge: Senecan drama and the discovery of the tragic in Kyd and Shakespeare', PhD dissertation, University of York, 2001.

Crosbie, C. J., 'Philosophies of retribution: Kyd, Shakespeare, Webster and the revenge tragedy genre', PhD dissertation, Rutgers, The State University of New Jersey – New Brunswick, 2007.

Degenhardt, J. H., 'Faith, embodiment, and "turning Turk": Islamic conversion on the early modern stage and the production of religious and racial identity', PhD dissertation, University of Pennsylvania, 2005.

Deutermann, A. K., 'Hearing and listening in early modern drama', PhD dissertation, Columbia University, 2008.

Griffin, E., 'The temper of Spain: The forging of anti-Hispanic sentiment in early modern England, 1492–1604', PhD dissertation, University of Iowa, 1998.

Jones, M., 'Alterity and nationalism on the Elizabethan stage: A study of the Spanish and Jewish other in the drama of Shakespeare and his contemporaries', PhD dissertation, Saint Louis University, Missouri, 2004.

Long, Z. C., 'The uncollected self: Memory, subjectivity, and cultural crisis in English Renaissance drama', PhD dissertation, University of Virginia, 2006.

Oroval Martí, V. A., 'Semiotics of drama: A way and a proposal around Thomas Kyd's *The Spanish Tragedy* (c.1590)', PhD dissertation, University of Valencia, 1993.

Ortego, J. N., 'The mirror and the stage: theatrical reflections in the plays of Kyd, Shakespeare, and Jonson', PhD dissertation, University of Louisiana at Lafayette, 2004.

Pollard, A. R., '"Female" stage props: Visualizing the disappearing woman on the early modern stage', PhD dissertation, Rice University Texas, 2007.

Schott, H., 'The trials of orality in early modern England, 1550–1625', PhD dissertation, Harvard University, Massachusetts, 2004.

Smith, A. L., 'Performing marriage in early modern England: Wooing and wedding in *The Shoemaker's Holiday*, *The Taming of the Shrew*, *The Spanish Tragedy*, and *Titus Andronicus*', PhD dissertation, University of Illinois, Urbana, 2000.

Steenbergh, K., 'Wild justice: The dynamics of gender and revenge in early modern English drama', PhD dissertation, Utrecht University, 2007.

Turner, T. A., 'Torture and the drama of emergency: Kyd, Marlow, Shakespeare', PhD dissertation, University of Texas, Austin, 2011.

Waldron, J. E., 'Eloquence of the body: Aesthetics, theology, and English Renaissance theater', PhD dissertation, Princeton University, New Jersey, 2004.

Walker, J. A., 'Reading material [for] performance theater and textuality in the English Renaissance', PhD dissertation, University of Illinois at Chicago, 2004.

REVIEWS OF STAGE PRODUCTIONS

Lazarus Theatre Company, Blue Elephant Theatre, London, dir. Ricky Dukes, 2013

Anderson, J., 'Review: *The Spanish Tragedy*', 29 September 2013, www.ayoungertheatre.com/review-the-spanish-tragedy-blue-elephant-theatre-lazarus-theatre-company/ [last accessed 30 January 2014].

Jameson, G., 'Exclusive: Lazarus to perform *The Spanish Tragedy*', 7 July 2013, www.entertainment-focus.com/theatre-section/theatre-news/exclusive-lazarus-to-perform-the-spanish-tragedy/ [last accessed 30 January 2014].

Jameson, G., '*The Spanish Tragedy* interviews', 25 September 2013, www.entertainment-focus.com/theatre-section/theatre-interviews/spanish-tragedy-interviews/. [last accessed 30 January 2014].

'Maria Alexe plays in "The Spanish Tragedy" by Thomas Kyd', 25 September 2013, www.romanianculturalcentre.org.uk/cultural-diary/2013/09/maria-alexe-plays-in-the-spanish-tragedy-by-thomas-kyd/ [last accessed 30 January 2014].

Radosavljevic, D., 'The Spanish Tragedy', 27 September 2013, www.thestage.co.uk/reviews/review.php/38954/the-spanish-tragedy. [last accessed 30 January 2014].

Thomas, M. F., 'The Spanish Tragedy', 30 September 2013, www.whatsonstage.com/london-theatre/reviews/09-2013/the-spanish-tragedy_32093.html [last accessed 30 January 2014].

Marin Shakespeare Company. Forest Meadows Amphitheatre, Dominican University, San Rafael, dir. Lesley Schisgall Currier, 2013

Hurwitt, R., 'The Spanish Tragedy review: Complicated revenge', 15 July 2013, www.sfgate.com/performance/article/The-Spanish-Tragedy-review-complicated-revenge-4666513.php [last accessed 30 January 2014].

Hurwitt, S., 'Theater review: Vengeful treat in "Spanish Tragedy" at Marin Shakes', 18 September 2013, www.marinij.com/ci_23673721/theater-review-vengeful-treat-spanish-tragedy-at-marin [last accessed 30 January 2014].

Planet Theatre Productions, Rose, London, dir. Adrian Brown, 2010

Finlay, L., 'Review', Ink Pellet, www.inkpellet.co.uk/2010/11/the-spanish-tragedy/ [last accessed 30 January 2014].

Goldie, A., 'Revenge is a sweet thing', 8 September 2010, www.remotegoat.com/uk/review_view.php?uid=5931#reviews [last accessed 30 January 2014].

Kirwan, P., 'The Spanish Tragedy (Planet Theatre Productions) @ The Rose, Bankside', The Bardathon, 11 September 2010, https://blogs.warwick.ac.uk/pkirwan/entry/the_spanish_tragedy/ [last accessed 30 January 2014].

Price, E., 'Reporting on The Spanish Tragedy', Research on Medieval and Renaissance Drama 50 (2012): 108–11.

Sladen, S. 'Review', British Theatre Guide, www.britishtheatreguide.info/reviews/span tragedyplanet-rev [last accessed 30 January 2014].

Whelan, B., 'Review', Extra! Extra!, September 2010, www.extraextra.org/Review_The_Spanish_Tragedy_2010.html [last accessed 30 January 2014].

Doublethink Theatre Company, Arcola Theatre, London, dir. Mitchell Moreno, 2009

Bassett, K., 'The Spanish Tragedy, Arcola, London, Annie Get Your Gun, Young Vic, London, Twelfth Night, Courtyard, Strat-

ford-Upon-Avon', *Independent on Sunday*, 25 October 2009.
'Review: *The Spanish Tragedy*', 16 October 2009 http://oughtto-beclowns.blogspot.com/2009/10/review-spanish-tragedy.html. [last accessed 30 January 2014].
'*The Spanish Tragedy* at the Arcola', 23 October 2009, http://intervaldrinks.blogspot.co.uk/2009/10/spanish-tragedy-at-arcola. html [last accessed 30 January 2014].
Tripney, N., '*The Spanish Tragedy*', *Stage*, 21 October 2009, www.thestage.co.uk/reviews/review.php/25956/the-spanish-tragedy [last accessed 30 January 2014].

The Rude Mechanicals Theatre Company, St Andrew's Episcopal Church in College Park, Maryland, dir. Charlene V. Smith, 2009
Follos, T., 'Vengeance for all: *The Spanish Tragedy*', www.expressnightout.com/2009/01/vengeance_is_everyones/ [last accessed 30 January 2014].

Oriel College, Oxford, dir. Will Maynard, 2–6 June 2009
'The Spanish Tragedie'. www.dailyinfo.co.uk/reviews/feature/4046/The_Spanish_Tragedie [last accessed 30 January 2014].

Captain Theatre, Assembly Rooms, Durham, dir. Narayani Menon, 2005
Badham, H., 'A Spanish triumph', 21 December 2005, www.durham21.co.uk/2005/12/a-spanish-triumph/ [last accessed 30 January 2014].

Loose Canon Theatre Company, Mint, Dublin, dir. Jason Byrne, 1997
Meany, H., 'The Play's the Thing', *The Irish Times*, 28 August 1997, 6.
Nowlan, D., 'Weighed down by serious intent', *The Irish Times*, 2 September 1997: 6.
'Projecting into the future', *The Irish Times*, 4 September 1997: 10.

Royal Shakespeare Company – The Swan, Stratford-upon-Avon, dir. Michael Boyd, 1997, transfer to Newcastle and London
Barr, G., 'Fasten your seatbelts for Siobhan's new role', *Newcastle Evening Chronicle*, 10 September 1997.
Bassett, K., 'From Elsinore to a Spanish court', *Daily Telegraph*, 10 December 1997.
Billen, A., 'The week in reviews: Theatre: So *Hamlet* drops the bullets from the gun. Then he gets the giggles', *Observer*, 11 May 1997.
Billington, M., 'Reviews: *The Spanish Tragedy*', *Guardian*, 12 May 1997.
Billington, M., 'Wild Justice [M. Billington chairs a debate in the Swan on the theme of revenge]', *RSC Magazine*, 15 (Summer 1997): 12–15.

B.N., 'The Spanish Tragedy', The Times, 29 November 1997.
Clark, D., 'The Spanish Tragedy', Newcastle Chronicle, 18 September 1997.
Curtis, N., 'Much madness and meathooks', Evening Standard, 8 May 1997.
Curtis, N., 'Red hot Redmond', Hot Tickets, 27 November 1997.
Darley, A., 'A tragedy if you don't make the effort to see this', Wembley Brent Times, 11 December 1997.
de Jongh, N., 'Royal skulduggery and revenge upon revenge', Evening Standard, 4 December 1997.
Dyson, S., 'Big spender', Evening Mail, 2 May 1997.
Edmonds, R., 'Blood and gore and clotted dialogue', Birmingham Post, 9 May 1997.
Eley, E., 'The Spanish Tragedy: Review', Midweek, 15 December 1997.
FitzGerald, A., 'Cuts too deep for this Hamlet: Hamlet and The Spanish Tragedy', Stage, 15 May 1997.
Grant, S., Time Out, 12 May 1997.
Gross, J., Sunday Telegraph, 11 May 1997.
Hagerty, B., News of the World, 11 May 1997.
'Hamlet and The Spanish Tragedy: Review', Stratford Journal, 22 May 1997.
Hanks, R., 'Theatre: The Spanish Tragedy', Independent, 7 December 1997.
Happé, P., 'The Spanish Tragedy – Review of the 1997 RSC production', in 'Census of Renaissance Drama Production' compiled by Elizabeth Schafer (63–78), Research Opportunities in Renaissance Drama, 37 (1998): 69–71.
Hemming, S., 'A sparkling evening in hell', Financial Times, 10 December 1997.
Hodgson, B., 'It's not for the faint-hearted', N Shields New Guardian, 18 September 1997.
Kingsley, L., 'The Spanish Tragedy', This Is London, 12 December 1997.
Kingston, J., 'More gore than Hamlet', The Times, 5 December 1997.
Lapworth, P., 'Variety is the spice of death', Stratford Herald, 15 May 1997.
Macaulay, A., 'A grievous attack of nobility', Financial Times, 9 May 1997.
Marlowe, S., 'The Spanish Tragedy', What's On, 10 December 1997.

Nightingale, B., 'First to cry for revenge', *The Times*, 9 May 1997.
Newton, K., 'What a lively form of death', *Middlesbrough Evening Gazette*, 17 September 1997.
Peacocke, H., 'Welcome revival for a Tudor classic', *Oxford Times*, 22 August 1997.
Peter, J. and R. Hewison, 'The Spanish Tragedy', *Sunday Times*, 11 May 1997.
'Rab C to RSC', *Middlesbrough Gazette*, 23 May 1997.
'Revenge is sweet, but tends to get a bit messy: Interview with Peter Wight', *Middlesbrough Evening Gazette*, 12 September 1997.
'Review,' *Northern Echo*, 15 May 1997.
Rhodes, P., 'A touch of the gore blimeys', *Express Star*, 8 May 1997.
Roe, C., 'Heightened emotion and horror', *Evening News*, 12 May 1997.
'RSC thrives on tragedy', *Daily Mail*, 27 June 1997.
Salisbury, M., 'Tragic tale steps out of shadows', *Kenilworth Observer*, 15 May 1997.
Smith, P. J. and G. Walker, 'The Spanish Tragedy, directed by Michael Boyd for the RSC', *Cahiers Élisabéthains: Études sur la Pré-Renaissance et la Renaissance Anglaises*, 52 (1997), 113–14.
'The Spanish Tragedy and Hamlet: Review', *Blackmore Vale Magazine*, 7 November 1997.
'The Spanish Tragedy: Preview', *Time Out*, 22 May 1997.
Spencer, C., 'RSC's triumph over tragedy', *Daily Telegraph*, 9 May 1997; reprinted in *The Theatre Record* (7–20 May 1997), 631–4.
Stratton, K., 'The Spanish Tragedy', *Time Out*, 10 December 1997.
Taylor, P., 'More matter, less art', *The Independent*, 10 May 1997.
Treadwell, J., 'Sweet is revenge', *Spectator*, 17 May 1997.
Upshon, K., 'RSC pitches its tent', *North Devon Journal*, 22 May 1997.
The Voice of the Westcountry, 'Peasants we are not, dear critic', *Western Morning News*, 14 May 1997.
Ward, J., 'A very Spanish sort of tragedy', *Hartlepool Mail*, 18 September 1997.
'Welcome to the world's greatest theatre company: The RSC season Plymouth, October–November 1997,' *Western Morning News*, 26 October 1997.
Whetstone, D., 'The power and the gory', *Newcastle Journal*, 17 July 1997.

Whetstone, D., 'A noble ambition is realized: The 21st RSC Newcastle season in full', *Newcastle Journal*, 11 September 1997.
White, C., 'Spanish swashbuckler's bodycount to blanch at', *Metro News*, 1 May 1997.
'Why playing love scenes can be tricky for Siobhan', *Plymouth Extra*, 22 May 1997.
Willing Suspension Productions, Boston University, Boston, dir. Andrew J. Hartley, 1994
Hartley, A. J., 'Social consciousness: Spaces for characters in *The Spanish Tragedy*', *Cahiers Élisabéthains: Late Medieval and Renaissance Studies* 58 (2000): 1–14.

ONLINE RESOURCES

Cinpoeş, N., *The Jacobethans*, www2.warwick.ac.uk/fac/arts/ren/elizabethan_jacobean_drama/kyd/ [last accessed 30 January 2014].
Smith, E., http://writersinspire.org/content/spanish-tragedy-thomas-kyd [last accessed 30 January 2014].
http://en.wikipedia.org/wiki/The_Spanish_Tragedy [last accessed 30 January 2014].
www.sparknotes.com/drama/spanishtragedy/ [last accessed 30 January 2014].
www.gradesaver.com/the-spanish-tragedy/study-guide/section1/ [last accessed 30 January 2014].
www.enotes.com/topics/spanish-tragedy [last accessed 30 January 2014].
www.theatredatabase.com/16th_century/thomas_kyd_001.html [last accessed 30 January 2014].
www.theatrehistory.com/british/kyd002.html [last accessed 30 January 2014].

INDEX

Additions: 1602, the Painter Scene 2, 61–2, 82, 84–5, 90, 91, 93, 94–9, 104n9, 105n17, 105n19, 149, 171, 174–5, 183
Aeschylus 45
  Oresteia, The 45
Alençon, Duke of 122, 130, 131
Alleyn, Edward 1, 37, 66
alliance, marital 113, 119–21, 125
alterity 112, 113–17, 125
anxiety 118, 120, 121–2
Arcola Theatre 4, 173, 189, 191
Ardolino, Frank 7, 111, 112, 117, 126n2, 126n15, 127n16, 141n5, 216, 222–3
Atey, Arthur 134–5, 137, 140
  Pieces of the storye or Relaciones so called (by the) Peregrini their Authors 134–5
audience 3, 10, 31, 34, 34, 36–7, 40, 45, 46, 47, 61, 62, 63, 64–5, 67, 78–9, 112, 118, 122, 125, 132, 155, 156, 180, 181, 182, 184, 187, 189, 190, 195–6, 198–9
author, intentions of 83, 84, 89, 100, 103n7
author's text 94
  publisher's text and 89, 90, 100, 103

Babel 111, 129, 172, 180, 183, 186, 190
  see also languages, sundry
Babylon 111, 112, 129, 141, 180, 182, 206, 207

Barker, Simon 94, 215
Bate, Jonathan 96, 100, 126n14, 215
Bergh, Adriaen van den 147–8, 149, 150, 151–2, 161n15
  Jeronimo 147, 148, 151–2
  Polidoor 148
betrayal 130, 133, 135, 136, 140–1
Bevington, David 3, 89, 94
Boas, Frederick 3, 55, 82, 95, 96, 105n19, 144, 148, 159
Bogdanov, Michael 171, 173, 175–8, 179, 181–2, 183–4, 186, 192n24
boundaries, geographical 118–19
Boyd, Michael 171, 173, 174, 176–8, 179–80, 182, 183, 184–5, 192n15, 192n16
Brathwait, Richard 65–7
Broude, Ronald 129
Bryant, Michael 175–6, 178–9, 183, 184
Burbage, Richard 1, 66

cacophony 172, 180, 190, 197
Cairncross, Andrew Scott 3, 88, 95, 105n19, 151, 162n29
Calvo, Clara 11n12, 89, 90, 94, 216, 220
Castile, Joanna of 121
Charles I 154–5, 158, 159, 163n50
Charles II 144, 152, 153–6, 157, 158, 163n50, 163n53
Cinpoeş, Nicoleta 103n1, 223, 234
Clare, Janet 53, 54
colonialism 113, 116, 117–18, 122–5

comedy 25, 26–7, 30, 33, 40, 115, 176, 182, 187
compositors' errors 80, 91–3, 99–100, 102, 104n11
Conestaggio, Girolamo Franchi di 124
confession 138, 139, 183
conspiracy 38, 77, 126, 129, 137, 189, 206
Copie of a Leter, The 130, 131, 132–4
copy-text 90, 92, 93, 96, 102, 103
Cottesloe, National Theatre London 171, 172, 176, 182, 186, 191

Daniel, Samuel 38
Davies, Tod 215
difference, linguistic 115–16, 180, 190, 197, 198
Drake, William 58
drama, closet 38–9
Drury, Alan 171, 173, 174–5, 179, 181, 184
duality, human 39–40
Dudley, Robert 130, 132, 133, 145
Duke of Castile 17
dumbshow 34, 35, 118, 185
dynasty 113, 117, 118, 119–20, 121–2, 124, 125, 135, 136–8

editing 4, 75, 76, 82–3, 88, 90, 92, 94, 99–101
  not editing 88
  re-editing 77, 88
  unediting 88, 89
edition, original 147, 149, 151–2, 158, 159
Edwards, Philip 3, 85, 88, 89, 94, 101, 102, 111, 112, 124, 151, 162n29, 180, 216, 225
Elizabeth I 38, 64, 82, 84, 117, 118, 121, 122, 130, 131, 137, 145, 195
Escobedo, Juan de 134, 135, 136, 137, 138–9, 140–1
Essex, Earl of 38, 130, 134, 136

exile, royalist 152, 153, 158–9

fiction, reality and 61–2
First Part of Hieronimo, The 147, 161, 171, 174
foreignness 113, 115, 116, 125
Freeman, Arthur 99–100, 122, 123, 133

Gartland, Roger 177
Glasgow Citizens Theatre 171, 173, 174, 175, 180, 184
glossary 55, 80, 101
Gosson, Stephen 27, 28
  Plays confuted in Five Actions 27
Greenblatt, Stephen 18, 56
Greene, Robert 111, 118
  Spanish Masquerado, The 111, 112, 118
Greville, Fulke 38–9
  Mustapha 38
grief 59–60, 121, 155, 173, 178, 203, 204, 206, 207, 210

Hadfield, Andrew 112
Henslowe, Philip 1, 135
Heywood, Thomas 26, 61, 64
  Apology for Actors 26, 61, 146
Hicks, Greg 175, 176, 177, 184
hierarchy 78, 85
  authority 21, 27, 55, 56, 64–5, 79, 119, 198
  institutions 3, 28, 28, 36, 45, 56–7, 60, 63–4, 64, 67, 69n42, 79–80, 189, 195
  Knight Marshal 1, 37, 49, 50, 59, 62, 63, 134
  Magistrates 64
  patriarchal norm 55, 66
  privileged status 25–6, 63, 154
  social 4, 21, 25, 25, 40, 44, 56, 63, 65, 89, 176, 187, 195, 196, 198
  state and individual 21, 118
Hill, Eugene 129
Hinds, Hilary 75, 76, 79, 83, 94

INDEX

Hoenselaars, Ton 161n24, 220, 225
Horace 26
  Ars poetica 26
Howard, Tony 201

identity 35, 40, 116, 179, 191, 210
  geographical 117, 118, 119, 122
  linguistic 111, 115–16
  national 3, 112, 113–14, 115, 116–17, 125, 126n12
  political 118
  racial 112, 113–14
illusion, dramatic 37, 61, 125, 184
innovations 2, 45–6, 80, 91–2, 102
Inns of Court, the 38, 56–7, 63, 64, 67, 69
Interregnum 158, 159
invasion 111, 116, 117, 118, 123, 134, 153, 158, 186

justice 16, 17, 21, 36, 43, 45, 50, 51, 53, 79, 82, 129, 195, 196, 198, 199, 204, 205, 206
  divine 45
  human 49
  personal 17, 27
  private 64
  revenge and 43–4, 180, 201

Kane, Sarah 190
  4:48 Psychosis 210

languages, sundry 35, 36–7, 129, 172, 180, 181–2
  see also Babel
legacy 4, 20, 201, 202, 207
Leicester, Earl of 130–4
Leicester's Commonwealth 130, 131, 132
Letter of Estate, The 130, 133–4
libel 130, 131, 133–4
  libellous satire 131
Love, Patti 177, 192n10
Low Countries 2, 144–5, 146, 147, 148, 152, 159

MacDonald, Robert David 171, 173, 174, 175, 181, 188
Marlowe, Christopher 2, 10, 15, 17–18, 29, 30, 33, 35, 38, 78, 112, 145
  Doctor Faustus 39, 77, 112, 160
  Jew of Malta, The 1, 160
  Tamburlaine the Great 35, 112
masque 35, 69n43, 86n15, 117–18, 122, 123, 124–5, 185
Medici, Lorenzo de' 111, 117, 126n15
Middleton, Thomas 77, 86n15
  Revenger's Tragedy, The (also *Revengers' Tragedy* and *Revengers Tragedy*) 146, 149–50, 152, 154, 186, 200n4
Misfortunes of Arthur, The 56, 57
monarchy 113, 117, 118, 122, 125, 127n20
monologue 32, 183
morality play 2, 34, 45, 46, 122
Moreno, Mitchell 189–91
Mulryne, J. R. 3, 88, 89, 94, 101, 150

Naiambana, Patrice 176
nationalism 115, 125
Newton, Thomas 57–8
Nietzsche, Friedrich 43, 51
  Human, All Too Human 44
nightmare 181, 183, 184, 185, 201, 207, 208, 210

O'Casey, Sean 209
  Plough and the Stars, The 209
oration 182, 183–4, 187, 189
otherness 113
  racial 113–14, 116

Pamuk, Orhan 187, 189
  Snow 187–9, 190–1
Peele, George
  Battle of Alcazar, The 35, 124
Pérez, Antonio 130, 134–41
  Las Relaciones 130, 134–41

Philip II 112, 117, 121, 122, 123, 130, 134, 135, 136–41
Pickering, John 45
  History of Horestes 45
playlet 36–7, 46, 50, 63–4, 83–5, 129, 134, 138, 139, 172, 179, 182, 186, 197, 203, 206, 207
play-within-the-play 46, 54, 63, 67, 83, 119, 127n20, 180, 182, 190, 208
policy, editorial 91, 92, 93
Pollard, Tanya 60
props 35, 37, 50, 149, 173
  arbour, *see* tree
  axe 173
  box 35, 37, 51, 132
  corpse 10, 172, 203
  curtain 10, 37, 174, 181, 206, 207
  handkerchief 50, 203
  iron-maiden 172
  knife 36, 37, 183
  letter 50
  noose 183
  pen 35, 37, 183
  scarf 50
  sword 150–1
  torture instruments 172
  tree 50, 54, 62, 199, 201, 206, 207
Prynne, William 65
  Histriomastix 65
publisher's intentions 90, 92
publisher's text 93
Puttenham, George 25–7, 30
  Art of English Poesy, The 25

reading practices, early modern 58–9
Redmond, Siobahn 177–8, 182
religion 3, 18, 112, 117, 124, 144, 160, 173, 187, 188
  anti-Catholic 112, 137
  atheism 18, 112
  Catholic 19, 111, 112, 117, 127n15, 129, 130, 131, 135, 137

Catholic Church 112
Catholic dissidents 130
Christian 17, 18, 21, 40, 58, 79, 84, 112, 125, 179, 185
classical 58, 79
damnation 40, 180
Destiny 16, 17, 19, 20, 23
divine control 17, 20
divine guidance 15, 20
divine intervention 19, 156
divine justification 158
divine power 16–17, 79
divine right 160
doom 47–9
evil 21, 32, 130, 159
Fortune 27, 35, 84, 136
God 23, 55, 66, 139, 154, 155–6, 180
gods 17, 20, 22–3, 25, 32
hell 26, 35, 101, 174, 189, 205, 206
heresy 134
Protestant 38, 40, 56, 112, 117, 126n2, 126n7, 129, 130, 131, 132, 139
providence 15, 18, 20, 23, 24, 134, 135, 158
punishment 25, 31, 131
Purgatory 18–19, 26
Puritan 27, 28, 29, 30, 148, 152
redemption 26, 29
scepticism 18, 23–4
sin 23, 133, 156, 203
underworld 16, 36, 48–9, 50, 59, 79, 101, 159
vice 28, 29–30, 34, 38, 56, 173
virtue 28–9, 30, 34, 38, 185
reprint 3, 78, 91, 99
resistance, political 138
Restoration 2, 144, 148, 152, 156, 159, 160
restoration 89, 92, 93, 103n7
revenge tragedy 45, 53
  adaptations 56, 146–7, 149, 153, 158, 160, 174
  avenger, *see* revenger

INDEX

biblical prohibition of revenge 55
divine revenge 55, 154, 155
duty 53, 57, 62, 67
Elizabethan 4, 29, 31, 33, 35, 40, 43
feminine fury and masculine rationality 54, 59–61, 64–5, 67
feminine revenge and masculine justice 53, 54, 59–60
genre 4, 53, 63–5, 67, 144, 147, 151, 152, 154, 157, 159, 160
genres 26, 32
honour, *see* duty
irony 35, 46, 50
Jacobean 38
judge 44, 49, 64–5, 67
madness 28, 37, 53–4, 61–2, 66–7, 84, 181, 208–9
murder 28, 57, 112, 140
neo-Senecan 56, 65, 67
passion 15, 20, 28, 32, 55, 59–62, 65–6
personal revenge 45
poetic justice 183
political debate 3, 34, 46, 117–20, 123, 125, 130, 152–9, 186–7
power 23, 27, 49, 50, 60, 65, 112, 113, 117–18, 123, 125, 158, 173, 181
private revenge 54, 56–7, 58, 63, 64, 65
retaliation 145, 154, 187
retribution 51, 53, 58, 63, 204
retributive justice 49, 50
revenger 28, 40, 53, 59–60, 64, 67, 129, 155, 156, 157, 158
rhetoric 32, 33, 56, 67, 84, 111, 154, 171, 175, 176, 178
royalist revenge 157, 159, 160
royal revenge 144, 154–6
Senecan 17, 32, 34, 36, 38, 54–60, 63, 154, 156, 157, 183
sententiae 32
sexuality 140, 178

soliloquy 19, 33, 34, 39, 40, 55, 92
suicide 16, 17, 22, 40, 50, 54, 179, 189, 204, 207
vindictiveness 51, 54, 55, 57, 58, 59, 155, 205
rivalries, political 117
rivalries, romantic 141
Rodenburgh, Theodore 145, 146–7, 149–50, 152, 154, 157, 159, 161n24
Rowan, Dominic 190
royalists 144, 153, 154, 156–7, 158–9, 160

Seneca 2, 31–3, 38, 54–6, 66, 82, 179
Agamemnon 55
Hercules Furens 61
Hippolytus 33
Medea 17, 28, 59
Octavia 55
Shakespeare, William 1, 2, 3, 4, 10n3, 15, 18–24, 30, 33, 35, 38, 75, 76, 78, 82, 85, 88, 89, 99, 100, 145, 148, 160n3, 161n17, 188
Cymbeline 23
Hamlet 1, 5, 18–21, 29, 35, 39–40, 59, 78, 94, 96, 100, 103, 105n20, 105n27, 120, 122, 156, 157, 158, 159, 163n49, 173, 175, 185–6, 192n16, 207, 210
Henry V 115
Henry VI 1, 100, 153
Julius Caesar 34, 105n29
King Lear 21–3, 96, 174
Macbeth 21, 94, 208, 209
Merry Wives of Windsor, The 115–16
Midsummer Night's Dream, A 105n29, 177, 186
Pericles 23
Richard III 1, 30, 153, 158
Romeo and Juliet 15, 31, 201

Tempest, The 23
Titus Andronicus 1, 3, 18, 28, 31, 33, 35, 59, 96, 113–15, 116, 148, 153, 154, 158, 190, 201, 206, 210
Winter's Tale, The 37, 105n29
Shapiro, James 66
Sheridan, Richard Brinsley 208
 Critic, The 208–9
Sidney, Philip 28–9, 30, 33, 131, 145, 146
 Apology for Poetry 28
D'Silva, Darrell 182
Soliman and Perseda, see playlet
Somerville, John 175
source materials 80
Spain 111–13, 117–25, 129–30, 134–8
Spanish Armada 83, 84, 111, 112, 117–18, 123, 124, 129, 130, 135, 137, 208
Spanish Tragedy, The
 Balthazar 16, 37, 47, 48–9, 54, 60, 63, 104n12, 117, 119, 120, 121, 129, 136, 137, 140, 141, 175, 176, 180, 181, 182, 183, 187, 191n8, 197, 198, 205
 Bazulto 104n12, 174, 206
 Bel-imperia 15, 16, 17, 20, 37, 48, 49, 50, 53, 54, 59, 66, 92, 105n16, 116, 117, 119, 120, 121, 129, 136, 137, 138, 139, 140, 174, 176–7, 180, 181, 182, 187, 188, 191n5, 192n10, 192n24, 197, 201, 203, 205, 206
 editions, 1592 1, 2, 82, 90, 91, 104n8
 editions, 1602 2, 61, 82, 90, 150, 171, 174, 175, 183
 editions, 1615 62, 149, 151, 201, 202, 207
 editions, anthologies 3, 75, 76, 77, 78, 79, 81, 82, 84, 85
 editions, hypertextual 89
 editions, modern-spelling 89, 90
 editions, multi-textual 89
 editions, octavo-in-fours 82, 104n8
 editions, Q1 90–2, 93–6, 97, 98, 99–100, 101–3, 104n11, 104n12, 104n13, 104n14, 104n15, 105n16, 105n27
 editions, Q2 91, 93, 101, 102, 104n12, 104n13, 104n15
 editions, Q3 91, 92, 93, 99, 102, 104n12, 104n13, 104n15
 editions, Q4 90–4, 95–6, 97, 98, 99, 102–3, 104n11, 104n12, 104n13, 104n15, 105n18, 105n19
 editions, quarto 2, 3, 62, 90–1, 96, 104n8, 149, 150, 151, 162n29, 201
 editions, quarto in octavo 104n8
 Ghost of Don Andrea, The 16, 19, 20, 35–6, 46–9, 50, 54, 78–9, 101–2, 117, 120, 121, 140, 147, 149, 173, 174, 176, 184, 185, 204
 Hangman, the 122, 205
 Hieronimo 15, 16, 19, 35, 36–7, 49–51, 53, 54–5, 58–9, 60, 61–2, 63, 66–7, 69n31, 69n42, 69n43, 79, 83, 90, 92, 93, 102, 111, 112, 116, 117, 118, 119, 120, 122, 123, 124–5, 126n2, 126n15, 129, 133, 134, 138, 139, 149, 172, 173, 174–5, 178–85, 186–7, 190, 192n12, 192, 192n24, 196, 197, 198–9, 201, 203–5, 206–7
 Horatio 16, 48–9, 50, 51, 54, 67, 102, 117, 134, 136, 138, 140, 141, 172, 173, 174, 175, 176, 177–8, 182, 185, 196, 197, 199, 201, 203, 204, 205, 206, 207
 Isabella 50, 53–4, 91, 102, 117, 174, 179, 189, 191n5, 192n15, 199, 202, 203, 204–10

INDEX

King of Spain, the 46, 48, 95,
118–19, 120, 121, 123, 181,
196, 197, 198, 205, 206
Lorenzo 16, 21, 37, 47, 48, 51,
54, 63, 92, 101, 116, 117,
121, 127n15, 130, 132, 133,
134, 136, 137–8, 139, 175–6,
177, 179, 180, 181, 182, 187,
190, 191, 191n8, 196, 197,
198, 201, 204, 205, 206
Painter, the 62
Pedringano 49, 51, 117, 122,
130, 132, 133, 134, 136, 138,
139, 140–1, 141n5, 150, 151,
176, 191n7, 205
Pluto 16, 17, 19, 23, 48, 49
productions, amateur 2, 3, 10n10
productions, professional 3,
10n10, 180
productions, radio 3, 10, 171,
174, 175, 179, 181
productions, stage 2, 3, 4, 191n3
Proserpine 16, 17, 19, 23, 47, 48,
49
Revenge 16, 19, 32, 35–6, 46–9,
50, 51, 78–9, 119, 120, 147,
159, 172, 173–4, 184, 185
Serberine 117, 130, 132, 136,
140
Viceroy, the 117, 120, 121, 174
spectacle 10, 20, 33, 34, 37, 50,
183, 184, 185, 186, 189, 203,
207
stage directions 23, 62, 92, 93, 94,
101, 105, 149–51, 205, 207
descriptive 150, 151, 162n29
prescriptive 150, 151, 162n29
Stage of English Miseries, The 155,
156, 157
Steenbergh, Kristine 204, 229
Stoker, Bram 209
Dracula 209
structures, supernatural 16, 21–4
Ghost 16, 18–19, 20, 21, 32, 36,
46, 47, 48, 49, 50, 78, 173,
176, 185

ghosts 18, 32, 35, 36, 39, 44, 54
Weird Sisters 21
witches 21
substitution 95, 102, 104n9
succession crisis 119, 122
Swan, The – Royal Shakespeare
Company 3, 8, 145, 171, 172,
173, 175, 176, 177, 177, 180,
181, 182, 182, 191, 191n8,
192n14

text, base, *see* copy-text
text, 'illegal' 91, 101, 104n8
text, multiple 89
text, pirate, *see* text, 'illegal'
text, stable 89
text, surviving 90, 102
text, unstable 85
theatre, Dutch rhetoricians' 145,
146, 147
theatre, ideas against 28, 64–5
theatre, moral philosophy and 28–9
theatre, total 37, 51
torture 18, 112, 126n15, 138, 172,
183, 190, 198
tragedy 26–9
action and character 31–2, 34
Aristotle 26, 28, 30–1
catharsis 31, 184
Donatus, Aelius 26, 27, 30
dramatic event 26, 32, 34
hamartia 30, 31
linear plot 79
narrative structure 25, 26, 28, 32,
46, 68n23
personal 182
Plato 27, 28
plot 45–6, 47–50, 53, 54, 79,
157, 158
sub-plot 46
tragic ending 26, 184, 185
tragic fall 25–7, 28, 29, 30–1
tragic flaw 31
tragic hero 28, 31–2
Tragedy of Gorboduc, The 33, 34,
35, 56, 57, 118, 125

transposition 92, 95–6, 97, 104n9,
    105n19
Tronch, Jesús 11n12, 216

union 119–20

variants 82, 91–4, 104n11
    Folio 96, 105n20
    inherited 91, 93
    Quarto 96, 105n20
    substantive 91, 92, 101
    textual 80
version 1, 82, 83, 90, 93, 94, 96,
    103, 133, 144, 147–8, 149,
    150–1, 158, 159–60, 171,
    173, 174, 175, 183, 184, 185,
    187
villain 21, 32, 134
    Machiavellian 35, 111, 130,
    132–3, 135, 140, 176, 201,
    204
Virgil 16, 19
Vos, Jan 148, 153–4, 161n17
    Aran and Titus 147, 148, 152,
    157, 164n59
    Olivier Kromwel 153

war 3, 4, 31, 45, 83, 84, 112, 117,
    145, 196
    Anglo-Dutch 158
    Anglo-Spanish 46
    civil 57, 67, 118, 125, 152, 158,
    173
    Civil, English 156, 158
    ideological 130
Wight, Peter 178–9, 182, 183
Williams, Tennessee 209
    A Streetcar Named Desire 209